SPANISH
for travellers

By the staff of Berlitz Guides

How best to use this phrase book

● We suggest that you start with the **Guide to pronunciation** (pp. 6–8), then go on to **Some basic expressions** (pp. 9–15). This gives you not only a minimum vocabulary, but also helps you get used to pronouncing the language. The phonetic transcription throughout the book enables you to pronounce every word correctly.

● Consult the **Contents** pages (3–5) for the section you need. In each chapter you'll find travel facts, hints and useful information. Simple phrases are followed by a list of words applicable to the situation.

● Separate, detailed contents lists are included at the beginning of the extensive **Eating out** and **Shopping guide** sections (Menus, p. 39, Shops and services, p. 97).

● If you want to find out how to say something in Spanish, your fastest look-up is via the **Dictionary** section (pp. 164–189). This not only gives you the word, but is also cross-referenced to its use in a phrase on a specific page.

● If you wish to learn more about constructing sentences, check the **Basic grammar** (pp. 159–163).

● Note the **colour margins** are indexed in Spanish and English to help both listener and speaker. And, in addition, there is also an **index in Spanish** for the use of your listener.

● Throughout the book, this symbol ☛ suggests phrases your listener can use to answer you. If you still can't understand, hand this phrase book to the Spanish-speaker to encourage pointing to an appropriate answer. The English translation for you is just along-side the Spanish.

Library of Congress Catalog Card No. 85-81371

Second revised edition—3rd printing 1986
Printed in Switzerland

Contents

Acknowledgments
We are particularly grateful to José Carasa for his help in the prep-
aration of this book, and to Dr. T.J.A. Bennett who devised the
phonetic transcription.

Guide to pronunciation

This and the following chapter are intended to make you familiar with the phonetic transcription we devised and to help you get used to the sounds of Spanish.

As a minimum vocabulary for your trip, we've selected a number of basic words and phrases under the title "Some Basic Expressions" (pages 9–15).

An outline of the spelling and sounds of Spanish

You'll find the pronunciation of the Spanish letters and sounds explained below, as well as the symbols we're using for them in the transcriptions. Note that Spanish has some diacritical letters—letters with special markings—which we don't know in English.

The imitated pronunciation should be read as if it were English except for any special rules set out below. It is based on Standard British pronunciation, though we have tried to take into account General American pronunciation as well. Of course, the sounds of any two languages are never exactly the same; but if you follow carefully the indications supplied here, you'll have no difficulty in reading our transcriptions in such a way as to make yourself understood.

Letters written in bold should be stressed (pronounced louder).

Consonants

Letter	Approximate pronunciation	Symbol	Example	
f, k, l, m, n, p, t, x, y	as in English			
b	1) generally as in English	b	**bueno**	**bway**noa
	2) between vowels, a sound between **b** and **v**	bh	**bebida**	bay**bhee**dhah

c	1) before **e** and **i** like **th** in thin	th	**centro**	thayntroa
	2) otherwise, like **k** in kit	k	**como**	koamoa
ch	as in English	ch	**mucho**	moochoa
d	1) generally as in dog, although less decisive	d	**donde**	doanday
	2) between vowels and at the end of a word, like **th** in this	dh	**edad**	aydhahdh
g	1) before **e** and **i**, like **ch** in Scottish lo**ch**	kh	**urgente**	oorkhayntay
	2) between vowels and sometimes inside a word, a weak, voiced version of the **ch** in lo**ch**	g	**agua**	ahgwah
	3) otherwise, like **g** in go	g	**ninguno**	neengoonoa
h	always silent		**hombre**	ombray
j	like **ch** in Scottish lo**ch**	kh	**bajo**	bahkhoa
ll	like **lli** in million	ly	**lleno**	lyaynoa
ñ	like **ni** in onion	ñ	**señor**	sayñor
qu	like **k** in kit	k	**quince**	keenthay
r	more strongly trilled (like a Scottish **r**), especially at the beginning of a word	r	**río**	reeoa
rr	strongly trilled	rr	**arriba**	ahrreebhah
s	always like the **s** in sit, often with a slight lisp	s/ss	**vista** **cuantos**	beestah kwahntoass
v	1) tends to be like **b** in bad, but less tense	b	**viejo**	byaykhoa
	2) between vowels, more like English **v**	bh	**rival**	reebhahl
z	like **th** in thin	th	**brazo**	brahthoa

Vowels

a	like **ar** in cart, but fairly short	ah	**gracias**	grahthyahss
e	1) sometimes like **a** in late	ay	**de**	day
	2) less often, like **e** in get	eh	**llover**	lyoabhehr
i	like **ee** in feet	ee	**sí**	see

PRONUNCIATION

o	1) like **oa** in b**oa**t, but pronounced without moving tongue or lips	oa	**sopa**	**soa**pah
	2) sometimes like **o** in g**o**t	o	**dos**	doss
u	like **oo** in l**oo**t	oo	**una**	**oo**nah
y	only a vowel when alone or at the end of a word; like **ee** in f**ee**t	ee	**y**	ee

N.B. 1) In forming diphthongs, **a, e,** and **o** are strong vowels, and **i** and **u** (pronounced before a vowel like **y** in **y**es and **w** in **w**as) are weak vowels. This means that in diphthongs the strong vowels are pronounced more strongly than the weak ones. If two weak vowels form a diphthong, the second one is pronounced more strongly.

2) The acute accent (´) is used to indicate a syllable that is stressed, e.g., *río* = **ree**oa.

3) In words ending with a consonant, the last syllable is stressed, e.g., *señor* = say**ñor**.

4) In words ending with a vowel, the next to last syllable is stressed, e.g., *mañana* = mah**ñah**nah.

Pronunciation of the Spanish alphabet					
A	ah	**J**	**kho**atah	**R**	ayrray
B	bay	**K**	kah	**S**	ayssay
C	thay	**L**	ay**llay**	**T**	tay
CH	chay	**LL**	ay**lyay**	**U**	oo
D	day	**M**	aym**may**	**V**	bhay
E	ay	**N**	ayn**nay**	**W**	bhay **doa**blay
F	ayf**fay**	**Ñ**	ayn**yay**	**X**	ay**khees**s
G	gay	**O**	oa	**Y**	ee **gray**gah
H	ahchay	**P**	pay	**Z**	**thay**tah
I	ee	**Q**	koo		

Some basic expressions

Yes.	**Sí.**	see
No.	**No.**	noa
Please.	**Por favor.**	por fahbhor
Thank you.	**Gracias.**	grahthyahss
No, thank you.	**No, gracias.**	noa grahthyahss
Yes, please.	**Sí, por favor.**	see por fahbhor
Thank you very much.	**Muchas gracias.**	moochahss grahthyahss
That's all right/ Don't mention it.	**No hay de qué.**	noa igh day kay
You're welcome.	**De nada.**	day nahdhah

Greetings   *Saludos*

Good morning.	**Buenos días.**	bwaynoass deeahss
Good afternoon.	**Buenas tardes.**	bwaynahss tahrdayss
Good evening.	**Buenas tardes.**	bwaynahss tahrdayss
Good night.	**Buenas noches.**	bwaynahss noachayss
Good-bye.	**Adiós.**	ahdhyoss
See you later.	**Hasta luego.**	ahstah lwaygoa
This is Mr. ...	**Este es el Señor ...**	aystay ayss ayl sayñor
This is Mrs. ...	**Esta es la Señora ...**	aystah ayss lah sayñoarah
This is Miss ...	**Esta es la Señorita ...**	aystah ayss lah sayñoareetah
How do you do? (Pleased to meet you.)	**Encantado(a)* de conocerle.**	aynkahntahdhoa(ah) day koanoathayrlay

---

* A woman would say *encantada*

SOME BASIC EXPRESSIONS

How are you?	¿Cómo está usted?	koamoa aystah oostaydh
Very well. And you?	Muy bien. ¿Y usted?	mwee byayn. ee oostaydh
How's it going?	¿Cómo le va?	koamoa lay bah
Fine, thanks. And you?	Muy bien, gracias. ¿Y usted?	mwee byayn grahthyahss. ee oostaydh
I beg your pardon?	¿Perdóneme?	payrdoanaymay
Excuse me. (May I get past?)	Perdóneme.	payrdoanaymay
Sorry!	Lo siento.	loa syayntoa
You're welcome.	Está bien.	aystah byayn

Questions *Preguntas*

Where?	¿Dónde?	doanday
How?	¿Cómo?	koamoa
When?	¿Cuándo?	kwahndoa
What?	¿Qué?	kay
Why?	¿Por qué?	por kay
Who?	¿Quién?	kyayn
Which?	¿Cuál/Cuáles?	kwahl/kwahlayss
Where is ...?	¿Dónde está ...?	doanday aystah
Where are ...?	¿Dónde están ...?	doanday aystahn
Where can I find/get ...?	¿Dónde puedo encontrar/conseguir ...?	doanday pwaydhoa aynkontrahr/konsaygeer
How far?	¿A qué distancia?	ah kay deestahnthyah
How long?	¿Cuánto tiempo?	kwahntoa tyaympoa
How much?	¿Cuánto?	kwahntoa
How many?	¿Cuántos?	kwahntoass
How much does it cost?	¿Cuánto cuesta?	kwahntoa kwaystah
How do I get to ...?	¿Cómo puedo llegar a ...?	koamoa pwaydhoa lyaygahr ah

Expresiones generales

When does ... open/close?	¿Cuándo abren/cierran ...?	kwahndoa ahbrayn/thyayrrahn
What do you call this/that in Spanish?	¿Cómo se llama esto/eso en español?	koamoa say lyahmah aystoa/ayssoa ayn ayspahñol
What do you call these/those in Spanish?	¿Cómo se llaman estos/esos en español?	koamoa say lyahmahn aystoass/ayssoass ayn ayspahñol
What does this/that mean?	¿Qué quiere decir esto/eso?	kay kyayray daytheer aystoa/ayssoa
Is that correct?	¿Es correcto?	ayss koarrayktoa
Why are you laughing?	¿Por qué se ríe?	poar kay say reeay
Is my pronunciation that bad?	¿Es mala mi pronunciación?	ayss mahlah mee proanoonthyahthyon

Do you speak ...? *¿Habla usted ...?*

Do you speak English?	¿Habla usted inglés?	ahblah oostaydh eenglayss
Is there anyone here who speaks ...?	¿Hay alguien aquí que hable ...?	igh ahlgyayn ahkee kay ahblay
I don't speak much Spanish.	No hablo mucho español.	noa ahbloa moochoa ayspahñol
Could you speak more slowly?	¿Puede usted hablar más despacio?	pwaydhay oostaydh ahblahr mahss dayspahthyoa
Could you repeat that?	¿Podría usted repetir eso?	poadreeah oostaydh raypayteer ayssoa
Please write it down.	Por favor, escríbalo.	por fahbhor ayskreebhahloa
Can you translate this for me?	¿Puede usted traducírmelo?	pwaydhay oostaydh trahdhootheermayloa
Can you translate this for us?	¿Puede usted traducírnoslo?	pwaydhay oostaydh trahdhootheernoasloa
Please point to the word/phrase/sentence in the book.	Por favor, señale la palabra/la expresión/la frase en el libro.	por fahbhor sayñahlay lah pahlahbrah/lah ayksprayssyon/lah frahssay ayn ayl leebroa

Just a minute. I'll see if I can find it in this book.	**Un momento. Veré si lo puedo encontrar en este libro.**	oon moamayntoa. bayray see loa **pway**dhoa aynkoan**trahr** ayn **ays**tay **lee**broa
I understand.	**Comprendo/ Entiendo.**	koam**prayn**doa/ ayn**tyayn**doa
I don't understand.	**No comprendo.**	noa koam**prayn**doa
Do you understand?	**¿Comprende usted?**	koam**prayn**day oo**stay**dh

Can/May ...?   *¿Puede ...?*

Can I have ...?	**¿Puede darme ...?**	**pway**dhay **dahr**may
Can we have ...?	**¿Puede darnos ...?**	**pway**dhay **dahr**noass
Can you show me ...?	**¿Puede usted enseñarme ...?**	**pway**dhay oo**stay**dh aynsay**ñahr**may
I can't.	**No puedo.**	noa **pway**dhoa
Can you tell me ...?	**¿Puede usted decirme ...?**	**pway**dhay oo**stay**dh day**theer**may
Can you help me?	**¿Puede usted ayudarme?**	**pway**dhay oo**stay**dh ahyoo**dahr**may
Can I help you?	**¿Puedo ayudarle?**	**pway**dhoa ahyoo**dahr**lay
Can you direct me to ...?	**¿Puede usted indicarme la dirección a ...?**	**pway**dhay oo**stay**dh eendee**kahr**may lah deerehkt**hyon** ah

Wanting   *Deseos*

I'd like ...	**Quisiera ...**	kees**syay**rah
We'd like ...	**Quisiéramos ...**	kees**syay**rahmoass
What do you want?	**¿Qué desea usted?**	kay day**ssay**ah oo**stay**dh
Please give me ...	**Por favor, déme ...**	por fah**bhor day**may
Give it to me, please.	**Démelo, por favor.**	**day**mayloa por fah**bhor**
Bring me ...	**Tráigame ...**	**trigh**gahmay
Bring it to me.	**Tráigamelo.**	**trigh**gahmayloa

Show me ...	Enséñeme ...	aynsayñaymay
Show it to me.	Enséñemelo.	aynsayñaymayloa
I'm hungry.	Tengo hambre.	tayngoa ahmbray
I'm thirsty.	Tengo sed.	tayngoa saydh
I'd like something to eat/drink.	Quisiera algo para comer/beber.	keessyayrah ahlgoa pahrah koamayr/baybhayr
I'm tired.	Estoy cansado(a). *	aystoy kahnsahdhoa(ah)
I'm lost.	Me he perdido.	may ay payrdeedhoa
I'm looking for ...	Estoy buscando ...	aystoy booskahndoa
It's important.	Es importante.	ayss eempoartahntay
It's urgent.	Es urgente.	ayss oorkhayntay
Hurry up!	¡Dése prisa!	dayssay preessah

It is/There is ...   Es/Está/Hay ...

It is/It's ...	Es ...	ayss
Is it ...?	¿Es ...?	ayss
It isn't ...	No es ...	noa ayss
Isn't it ...?	¿No es ...?	noa ayss
Here it is.	Aquí está.	ahkee aystah
Here they are.	Aquí están.	ahkee aystahn
There it is.	Ahí está.	ahee aystah
There they are.	Ahí están.	ahee aystahn
There is/There are ...	Hay ...	igh
Is there/Are there ...?	¿Hay ...?	igh
There isn't/There aren't ...	No hay ...	noa igh
Isn't there/Aren't there ...?	¿No hay ...?	noa igh
There isn't/There aren't any ...	No hay ninguno(a)/ No hay ningu-nos(as) ...	noa igh neengoonoa(ah)/noa igh neengoonoass(ahss)

* A woman would say *cansada*

SOME BASIC EXPRESSIONS

It's ... *Es/Está ...*

big/small	**grande/pequeño***	grahnday/paykayñoa
quick/slow	**rápido/lento**	rahpeedhoa/layntoa
early/late	**temprano/tarde**	taymprahnoa/tahrday
cheap/expensive	**barato/caro**	bahrahtoa/kahroa
near/far	**cerca/lejos**	thehrkah/lehkhoss
hot/cold	**caliente/frío**	kahlyayntay/freeoa
full/empty	**lleno/vacío**	lyaynoa/bahtheeoa
easy/difficult	**fácil/difícil**	fahtheel/deefeetheel
heavy/light	**pesado/ligero**	payssahdhoa/leekhayroa
open/shut	**abierto/cerrado**	ahbhyehrtoa/thehrrahdhoa
free (vacant)/ occupied	**libre/ocupado**	leebray/oakoopahdhoa
right/wrong	**correcto/incorrecto**	koarrehktoa/eenkoarrehktoa
old/new	**viejo/nuevo**	byaykhoa/nwaybhoa
old/young	**viejo/joven**	byaykhoa/khoabhehn
next/last	**próximo/último**	proakseemoa/oolteemoa
beautiful/ugly	**bonito/feo**	boaneetoa/fehoa
good/bad	**bueno/malo**	bwaynoa/mahloa
better/worse	**mejor/peor**	mehkhor/pehor

Quantities *Cantidades*

a little/a lot	**un poco/mucho**	oon poakoa/moochoa
few/a few	**pocos/(alg)unos**	poakoass/(ahlg)oonoass
much/many	**mucho/muchos**	moochoa/moochoass
more than/less than	**más que/menos que**	mahss kay/maynoass kay
enough/too	**bastante/demasiado**	bahstahntay/daymah-ssyahdhoa
some	**unos/unas**	oonoass/oonahss
any	**alguno/alguna**	ahlgoonoa/ahlgoonah

___
* For feminine and plural forms, see grammar section page 159 (adjectives).

Expresiones generales

Some more useful words *Algunas palabras útiles*

at	**a/en**	ah/ayn
on	**sobre/en**	soabray/ayn
in	**en**	ayn
to	**a/para**	ah/pahrah
for	**por/para**	por/pahrah
from	**de/desde**	day/daysday
inside	**dentro**	dayntroa
outside	**fuera**	fwayrah
up/upstairs	**arriba**	ahreebha
down/downstairs	**abajo**	ahbhahkhoa
above	**encima**	ayntheemah
below	**debajo**	daybhahkhoa
under	**debajo**	daybhahkhoa
next to	**junto a**	khoontoa ah
between	**entre**	ayntray
with/without	**con/sin**	kon/seen
since	**desde**	daysday
and	**y**	ee
or	**o**	oa
not	**no**	noa
nothing	**nada**	nahdhah
never	**nunca**	noonkah
none	**ninguno/ninguna**	neengoonoa/neengoonah
very	**muy**	mwee
too (also)	**también**	tahmbyayn
soon	**pronto**	proantoa
perhaps	**quizá/tal vez**	keethah/tahl bayth
here	**aquí**	ahkee
there	**allí**	ahlyee
now	**ahora**	ahoarah
then	**entonces**	ayntoanthayss
yet	**todavía**	toadhahbheeah

Arrival

CONTROL DE PASAPORTES
PASSPORT CONTROL

Here's my passport.	**Aquí está mi pasaporte.**	ahkee aystah mee pahssahportay
I'll be staying …	**Me quedaré …**	may kaydahray
a few days	**unos días**	oonoas deeahss
a week	**una semana**	oonah saymahnah
I don't know yet.	**No lo sé todavía.**	noa loa say toadhahbheeah
I'm here on holiday/ business.	**Estoy aquí de vacaciones/ negocios.**	aystoy ahkee day bahkahthyoanayss/ naygothyoass
I'm just passing through.	**Estoy sólo de paso.**	aystoy soaloa day pahssoa

If things become difficult:

I'm sorry, I don't understand.	**Lo siento, no comprendo.**	loa syayntoa noa komprayndoa
Is there anyone here who speaks English?	**¿Hay alguien aquí que hable inglés?**	igh ahlgyayn ahkee kay ahblay eenglayss

ADUANA
CUSTOMS

After collecting your baggage at the airport (*el aeropuerto* —ayl ahehroa**pwayr**toa) you have a choice: follow the green arrow if you have nothing to declare. Or leave via a doorway marked with a red arrow if you have items to declare (in excess of those allowed).

artículos para declarar
goods to declare

nada que declarar
nothing to declare

The chart below shows what you can bring in duty-free.*

	Cigarettes	Cigars	Tobacco	Spirits (liquor)	Wine
Residents of European countries and Mediterranean countries of Africa and Asia	200 or	50 or	250 g.	1 l. or	2 l.
All others	400 or	100 or	500 g.	1 l. or	2 l.

I've nothing to declare.	**No tengo nada que declarar.**	noa **tayng**oa **nah**dhah kay dayklah**rahr**
I've a ...	**Tengo ...**	**tayng**oa
carton of cigarettes	**un cartón de cigarrillos**	oon kahr**ton** day theegahr-**reel**yoass
bottle of whisky	**una botella de whisky**	**oo**nah boa**tay**lyah day **wees**kee
bottle of wine	**una botella de vino**	**oo**nah boa**tay**lyah day **bee**noa
It's for my personal use.	**Es de mi uso personal.**	ayss day mee **oos**soa pehrsoa**nahl**
It's a gift.	**Es un regalo.**	ayss oon ray**gah**loa

Su pasaporte, por favor.	Your passport, please.
¿Tiene usted algo que declarar?	Do you have anything to declare?
Por favor, abra esta bolsa.	Please open this bag.
Tendrá que pagar impuestos por esto.	You'll have to pay duty on this.
¿Tiene usted más equipaje?	Do you have any more luggage?

Baggage—Porters   *Equipaje—Mozos*

You'll find porters to carry your luggage to taxi ranks or bus stops. Major airports have self-service luggage carts which can be found in the baggage claim area.

Porter!	¡Mozo!	moathoa
Please take this luggage.	Por favor, lleve este equipaje.	por fahbhor lyaybhay aystay aykeepahkhay
That's mine.	Eso es mío.	ayssoa ayss meeoa
That's my bag/ suitcase.	Esa es mi bolsa/ maleta.	ayssay eyss mee bolsah/ mahlaytah
There is one piece missing.	Falta un bulto.	fahltah oon booltoa
Please take this/my luggage to the ...	Por favor, lleve este/ mi equipaje ...	por fahbhor lyaybhay aystay/mee aykeepahkhay
bus	al autobús	ahl owtoabhooss
luggage lockers	a la consigna automática	ah lah konseegnah owtoamahteekah
taxi	al taxi	ahl tahksee
How much is that?	¿Cuánto es?	kwahntoa ayss
Where are the baggage trolleys (carts)?	¿Dónde están los carritos de equipaje?	doanday aystahn los kahr-reetoss day aykeepahkhay

Changing money   *Cambio de moneda*

Where's the nearest currency exchange office?	¿Dónde está la oficina de cambio más cercana?	doanday aystah lah oafee-theenah day kahmbyoa mahss thayrkahnah
Can you change these traveller's cheques (checks)?	¿Puede cambiarme estos cheques de viajero?	pwaydhay kahmbyahrmay aystoass chaykayss day byahkhayroa
I want to change some ...	Quiero cambiar ...	kyayroa kahmbyahr
dollars	dólares	doalahrayss
pounds	libras	leebrahss
Can you change this into pesetas?	¿Puede cambiarme esto en pesetas?	pwaydhay kahmbyahrmay aystoa ayn payssaytahss
What's the exchange rate?	¿A cuánto está el cambio?	ah kwahntoa aystah ayl kahmbyoa

TIPPING, see inside back-cover

Where is ...? *¿Dónde está ...?*

Where is/are the ...?	**¿Dónde está/ están ...?**	doanday aystah/aystahn
booking office	**la oficina de reservas**	lah oafeetheenah day rayssayrbahss
car hire	**la agencia de alqui- ler de coches**	lah ahkhaynthyah day ahl- keelayr day koachayss
currency-exchange office	**la oficina de cambio de moneda**	lah oafeetheenah day kahm- byoa day moanaydhah
duty-free shop	**la tienda libre de impuestos**	lah tyayndah leebray day eempwaysstoass
luggage lockers	**la consigna auto- matica**	lah konseegnah owto- mahteekah
newsstand	**el quiosco de perió- dicos**	ayl kyoskoa day payrryodheekoass
restaurant	**el restaurante**	ayl raystowrahntay
toilets	**los servicios**	loss sehrbeethyoass
How do I get to ...?	**¿Cómo podría ir a ...?**	koamoa poadreeah eer ah
Is there a bus into town?	**¿Hay un autobús que va al centro?**	igh oon owtoabhooss kay bah ahl thayntroa
Where can I get a taxi?	**¿Dónde puedo coger un taxi?**	doanday pwaydhoa koakhayr oon tahksee

Hotel reservation *Reserva de hotel*

Do you have a hotel guide?	**¿Tiene una guía de hoteles?**	tyaynay oonah geeah day oatehlayss
Could you please reserve a room for me at a hotel/ boarding-house?	**¿Podría reservarme una habitación en un hotel/una pensión, por favor?**	poadreeah rayssayrbahr- may oonah ahbheetahthyon ayn oon oatehl/oonah paynsyon por fahbor
in the centre	**en el centro**	ayn ayl thayntroa
near the railway station	**cerca de la estación de ferrocarril**	thayrkah day lah aystah- thyon day fehrrokahrreel
a single room	**una habitación sencilla**	oonah ahbheetahthyon sayntheelyah
a double room	**una habitación doble**	oonah ahbheetahthyon doablay
not too expensive	**no muy cara**	noa mwee kahrah
Where is the hotel/ boarding-house?	**¿Dónde está el hotel/ la pensión?**	doanday aystah ayl oatehl/ lah paynsyon

HOTEL, see page 22

Car hire (rental) *Alquiler de coches*

Normally you must be over 21 and hold an international driving licence. In practice, British, American and European licences are accepted in almost all situations.

I'd like to hire (rent) a ...	**Quisiera alquilar un ...**	keessyayrah ahlkeelahr oon
car	**coche**	koachay
small car	**coche pequeño**	koachay paykayñoa
medium-sized car	**coche no de lujo**	koachay noa day lookhoa
large car	**coche grande**	koachay grahnday
automatic car	**coche automático**	koachay owtoamahteekoa
I'd like it for ...	**Lo quisiera para ...**	loa keessyayrah pahrah
a day	**un día**	oon deeah
a week	**una semana**	oonah saymahnah
Are there any weekend arrangements?	**¿Hay condiciones especiales para los fines de semana?**	igh koandeethyonayss ayspaythyahlayss pahrah loass feenayss day saymahnah
Do you have any special rates?	**¿Tienen tarifas especiales?**	tyaynayn tahreefahss ayspaythyahlayss
What's the charge per day/week?	**¿Cúanto cobran por día/semana?**	kwahntoa koabrahn por deeah/saymahnah
Is mileage included?	**¿Está incluido el kilometraje?**	aystah eenklooeedhoa ayl keeloamaytrahkhay
Is petrol (gasoline) included?	**¿Está incluida la gasolina?**	aystah eenklooeedhah lah gahssoaleenah
What's the charge per kilometre?	**¿Cúanto cobran por kilómetro?**	kwahntoa koabrahn por keeloamaytroa
I want to hire the car here and leave it in ...	**Quiero alquilar un coche aquí y entregarlo en ...**	kyayroa ahlkeelahr oon koachay ahkee ee ayntraygahrloa ayn
I want full insurance.	**Quiero un seguro a todo riesgo.**	kyayroa oon saygooroa ah toadhoa ryaysgoa
What's the deposit?	**¿Cuál es el depósito?**	kwahl ayss ayl daypoasseetoa
I've a credit card.	**Tengo una tarjeta de crédito.**	tayngoa oonah tahrkhaytah day kraydheetoa
Here's my driving licence.	**Este es mi permiso de conducir.**	aystay ayss mee pehrmeessoa day kondootheer

CAR, see page 75

Taxi *Taxi*

Taxis in major towns are fitted with meters. The figure displayed at the end of your trip may not be the full price. Legitimate added charges are compounded for night and holiday travel, pickups at railway stations, theatres or bull-rings, and for baggage. It's usually best to ask the approximate fare beforehand.

Where can I get a taxi?	¿Dónde puedo coger un taxi?	doanday pwaydhoa koakhehr oon tahksee
Please get me a taxi.	Pídame un taxi, por favor.	peedhahmay oon tahksee por fahbhor
What's the fare to ...?	¿Cuánto es la tarifa a ...?	kwahntoa ayss lah tahreefah ah
How far is it to ...?	¿Cuánto se tarda a ...?	kwahntoa say tahrdah ah
Take me to ...	Lléveme ...	lyaybhaymay
this address	a estas señas	ah aystahss sayñahss
the airport	al aeropuerto	ahl ahehropwayrto
the air terminal	a la terminal aérea	ah lah tehrmeenahl ahayrayah
the railway station	a la estación de ferrocarril	ah lah aystahthyon day fehrrokahrreel
the town centre	al centro de la ciudad	ahl thayntroa day lah thyoodhahdh
the ... Hotel	al hotel ...	ahl oatehl
Turn ... at the next corner.	Doble ... en la próxima esquina.	doablay ... ayn lah prokseemah ayskeenah
left	a la izquierda	ah lah eethkyayrdah
right	a la derecha	ah lah dayraychah
Go straight ahead.	Siga derecho.	seegah dayraychoa
Please stop here.	Pare aquí, por favor.	pahray ahkee por fahbhor
I'm in a hurry.	Tengo mucha prisa.	tayngoa moochah preessah
Could you drive more slowly?	¿Puede usted ir más despacio?	pwaydhay oostaydh eer mahss dayspahthyoa
Could you help me carry my bags?	¿Podría ayudarme a llevar mi equipaje?	poadreeah ahyoodhahrmay ah lyaybhahr mee aykeepahkhay
Would you please wait for me?	¿Puede esperarme, por favor?	pwaydhay ayspayrahrmay por fahbhor

TIPPING, see inside back-cover

Hotel—Other accommodation

Early reservation (and confirmation) is essential in most major tourist centres in the high season. Most towns and arrival points have a tourist information office, and that's the place to go if you're stuck without a room.

Hotel
(oatehl)

There are five official categories of hotels: luxury, first class A, first class B, second class and third class. There may be price variations within any given category, depending on the location and the facilities offered. There are also, of course, plenty of unclassified hotels where you will find clean, simple accommodation and good food.

Hostal
(oastahl)

Modest hotels, often family concerns, graded one to three stars.

Residencia
(rayssee-
daynthyah)

When referred to as *hostal-residencia* or *hotel-residencia,* this term indicates a hotel without a restaurant.

Pensión
(paynsyon)

This roughly corresponds to a boarding house. Usually divided into four categories, it offers *pensión completa* (full board) or *media pensión* (half board). Meals are likely to be from a set menu.

Albergue
(ahlbehrgay)

Modern country inns, catering especially to the motorist.

Parador
(pahrahdhor)

Palaces, country houses or castles that have been converted into hotels and are under government supervision.

Refugio
(rehfookhyoa)

Small inns in remote and mountainous regions. They're often closed in winter.

**Apartamento
amueblado**
(ahpahrtah-
mayntoa ah-
mwayblahdhoa)

A furnished flat (apartment) mainly in resorts. Available from specialized travel agents or directly from the landlord (look for the sign *se alquila*—to let, for rent).

**Albergue de
juventud**
(ahlbehrgay day
khoobehntoodh)

Youth hostel. Foreign tourists wishing to use them should be members of the international Youth Hostels Association.

CAMPING, see page 32

Hotel

Checking in—Reception *Recepción*

My name is ...	**Mi nombre es ...**	mee noambray ayss
I've a reservation.	**He hecho una reserva.**	eh aychoa oonah rayssayrbah
We've reserved two rooms.	**Hemos reservado dos habitaciones.**	ehmoass rayssayrbahdhoa doss ahbheetahthyonayss
Here's the confirmation.	**Aquí está la confirmación.**	ahkee aystah lah konfeermahthyon
Do you have any vacancies?	**¿Tiene habitaciones libres?**	tyaynay ahbheetahthyonayss leebhrayss
I'd like a single/double room.	**Quisiera una habitación sencilla/doble.**	keessyayrah oonah ahbheetahthyon sayntheelyah/doablay
I'd like a room ...	**Quisiera una habitación ...**	keessyayrah oonah ahbheetahthyon
with twin beds	**con dos camas**	kon doss kahmahss
with a double bed	**con una cama matrimonial**	kon oonah kahmah mahtreemoanyahl
with a bath	**con baño**	kon bahñoa
with a shower	**con ducha**	kon doochah
with a balcony	**con balcón**	kon bahlkon
with a view	**con vista**	kon beestah
in the front	**en la parte delantera**	ayn lah pahrtay daylahntayrah
at the back	**en la parte trasera**	ayn lah pahrtay trahssayrah
facing the sea	**con vista al mar**	kon beestah ahl mahr
facing the courtyard	**con vista al patio**	kon beestah ahl pahtyoa
It must be quiet.	**Tiene que ser tranquila.**	tyaynay kay sayr trahnkeelah
Is there ...?	**¿Hay ...?**	igh
air conditioning	**aire acondicionado**	ighray ahkondeethyoanahdhoa
heating	**calefacción**	kahlayfahkthyon
a radio/a television in the room	**radio/televisión en la habitación**	rahdhyoa/taylaybheessyon ayn lah ahbheetahthyon
laundry/room service	**servicio de lavado/de habitación**	sehrbeethyoa day lahbhahdhoa/day ahbheetahthyon
hot water	**agua caliente**	ahgwah kahlyayntay
running water	**agua corriente**	ahgwah korryayntay
a private toilet	**water particular**	wahtayr pahrteekoolahr

CHECKING OUT, see page 31

How much? *¿Cuánto cuesta?*

What's the price ...?	**¿Cuánto cuesta ...?**	kwahntoa kwaystah
per night/per week	**por noche/por semana**	por noachay/por saymahnah
for bed and breakfast	**por dormir y desayunar**	por dormeer ee dayssahyoonahr
excluding meals	**excluyendo las comidas**	aykslooyayndoa lahss koameedhahss
for full board (A.P.)	**por pensión completa**	por paynsyon komplaytah
for half board (M.A.P.)	**por media pensión**	por maydhyah paynsyon
Does that include service/breakfast?	**¿Está incluido el servicio/el desayuno?**	aystah eenklooeedhoa ayl sehrbeethyoa/ayl dayssahyoonoa
Is tax included?	**¿Están incluidos los impuestos?**	aystahn eenklooeedhoass loss eempwaystoass
Is there any reduction for children?	**¿Hay algún descuento para los niños?**	igh ahlgoon dayskwayntoa pahrah loss neeñoass
Do you charge for the baby?	**¿Cobran ustedes por el bebé?**	koabrahn oostaydhayss por ayl baybay
That's too expensive.	**Eso es demasiado caro.**	ayssoa ayss daymahssyahdhoa kahroa
Haven't you anything cheaper?	**¿No tiene usted nada más barato?**	noa tyaynay oostaydh nahdhah mahss bahrahtoa

Decision *Decisión*

May I see the room?	**¿Puedo ver la habitación?**	pwaydhoa behr lah ahbheetahthyon
No, I don't like it.	**No, no me gusta.**	noa noa may goostah
It's too ...	**Es demasiado ...**	ayss daymahssyahdhoa
cold/hot	**fría/caliente**	freeah/kahlyayntay
dark/small	**oscura/pequeña**	oskoorah/paykayñah
noisy	**ruidosa**	rweedhoassah
I asked for a room with a bath.	**Yo había pedido una habitación con baño.**	yoa ahbheeah paydheedhoa oonah ahbheetahthyon kon bahñoa

NUMBERS, see page 147

Hotel

Do you have anything ...?	¿Tiene usted algo ...?	tyaynay oostaydh ahlgoa
better/bigger	mejor/más grande	mehkhor/mahss grahnday
cheaper	más barato	mahss bahrahtoa
quieter	más tranquilo	mahss trahnkeeloa
higher up/lower down	más arriba/más abajo	mahss ahrreebhah/mahss ahbhahkhoa
Do you have a room with a better view?	¿Tiene usted una habitación con una vista mejor?	tyaynay oostaydh oonah ahbheetahthyon kon oonah beestah mehkhor
That's fine, I'll take it.	Muy bien, la tomaré.	mwee byayn lah toamahray

Registration *Inscripción*

Upon arrival at a hotel or boarding house you'll be asked to fill in a registration form *(una ficha)*.

Apellido/Nombre	Name/First name
Domicilio/Calle/nº	Home address/Street/No.
Nacionalidad/Profesión	Nationality/Profession
Fecha de nacimiento	Date of birth
Lugar	Place
Fecha	Date
Firma	Signature

| What does this mean? | ¿Qué quiere decir esto? | kay kyayray daytheer aystoa |

¿Me deja ver su pasaporte?	May I see your passport?
¿Le importa llenar esta ficha?	Would you mind filling in this registration form?
Firme aquí, por favor.	Please sign here.
¿Cuánto tiempo va a quedarse?	How long will you be staying?

We'll be staying …	**Nos quedaremos …**	noss kaydhahraymoass
overnight only	**sólo una noche**	soaloa oonah noachay
a few days	**algunos días**	ahlgoonoass deeahss
a week (at least)	**una semana (por lo menos)**	oonah saymahnah (por loa maynoass)
I don't know yet.	**No lo sé todavía.**	noa loa say toadhahbheeah

Hotel staff *Personal del hotel*

hall porter	**el conserje**	ayl koansayrkhay
maid	**la camarera**	lah kahmahrayrah
manager	**el director**	ayl deerehktoar
page (bellboy)	**el botones**	ayl boatoanayss
porter	**el mozo**	ayl moathoa
receptionist	**el recepcionista**	ayl raythaypthyoneestah
switchboard operator	**la telefonista**	lah taylayfoaneestah
waiter	**el camarero**	ayl kahmahrayroa
waitress	**la camarera**	lah kahmahrayrah

General requirements *Peticiones generales*

What's my room number?	**¿Cuál es el número de mi habitación?**	kwahl ayss ayl noomayroa day mee ahbheetahthyon
The key, please.	**La llave, por favor.**	lah lyahbhay por fahbhor
Where can I park my car?	**¿En dónde puedo aparcar mi coche?**	ayn doanday pwaydhoa ahpahrkahr mee koachay
Does the hotel have a garage?	**¿Tiene garaje el hotel?**	tyaynay gahrahkhay ayl oatehl
Will you have our luggage sent up?	**¿Puede usted encargarse de que suban nuestro equipaje?**	pwaydhay oostaydh aynkahrgahrsay day kay soobhahn nwaystroa aykeepahkhay
Is there a bath on this floor?	**¿Hay baño en este piso?**	igh bahñoa ayn aystay peessoa
Where's the socket (outlet) for the shaver?	**¿Dónde está el enchufe para la máquina de afeitar?**	doanday aystah ayl aynchoofay pahrah lah mahkeenah day ahfaytahr

Can we have breakfast in our room?	**¿Podemos desayunar en nuestra habitación?**	poadhaymoass dayssahyoonahr ayn nwaystrah ahbheetahthyon
I'd like to leave this in your safe.	**Me gustaría dejar esto en su caja fuerte.**	may goostahreeah daykhahr aystoa ayn soo kahkhah fwehrtay
Can you find me a ...?	**¿Podría buscarme ...?**	poadreeah booskahrmay
baby-sitter	**una niñera**	oonah neeñayrah
secretary	**una secretaria**	oonah saykraytahryah
typewriter	**una máquina de escribir**	oonah mahkeenah day ayskreebheer
Will you please wake me up at ...	**Por favor, ¿puede despertarme a las ...?**	por fahbhor pwaydhay dayspayrtahrmay ah lahss
May I have a/an/ some ...?	**¿Me puede dar ...?**	may pwaydhay dahr
ashtray	**un cenicero**	oon thayneethayroa
bath towel	**una toalla de baño**	oonah toaahlyah day bahñoa
(extra) blanket	**una manta (más)**	oonah mahntah (mahss)
envelopes	**unos sobres**	oonoass soabrayss
hot-water bottle	**una botella de agua caliente**	oonah bhoataylyah day ahgwah kahlyayntay
(more) hangers	**(más) perchas**	(mahss) pehrchahss
ice cubes	**cubitos de hielo**	koobheetoass day yayloa
needle and thread	**una aguja e hilo**	oonah ahgookha ay eeloa
(extra) pillow	**una almohada (más)**	oonah ahlmoaahdhah (mahss)
reading-lamp	**una lámpara para leer**	oonah lahmpahrah pahrah layehr
soap	**jabón**	khahbhon
writing-paper	**papel de escribir**	pahpehl day ayskreebheer
Where's the ...?	**¿Dónde está ...?**	doanday aystah
beauty salon	**el salón de belleza**	ayl sahlon day baylyaythah
dining-room	**el comedor**	ayl koamaydhor
emergency exit	**la salida de emergencia**	lah sahleedhah day aymayrkhaynthyah
hairdresser's	**la peluquería**	lah paylookayreeah
lift (elevator)	**el ascensor**	ayl ahsthaynsoar
restaurant	**el restaurante**	ayl raystowrahntay
television room	**la sala de televisión**	lah sahlah day taylaybheessyon
toilet	**el servicio**	ayl sayrbeethyoa

BREAKFAST, see page 38

Telephone—Post (mail) *Teléfono – Correo*

Can you get me Madrid 123-45-67?	**¿Puede comunicarme con el número 123-45-67 de Madrid?**	pwaydhay komoonee-kahrmay kon ayl noomayroa 123-45-67 day mahdreedh
Do you have any stamps?	**¿Tiene usted sellos?**	tyaynay oostaydh saylyoass
Would you please mail this for me?	**Por favor, ¿mandaría usted esto por correo?**	por fahbhor mahndahreeah oostaydh aystoa por korrehoa
Are there any messages for me?	**¿Hay algún recado para mí?**	igh ahlgoon raykahdhoa pahrah mee
How much are my telephone charges?	**¿Cuánto debo de llamadas telefónicas?**	kwahntoa dayboa day lyahmahdahss taylayfoa-neekahss

Difficulties *Dificultades*

The ... doesn't work.	**... no funciona.**	... noa foonthyoanah
air conditioner	**el acondicionador de aire**	ayl ahkondeethyoanah-dhor day ighray
fan	**el ventilador**	ayl baynteelahdhor
heating	**la calefacción**	lah kahlayfahkthyon
light	**la luz**	lah looth
radio	**la radio**	lah rahdhyoa
toilet	**los servicios**	loss sehrbeethyoass
television	**el televisor**	ayl taylaybheessoar
The window is jammed.	**La ventana está atrancada.**	lah bayntahnah aystah ahtrahnkahdha
The curtain is stuck.	**La cortina está atrancada.**	lah koarteenah aystah ahtrahnkahdhah
There's no (hot) water.	**No hay agua (caliente).**	noa igh ahgwah (kahlyayntay)
The wash-basin is clogged.	**El lavabo está atascado.**	ayl lahbhahbhoa aystah ahtahskahdhoa
The tap (faucet) is dripping.	**El grifo está goteando.**	ayl greefoa aystah goatayahndhoa
My bed hasn't been made up yet.	**Aún no me han hecho la cama.**	ahoon noa may ahn aychoa lah kahmah

POST OFFICE AND TELEPHONE, see page 132–135

The bulb is burnt out.	**La bombilla está fundida.**	lah bombeelyah aystah foondeeddah
The ... is broken.	**... está roto (rota).**	... aystah rotoa (rotah)
blind	**la persiana**	lah pehrsyahnah
lamp	**la lámpara**	lah lahmpahrah
plug	**una clavija de enchufe**	oonah klahbheekhah day aynchoofay
shutter	**el postigo**	ayl posteegoa
switch	**el interruptor**	ayl eentehrrooptor
Can you get it repaired?	**¿Puede usted arreglarlo(la)?**	pwayday oostaydh ahrrayglahrloa(lah)

Laundry—Dry cleaner's *Lavandería—Tintorería*

I want these clothes ...	**Quiero que ... esta ropa.**	kyayroa kay ... aystah roapah
cleaned	**limpien**	leempyayn
ironed/pressed	**planchen**	plahnchayn
washed	**laven**	lahbhayn
When will it be ready?	**¿Cuándo estará lista?**	kwahndoa aystahrah leestah
I need it ...	**La necesito para ...**	lah naythaysseetoa pahrah
today	**hoy**	oy
tonight	**esta noche**	aystah noachay
tomorrow	**mañana**	mahñahnah
before Friday	**antes del viernes**	ahntayss dayl byehrnayss
Can you mend/sew this?	**¿Puede usted remendar/coser esto?**	pwayday oostaydh rehmayndahr/koassayr aystoa
Can you sew on this button?	**¿Puede usted coser este botón?**	pwayday oostaydh koassayr aystay boaton
Can you get this stain out?	**¿Puede usted quitar esta mancha?**	pwayday oostaydh keetahr aystah mahnchah
This isn't mine.	**Esto no es mío.**	aystoa noa ayss meeoa
There's one piece missing.	**Falta una prenda.**	fahltah oonah prayndah
There's a hole in this.	**Hay un hoyo aquí.**	igh oon oayoa ahkee
Is my laundry ready?	**¿Está lista mi ropa?**	aystah leestah mee roapah

Hairdresser's—Barber's   *Peluquería—Barbería*

Is there a hairdresser/ beauty salon in the hotel?	¿Hay una peluquería/ un salón de belleza en el hotel?	igh oonah paylookayreeah/ oon sahlon day baylyaythah ayn ayl oatehl
Can I make an appointment for this afternoon?	¿Puedo pedir hora para esta tarde?	pwaydhoa paydheer oarah pahrah aystah tahrdhay
I want a haircut, please.	Quiero un corte de pelo, por favor.	kyayroa oon kortay day pehloa por fahbhor
I'd like a shave.	Quisiera que me afeitaran.	keessyayrah kay may ahfaytahrahn

I want (a) ...	Quiero ...	kyayroa
bleach	un aclarado	oon ahklahrahdhoa
blow dry	un modelado	oon moadaylahdhoa
colour rinse	unos reflejos	oonoass rehflaykhoass
dye	una tintura	oonah teentoorah
fringe (bangs)	un flequillo	oon flaykeelyoa
manicure	una manicura	oonah mahneekoorah
parting (part)	una raya	oonah rahyah
left/right/ in the middle	a la izquierda/ derecha/en medio	a lah eethkyayrdhah/ dayraychah/ayn maydhyoa
permanent wave	una permanente	oonah pehrmahnayntay
setting lotion	un fijador	oon feekhadhoar
shampoo and set	lavado y marcado	lahbhahdhoa ee mahrkahdhoa

I'd like a shampoo for ... hair.	Quisiera un champú para cabello ...	keessyayrah oon chahmpoo pahrah kahbhaylyoa
dry	seco	saykoa
greasy (oily)	graso	grahssoa
normal	normal	normahl

Do you have a colour chart?	¿Tiene usted un muestrario?	tyaynay oostaydh oon mwaystrahryoa
Don't cut it too short.	No me lo corte mucho.	noa may loa koartay moochoa
That's enough off.	Eso es bastante.	ayssoa ayss bahstahntay
A little more off the ...	Un pocco más ...	oon poakoa mahss
back	por detrás	por daytrahss
neck	en el cuello	ayn ayl kwaylyoa
sides	en los lados	ayn loss lahdhoass
top	arriba	ahrreebhah

DAYS OF THE WEEK, see page 151

Please don't use any oil/hairspray.	**Por favor, no me dé ningún aceite/laca.**	por fahbhor noa may day neengoon ahthaytay/lahkah
Would you please trim my ...?	**¿Quiere usted recortarme ...?**	kyayray oostaydh rehkortahrmay
beard	**la barba**	lah bahrbah
moustache	**al bigote**	ayl beegoatay
sideboards (sideburns)	**las patillas**	lahss pahteelyahss

Checking out *Al marcharse*

May I have my bill, please?	**Por favor, ¿puede darme mi cuenta?**	por fahbhor pwaydhay dahrmay mee kwayntah
I'm leaving early in the morning. Please have my bill ready.	**Me marcho por la mañana, temprano. Por favor, tenga mi cuenta preparada.**	may mahrchoa por lah mahñahnah taymprahnoa. por fahbhor tayngah mee kwayntah praypahrahdhah
What time must I check out?	**¿A qué hora debo desocupar la habitación?**	ah kay oarah daybhoa dayssoakoopahr lah ahbheetahthyon
Would you call a taxi, please?	**¿Quiere llamar un taxi, por favor?**	kyayray lyahmahr oon tahksee por fahbhor
I must leave at once.	**Debo marcharme ahora mismo.**	daybhoa mahrchahrmay ahorah meesmoa
Is everything included?	**¿Está todo incluido?**	aystah toadhoa eenklooeedhoa
Do you accept credit cards?	**¿Acepta tarjetas de crédito?**	ahthayptah tahrkhaytahss day kraydheetoa
You've made a mistake in this bill, I think.	**Creo que se ha equivocado usted en esta cuenta.**	krehoa kay say ah aykeebhoakahdhoa oostaydh ayn aystah kwayntah
Would you send someone to bring down our luggage?	**¿Quiere usted mandar a alguien para bajar nuestro equipaje?**	kyayray oostaydh mahndahr ah ahlgyayn pahrah bahkhahr nwaystroa aykeepahkhay
Here's my forwarding address.	**Remita mis cartas a esta dirección.**	raymeetah meess kahrtahss ah aystah deeraykthyon
It's been a very enjoyable stay.	**Ha sido una estancia muy agradable.**	ah seedhoa oonah aystahnthyah mwee ahgrahdhahblay

TAXI, see page 21

Camping *Camping*

Camping facilities vary, but most sites have electricity and running water. Many have shops and children's playgrounds, and some even laundrettes and restaurants. For a complete list of camp sites consult any Spanish National Tourist Office.

Is there a camp site near here?	**¿Hay algún camping cerca de aquí?**	igh algooŋ **kah**mpeeng thehr**kah** day ah**kee**
Can we camp here?	**¿Podemos acampar aquí?**	poad**hay**moass ahkahm**pahr** ah**kee**
Have you room for a caravan (trailer)/tent?	**¿Tiene sitio para una tienda/caravana?**	tyay**nay see**tyo **pah**rah **oo**nah tyay**ndah**/kahrah**bhah**nah
What's the charge ...?	**¿Cuál es el precio ...?**	kwahl ayss ayl **pray**thyoa
per day/person	**por día/persona**	por **dee**ah/pehr**soa**nah
for a car/tent	**por coche/tienda**	por **koa**chay/**tyay**ndah
for a caravan (trailer)	**por caravana**	por kahrah**bhah**nah
May we light a fire?	**¿Podemos encender una hoguera?**	poad**hay**moass aynthayn**dehr oo**nah oa**geh**rah
Is there/Are there (a) ...?	**¿Hay ...?**	igh
drinking water	**agua potable**	**ah**gwah poa**tah**blay
electricity	**electricidad**	aylayktreethee**dhahd**
playground	**un campo de juego**	oon **kah**mpoa day **khway**goa
restaurant	**un restaurante**	oon raystow**rahn**tay
shopping facilities	**tiendas**	**tyay**ndahss
swimming pool	**una piscina**	**oo**nah pees**thee**nah
Where are the showers/toilets?	**¿Dónde están las duchas/los servicios?**	**doan**day ays**tahn** lahss **doo**chahss/loass sayr**bee**thyoass
Where can I get butane gas?	**¿Dónde puedo conseguir gas butano?**	**doan**day **pway**dhoa konsay**geer** gahss boo**tah**noa

PROHIBIDO ACAMPAR NO CAMPING	**PROHIBIDO ACAMPAR CON CARAVANA** NO CARAVANS (TRAILERS)

CAMPING EQUIPMENT, see page 106

Eating out

There are many different places where you can eat and drink in Spain.

Albergue de carretera
(ahlbehrgay day kahrrehtayrah)

Motel; strategically located on main roads; snacks and full meals offered, quick service

Bar
(bahr)

Bar; drinks and *tapas* (see page 63) served, sometimes hot beverages, too

Café
(kahfay)

As in all Mediterranean countries, *cafés* can be found on virtually every street corner. An indispensable part of everyday life, the *café* is where people get together for a chat over a coffee, soft drink or glass of wine.

Cafetería
(kahfaytayreeah)

Coffee shop; not to be confused with the English word cafeteria; there's counter service or —for a few pesetas extra—you can choose a table. The set menu is often very good.

Casa de comidas
(kahssah day koameedhahss)

Simple inn serving cheap meals

Fonda
(fondah)

Typical Spanish inn

Hostería
(ostayreeah)

Restaurant; often specializing in regional cooking

Merendero
(mayrayndayroa)

Seaside fish restaurant; you can usually eat out-of-doors

Parador
(pahrahdhor)

A government-supervised establishment located in a historic castle, palace or former monastery. A *parador* is usually noted for excellent regional dishes served in a dining room with handsome Spanish decor.

Pastelería/ Confitería
(pahstaylayreeah/ konfeetayreeah)

Pastry shop; some serve coffee, tea and drinks

Posada
(poassahdhah)

A humble version of a *fonda;* the food is usually simple but good

Refugio (rehf**oo**khyoa)	Mountain lodge serving simple meals
Restaurante (raystow**rahn**tay)	Restaurant; these are classified by the government but the official rating has more to do with the decor than with the quality of cooking
Salón de té (sah**lon** day tay)	Tearoom; at bit exclusive
Taberna (tah**beh**rnah)	Similar to an English pub or American tavern in atmosphere; always a variety of *tapas* on hand as well as other snacks
Tasca (**tahs**kah)	Similar to a *bar*; drinks and *tapas* are served at the counter; standing only

Meal times *Horas de comida*

Breakfast (*el desayuno*—ayl dayssah**yoo**noa) is generally served from 7 to 10 a.m.

Lunch (*el almuerzo*—ayl ahl**mwayr**thoa) is generally served from around 2 or 3 p.m.

Dinner (*la cena*—lah **thay**nah) is served far later than at home, from about 8 p.m. in tourist areas, elsewhere from about 9.

The Spaniards like to linger over a meal, so service may seem on the leisurely side.

Spanish Cuisine *Cocina española*

The history of Spain has had much to do with the wealth and variety of Spanish cuisine. The Celtic tribes which settled Galicia cooked with animal fats, in particular pork fat. The Romans introduced garlic, as well as olive oil, which is today the basic ingredient of Spanish cooking. The conquering Arabs brought lemons, oranges, saffron, dates and rice. And the discovery of America in 1492 further enriched Spanish cuisine with the potato, pimentos, pepper and cocoa.

In addition, Spain's 5,000 kilometres of coastline offer, at all seasons, a profusion of Atlantic and Mediterranean seafood.

¿Qué desea?	What would you like?
Le recomiendo esto.	I recommend this.
¿Qué desea beber?	What would you like to drink?
No tenemos ...	We haven't got ...
¿Desea ...?	Do you want ...?

Hungry?   *¿Hambre?*

I'm hungry/I'm thirsty.	**Tengo hambre/ Tengo sed.**	tayngoa ahmbray/ tayngoa saydh
Can you recommend a good restaurant?	**¿Puede recomendarme un buen restaurante?**	pwaydhay raykoamayndahrmay oon bwayn raystowrahntay
Where can we get a typical Spanish meal?	**¿Dónde podemos encontrar comidas típicas de España?**	doanday poadhaymoass aynkontrahr koameedhahss teepeekahss day ayspahñah
Are there any inexpensive restaurants around here?	**¿Hay restaurantes no muy caros cerca de aquí?**	igh raystowrahntayss noa mwee kahroass thehrkah day ahkee

If you want to be sure of getting a table in well-known restaurants, it may be better to telephone in advance. Some of them close one day a week (usually a Monday).

I'd like to reserve a table for 4.	**Quiero reservar una mesa para 4.**	kyayroa rehssayrbahr oonah mayssah pahrah 4
We'll come at 8.	**Vendremos a las 8.**	bayndraymoass ah lahss 8

TIPPING, see inside back-cover

EATING OUT

Asking and ordering *Preguntando y pidiendo*

Good evening, I'd like a table for 3.	**Buenas tardes, quisiera una mesa para 3.**	bwaynahss tahrdayss keessyayrah oonah mayssah pahrah 3
Could we have a table ...?	**¿Nos puede dar una mesa ...?**	noss pwaydhay dahr oonah mayssah
in the corner	**en el rincón**	ayn ayl reenkon
by the window	**al lado de la ventana**	ahl lahdhoa day lah behntahnah
in a non-smoking area	**en la sección de no fumadores**	ayn lah sekthyon day noa foomahdhorayss
outside/on the patio	**fuera/en el patio**	fwayrah/ayn ayl pahtyoa
Waiter!/ Waitress!	**¡Camarero!/ ¡Camarera!**	kahmahrayroa/ kahmahrayrah
I'd like something to eat/drink.	**Quisiera algo de comer/beber.**	keessyayrah ahlgoa day koamayr/behbhayr
What do you recommend?	**¿Qué me aconseja?**	kay may ahkoansehkhah
May I please have the menu?	**¿Puedo ver la carta, por favor?**	pwaydhoa behr lah kahrtah por fahbhor
What's this?	**¿Qué es esto?**	kay ayss aystoa
Do you have ...?	**¿Tienen ...?**	tyaynayn
a set menu/local dishes	**platos combinados/ especialidades locales**	plahtoass koambeenah-dhoass/ayspaythyahlee-dhahdhayss loakahlayss
I'd like a supplement.	**Quisiera otra ración.**	keessyayrah oatrah rahthyon
Nothing more, thanks.	**Nada más, gracias.**	nahdhah mahss grahthyahss
Can we have a/an ..., please?	**¿Puede darnos ..., por favor?**	pwaydhay dahrnoass ... por fahbhor
ashtray	**un cenicero**	oon thayneethayroa
(extra) chair	**una silla (más)**	oonah seelyah (mahss)
cup	**una taza**	oonah tahthah
fork	**un tenedor**	oon taynaydhoar
glass	**un vaso**	oon bahssoa
knife	**un cuchillo**	oon koocheelyoa
napkin (serviette)	**una servilleta**	oonah sehrbeelyaytah
plate	**un plato**	oon plahtoa
spoon	**una cuchara**	oonah koochahrah

COMPLAINTS, see page 61

Comidas y bebidas

I'd like some ...	Quisiera ...	keessyayrah
bread	pan	pahn
butter	mantequilla	mahntaykeelyah
ketchup	salsa de tomate	sahlsah day toamahtay
lemon	limón	leemon
mustard	mostaza	moastahthah
oil	aceite	athaytay
olive oil	aceite de oliva	athaytay day oaleebhah
pepper	pimienta	peemyayntah
rolls	panecillos	pahnaytheelyoass
salt	sal	sahl
seasoning	condimentos	kondeemyayntoass
sugar	azúcar	ahthookahr
vinegar	vinagre	beenahgray

Some useful expressions if you have to follow a diet:

I have to live on a diet.	Tengo que guardar dieta.	tayngoa kay gwahrdahr dyaytah
I mustn't eat food containing ...	No debo comer alimentos que contengan ...	noa daybhoa koamayr ahleemayntoass kay koantayngahn
flour/fat	harina/grasa	ahreenah/grahssah
salt/sugar	sal/azúcar	sahl/ahthookahr
Do you have ... for diabetics?	¿Tiene ... para diabéticos?	tyaynay ... pahrah dyahbhayteekoass
cakes	pasteles	pahsstaylayss
fruit juice	jugo de frutas	khoogoa day frootahss
special menus	menús especiales	maynooss aysspaythyahlayss
Do you have vegetarian dishes?	¿Tiene platos vegetarianos?	tyaynay plahtoass baykhaytahryahnoass
Could I have ... instead of the dessert?	¿Podría tomar ... en lugar del postre?	poadhryah toamahr ... ayn loogahr dayl poasstray
cheese	queso	kayssoa
fruit	fruta	frootah
Can I have an artificial sweetener?	¿Puede darme un edulcorante?	pwaydhay dahrmay oon aydhoolkoarahntay

Breakfast *Desayuno*

Most Spaniards eat continental breakfast: coffee, bread or rolls and jam. However, many of the larger hotels also provide a full breakfast (*el desayuno completo*—ayl days-sah**yoo**noa kom**play**toa) with fruit juice and eggs.

I'd like breakfast, please.	**Quisiera desayunar, por favor.**	keess**yay**rah dayssahyoo-**nahr** por fah**bhor**
I'll have a/an/ some ...	**Tomaré ...**	toamah**ray**
bacon and eggs	**huevos con tocino**	**way**bhoass kon toa**thee**noa
cereal	**cereales**	thayrah**yah**layss
boiled egg	**huevo cocido**	**way**bhoa koa**theed**hoa
soft	**pasado por agua**	pahs**sahd**hoa por **ah**gwah
medium	**blando (mollet)**	**blahn**doa (moa**lyayt**)
hard	**duro**	**doo**roa
fried eggs	**huevos fritos**	**way**bhoass **free**toass
fruit juice	**un jugo de fruta**	oon **khoo**goa day **froo**tah
grapefruit	**pomelo**	poa**may**loa
orange	**naranja**	nah**rahn**khah
ham and eggs	**huevos con jamón**	**way**bhoass kon khah**mon**
jam	**mermelada**	mehrmay**lahd**hah
marmalade	**mermelada amarga de naranjas**	mehrmay**lahd**hah ah**mahr**-gah day nah**rahn**khahss
scrambled eggs	**huevos revueltos**	**way**bhoass raybh**wayl**toass
toast	**tostadas**	toast**ahd**hahss
May I have some ...?	**¿Podría darme ...?**	poad**reeah dahr**may
bread	**pan**	pahn
butter	**mantequilla**	mahntay**keel**yah
(hot) chocolate	**chocolate (caliente)**	choakoa**lah**tay (kah**lyayn**tay)
coffee	**café**	kah**fay**
caffein-free	**descafeinado**	dayskahfayee**nahd**hoa
black	**solo**	**soa**loa
with milk	**con leche**	kon **lay**chay
honey	**miel**	myehl
milk	**leche**	**lay**chay
cold/hot	**fría/caliente**	**free**ah/kah**lyayn**tay
pepper	**pimienta**	peem**yayn**tah
salt	**sal**	sahl
tea	**té**	tay
with milk	**con leche**	kon **lay**chay
with lemon	**con limón**	kon lee**mon**
(hot) water	**agua (caliente)**	**ah**gwah (kah**lyayn**tay)

What's on the menu?   *¿Qué hay en el menú?*

Under the headings below you'll find alphabetical lists of dishes that might be offered on a Spanish menu with their English equivalent. You can simply show the book to the waiter. If you want some fruit, for instance, let *him* point to what's available on the appropriate list. Use pages 36 and 37 for ordering in general.

In addition to various à la carte dishes, restaurants usually offer one or more set menus *(platos combinados)* or a dish of the day *(plato del día)* which provide a good meal at a fair price.

Reading the menu *Leyendo la carta*

Especialidades de la casa	Specialities of the house
Especialidades locales	Local specialities
Plato del día	Dish of the day
Platos fríos	Cold dishes
Platos típicos	Specialities
Recomendamos	We recommend
Suplemento sobre ...	... extra

agua mineral	ahgwah meenayrahl	mineral water
aperitivos	ahpayreeteebhoass	apéritifs
arroces	ahrrothayss	rice
asados	ahssahdhoass	roasts
aves	ahbhayss	poultry
bebidas	baybheedhahss	drinks
carnes	kahrnayss	meat
caza	kahthah	game
cerveza	thehrbaythah	beer
entremeses	ayntraymayssayss	starters (appetizers)
ensaladas	aynsahlahdhahss	salads
frutas	frootahss	fruit
granizados	grahneethahdhoass	iced drinks
helados	aylahdhoass	ice-cream
huevos	waybhoass	egg dishes
jugo	khoogoa	fresh juice
legumbres	laygoombrayss	vegetables
mariscos	mahreeskoass	seafood
parrilladas	pahrreelyahdhass	grills
pastas	pahsstahss	pastas
pastelería	pahsstaylayreeah	pastries
patatas	pahtahtahss	potatoes
pescados	payskahdhoass	fish
postres	poastrayss	dessert
quesos	kayssoass	cheese
refrescos	rayfraysskoass	cold drinks
sopas	soapahss	soups
verduras	bayrdoorahss	vegetables
vinos	beenoass	wine
zumo	thoomoa	fresh juice

Starters (Appetizers) *Entremeses*

If you are planning to eat a three-course meal try not to tuck into too many of the great variety of *tapas* (see page 63) over your apéritif.

I'd like a starter (appetizer).	**Quisiera unos entremeses.**	keessyayrah oonoass ayntray**may**ssayss
What do you recommend?	**¿Qué me aconseja?**	kay may ahkon**say**khah

aceitunas (rellenas)	ahthay**too**nahss (ray-**lyay**nahss)	(stuffed) olives
aguacate	ah wah**kah**tay	avocado
alcachofas	ahlkah**choa**fahss	artichoke
almejas	ahl**meh**khahss	clams
a la marinera	ah lah mahree**nay**rah	in paprika sauce
anchoas	ahn**choa**hss	anchovies
anguila ahumada	ahn**gee**lah ahoo**mah**dhah	smoked eel
arenque (ahumado)	ah**rehn**kay (ahoo**mah**dhoa)	(smoked) herring
atún	ah**toon**	tunny (tuna)
cabeza	kah**beh**thah	brawn (headcheese)
de cordero	day koar**day**roa	lamb's
de ternera	day tehr**nay**rah	calf's
calamares	kahlah**mah**rayss	squid
a la romana	ah lah roa**mah**nah	deep-fried
callos	**kah**lyoass	tripe (usually in hot paprika sauce)
caracoles	kahrah**koa**layss	snails
carne de cangrejo	**kahr**nay day kahn**greh**khoa	crabmeat
champiñones	chahmpee**ño**anayss	button mushrooms
chorizo	choa**ree**thoa	spicy sausage made of pork, garlic and paprika
cigalas	thee**gah**lahss	Dublin Bay prawns (sea crayfish)
entremeses variados	ayntray**may**ssayss bah**ryah**dhoass	assorted appetizers
espárragos (puntas de)	ays**par**rahgoass (**poon**tahss day)	asparagus (tips)
fiambres	**fyahm**brayss	cold cuts
gambas	**gahm**bahss	prawns (shrimps)
al ajillo	ahl ah**khee**lyoa	with garlic
a la plancha	ah lah **plahn**chah	grilled
higaditos de pollo	eegah**dhee**toass day **poal**yoa	chicken livers

huevos duros	waybhoass dooroass	hard-boiled eggs
jamón	khahmon	ham
en dulce	ayn **dool**thay	boiled
serrano	sayrrahnoa	cured
langosta	lahn**goas**tah	spiny lobster
langostinos	lahngoas**teen**oass	prawns (shrimps)
mejillones	mehkhee**lyoa**nayss	mussels
melón	may**lon**	melon
ostras	**oas**trahss	oysters
palitos de queso	pah**lee**toass day **kays**soa	cheese sticks (straws)
pepinillos	paypee**neel**yoass	gherkins
pepino	pay**pee**noa	cucumber
percebes	pehr**thay**bhayss	goose barnacles
pimientos	peem**yayn**toass	peppers
quisquillas	kees**keel**yahss	common prawns (shrimps)
rábanos	**rahbh**anoass	radishes
salchichón	sahlchee**chon**	salami
salmón (ahumado)	sahl**mon** (ahoo**mahdh**oa)	(smoked) salmon
sardinas	sahr**deen**ahss	sardines
zumo de fruta	**thoom**oa day **froot**ah	fruit juice
piña/tomate	**peeñ**ah/toa**mah**tah	pineapple/tomato
pomelo/naranja	poa**may**loa/nah**rahn**khah	grapefruit/orange

If you feel like something more ambitious and are prepared to leave the gastronomic beaten track, some of these may tempt you:

albóndigas (ahl**bond**ee ahss)	spiced meatballs
banderillas (bahnday**reel**yahss)	similar to *palitos* but with gherkins
buñuelitos (booñway**lee**toass)	small fritters made with ham, fish, egg or a wide variety of other fillings
empanadillas (aympahnah**dheel**yahss)	small savoury pasties stuffed with meat or fish
palitos (pah**lee**toass)	ham, cheese, pâté, smoked anchovy, trout or eel on a skewer
pinochos, pinchitos (pee**noa**choass, peen**chee**toass)	grilled skewered meat
tartaletas (tahrtah**lay**tahss)	small open tarts filled with fish, meat, vegetables or cheese

Salads *Ensaladas*

What salads do you have?	¿Qué clase de ensaladas tienen?	kay **klah**ssay day aynsah-**lah**dhahss tyaynayn
Can you recommend a local speciality?	¿Puede aconsejarnos una especialidad local?	**pway**dhay ahkonsay**khahr**noass oonah ayspaythyah-leed**hahdh** loakahl

ensalada	aynsah**lah**dhah	salad
de gambas	day **gahm**bahss	shrimp
de lechuga	day lay**choo**gah	green
de patata	day pah**tah**tah	potato
de pepino	day pay**pee**noa	cucumber
del tiempo	dayl **tyaym**poa	(in) season
de tomate	day toa**mah**tay	tomato
valenciana	balayn**thyah**nah	with green peppers, lettuce and oranges

Soups *Sopas*

In Spain, soup is undoubtedly the most popular first course. There is a great variety of soups ranging from the simple *sopa de ajo* to the filling *sopa de mariscos*. Here are a few that you're sure to find on the menu during your trip.

consomé al jerez	konsoa**may** ahl khay**rayth**	chicken broth with sherry
sopa de ajo	soapah day **ah**khoa	garlic soup
sopa de arroz	soapah day ar**roth**	rice soup
sopa de cangrejos	soapah day kahn**greh**khoass	crayfish soup
sopa de cebolla	soapah day thay**boal**yah	onion soup
sopa de cocido	soapah day koa**thee**dhoa	a kind of broth
sopa de espárragos	soapah day ayspah**rrah**goass	asparagus soup
sopa de fideos	soapah day fee**dhay**oass	noodle soup
sopa Juliana	soapah joo**lyah**nah	bouillon of finely shredded vegetables
sopa de mariscos	soapah day mah**rees**koass	seafood soup
sopa de patatas	soapah day pah**tah**tahss	potato soup
sopa de pescado	soapah day pays**kah**dhoa	fish soup
sopa de tomate	soapah day toa**mah**tay	tomato soup
sopa de tortuga	soapah day tor**too**gah	turtle soup
sopa de verduras	soapah day bayr**doo**rahss	vegetable soup

caldo gallego		meat and vegetable broth
(**kahl**doa gahlyehgoa)		
gazpacho		a cold soup of cucumber, tomato, green
(gahth**pah**choa)		pepper, bread, onion and garlic

Omelets *Tortillas*

The Spanish omelet is more likely to be round rather than the rolled form of the classic French *omelette*. Here are the names of a few of the more common egg dishes you'll find on the menu:

tortilla	toar**tee**lyah	omelet
de alcachofa	day ahlkah**choa**fah	artichoke omelet
de cebolla	day thay**boa**lyah	onion omelet
de espárragos	day ays**pahrr**ahgoass	asparagus omelet
gallega	gah**lyeh**gah	potato omelet with ham, chili peppers and peas
de jamón	day kha**mon**	ham omelet
paisana	pahee**ssah**nah	omelet with potatoes, peas, prawns or ham
de patatas	day pah**tah**tahss	potato omelet
de queso	day **kay**ssoa	cheese omelet
al ron	ahl ron	rum omelet
de setas	day **say**tahss	mushroom omelet

... and other egg dishes:

huevos a la flamenca	eggs baked with tomato, onion and diced
(**way**bhoass ah lah flah**mayn**kah)	ham; often garnished with asparagus tips, red peppers or slices of spicy pork sausage
huevos al nido	"eggs in the nest"; egg yolks set in small,
(**way**bhoass ahl **need**hoa)	soft rolls; fried and then covered in egg white
huevos al trote	boiled eggs filled with tunny (tuna) fish and
(**way**bhoass ahl **troa**tay)	dressed with mayonnaise
huevos revueltos al pisto	scrambled eggs with vegetables
(**way**bhoass ray**wayl**toass ahl **pees**toa)	

Paella

An immensely popular dish along Spain's Mediterranean coast, *paella* actually refers to the large metal pan traditionally used for making rice dishes in the Valencia region. Basically, the *paella* dish is made of golden saffron rice garnished with meat, fish, seafood and/or vegetables. Here are four of the most popular ways of preparing *paella* (pah**ay**lyah):

catalana (kahtah**lah**nah)	spicy pork sausages, pork, squid, tomato, chili pepper, peas; the same dish is sometimes referred to as *arroz a la catalana*
marinera (mahree**nay**rah)	fish and seafood only
valenciana (bahlayn**thyah**nah)	chicken, shrimp, mussels, prawns, squid, peas, tomato, chili pepper, garlic—it's the classic *paella*
zamorana (thamoa**rah**nah)	ham, pork loin, pig's trotters (feet), chili pepper

Another rice dish is called *arroz a la cubana* (ahr**roth** ah lah koo**bah**nah) made with white rice, fried eggs and bananas and a savoury tomato sauce.

Fish and seafood   *Pescado y mariscos*

Don't miss the opportunity to sample some of the wide variety of fresh fish and seafood in coastal areas.

I'd like some fish.	**Quisiera pescado.**	keess**yay**rah payss**kah**dhoa
What kind of seafood do you have?	**¿Qué tipo de mariscos tiene usted?**	kay **tee**poa day mah**reess**koass **tyay**nay oos**taydh**
almejas	ahl**mehk**hahss	clams
arenques	ah**rehn**kayss	herring
atún	ah**toon**	tunny (tuna)
bacalao	bahkah**lah**oa	cod
besugo	bay**ssoo**goa	(sea) bream
bonito	boa**nee**toa	tunny (tuna)
boquerones	boakayroa**nayss**	whitebait
caballa	kah**bah**lyah	mackerel

calamares	kahlah**mah**rayss	squid
cangrejo	kahn**greh**khoa	crab/crayfish
chipirones	cheepeero**a**nayss	baby squid
cigalas	thee**gah**lahss	Dublin Bay prawns (sea crayfish)
congrio	**koan**gryoa	conger eel
escarcho	ays**kahr**choa	roach
lampresas	lahm**preh**ssahss	lamprey
langosta	lahn**goas**tah	spiny lobster
langostinos	lahngoas**tee**noass	prawns (shrimps)
lenguado	layng**wah**dhoa	sole
merluza	mayr**loo**thah	hake
mero	**meh**roa	seabass
mú.jol	**mook**hoal	mullet
ostras	**os**trahss	oysters
perca	**pehr**kah	perch
percebes	pehr**thay**bhayss	goose barnacles
pescadilla	payskah**dheel**yah	whiting
pez espada	payth ays**pah**dhah	swordfish
pulpitos	pool**pee**toass	baby octopus
pulpo	**pool**poa	octopus
quisquillas	kees**keel**yahss	common prawns (shrimps)
rape	**rah**pay	monkfish
rodaballo	roadhah**bhah**lyoa	turbot
salmón	sahl**mon**	salmon
salmonetes	sahlmoa**nay**tayss	red mullet
sardinas	sahr**dee**nahss	sardines
pequeñas	pay**kay**ñahss	sprats
trucha	**troo**chah	trout
veneras	bay**nay**rah	scallops

You'll want to try the spicy fish and seafood stew called *zarzuela* (thahr**thway**lah)—the pride of Catalonia.

baked	**al horno**	ahl **oar**noa
cured	**en salazón**	ayn sahlah**thon**
deep fried	**a la romana**	ah lah roa**mah**nah
fried	**frito**	**free**toa
grilled	**a la parrilla**	ah lah pahr**reel**yah
marinated	**en escabeche**	ayn ayskahb**bhay**chay
poached	**hervido**	ayr**bee**dhoa
sautéed	**salteado**	sahlteh**ah**dhoa
smoked	**ahumado**	ahoo**mah**dhoa
steamed	**cocido al vapor**	koa**thee**dhoa ahl bah**por**

Meat *Carne*

Although fish and rice dishes predominate, meat also has a place in the cuisine of Spain—especially pork.

I'd like some ...	Quisiera ...	keessyayrah	
beef	**carne de buey**	**kahr**nay day bway	
lamb	**carne de cordero**	**kahr**nay day koar**day**roa	
pork	**carne de cerdo**	**kahr**nay day **thehr**doa	
veal	**carne de ternera**	**kahr**nay day tehr**nay**rah	
biftec	beef**tayk**		beef steak
cabrito	kah**bree**toa		kid
carne picada	**kahr**nay pee**kah**dhah		minced meat
carnero	kahr**nay**roa		mutton
chuletas	choo**lay**tahss		chops
corazón	koarah**thon**		heart
criadillas	kreeahdh**ee**lyahss		sweetbreads
filete	fee**lay**tay		steak
hígado	ee**gah**dhoa		liver
jamón	khah**mon**		ham
lechón	lay**chon**		suck(l)ing pig
morcilla	moar**thee**lyah		black pudding (blood sausage)
paletilla	pahlay**tee**lyah		shank
patas	**pah**tahss		trotters (feet)
pierna	**pyehr**nah		leg
rabo de buey	**rah**bhoa day bway		oxtail
riñones	ree**ñoa**nayss		kidneys
salchichas	sahl**chee**chahss		sausages
sesos	**say**ssoass		brains
solomillo de cerdo	soaloa**mee**lyoa day **thehr**doa		tenderloin of pork
tocino	toa**thee**noa		bacon

callos a la madrileña (**kah**lyoass ah lah mahdree**lay**ñah)	tripe in piquant sauce with spicy pork sausage and tomatoes
cochifrito de cordero (koachee**free**toa day koar**day**roa)	highly seasoned stew of lamb or kid
cochinillo asado (koachee**nee**lyoa ah**ssah**dhoa)	crispy roasted Castillian suck(l)ing pig
empanada gallega (aympah**nah**dhah gah**lyay**gah)	tenderloin of pork, onions and chili peppers in a pie
magras al estilo de Aragón (**mah**grahss ahl ays**tee**loa day ahrah**gon**)	cured ham in tomato sauce

pimientos a la riojana
(peemyayntoass ah lah ryoakhahnah)

sweet peppers stuffed with minced meat

riñones al jerez
(reeñyoanayss ahl khehrayth)

kidneys braised in sherry

baked	**al horno**	ahl oarnoa
boiled	**hervido**	ayrbheedhoa
braised	**estofado**	aystoafahdhhoa
braised in casserole	**en salsa**	ayn sahlssah
fried	**frito**	freetoa
grilled (broiled)	**a la parrilla**	ah lah pahrreelyah
pot roasted	**en su jugo**	ayn soo khoogoa
roast	**asado**	ahssahdhoa
sautéed	**salteado**	sahltehahdhoa
stewed	**estofado**	aystoafahdhoa
underdone (rare)	**poco hecho**	poakoa aychoa
medium	**regular**	rehgoolahr
well-done	**muy hecho**	mwee aychoa

Poultry and game *Aves y carne de caza*

Chicken is prepared in scores of ways in Spain. In the north, rabbit is a favourite dish—sometimes even prepared with chocolate!

I'd like some game.	**Quisiera carne de caza.**	keessyayrah kahrnay day kahthah
What poultry dishes do you have?	**¿Qué tipo de ave tiene usted?**	kay teepoa day ahbhay tyaynay oostaydh
becada	baykahdhah	woodcock
capón	kahpon	capon
codorniz	koadoarneeth	quail
conejo	koanaykhoa	rabbit
conejo de monte	koanaykhoa day moantay	wild rabbit
corzo	koarthoa	deer
faisán	fighssahn	pheasant
gallina	gahlyeenah	hen
ganso	gahnsoa	goose
higaditos de pollo	eegahdheetoass day poalyoa	chicken liver

jabalí	khahbhahlee	wild boar
lavanco	lahbhahnkoa	wild duck
liebre	lyehbray	hare
pato	pahtoa	duck/duckling
pavo	pahbhoa	turkey
perdiz	pehrdeeth	partridge
pichón	peechon	pigeon
pollo	poalyoa	chicken
muslo de pollo	moosloa day poalyoa	chicken leg
pechuga de pollo	paychoogah day poalyoa	breast of chicken
pollo asado	poalyoa ahssahdhoa	roast chicken
pollo a la brasa	poalyoa ah lah brahssah	grilled chicken
venado	baynahdhoa	venison

conejo al ajillo
(koanaykhoa ahl
ahkheelyoa)
rabbit with garlic

menestra de pollo
(maynaystrah day
poalyoa)
casserole of chicken and vegetables

perdices estofadas
(pehrdeethayss
aystoafahdhahss)
partridges served in a white-wine sauce

Sauces *Salsas*

Many meat, fish or vegetable dishes are dressed or braised
in a light, delicate sauce. Here are the names of some well-
known preparations:

salsa allioli
(sahlsah ahlyoalee)
garlic sauce

a la catalana
(ah lah kahtahlahnah)
sauce of tomatoes and green peppers

en escabeche
(ayn ayskahbhaychay)
sweet and sour sauce

salsa romesco
(sahlsah roamayskoa)
green peppers, pimentos, garlic; popular
chilled dressing for fish on the east cost
around Tarragona

a la vasca
(ah lah bahskah)
parsley, peas, garlic; a delicate green dressing for fish in the Basque country

Vegetables *Verduras*

What vegetables do you recommend?	**¿Qué verduras me aconseja?**	kay bayrdoorahss may ahkoansaykhah
I'd prefer a salad.	**Prefiero una ensalada.**	prayfyayroa oonah aynsahlahdah

achicoria	ahcheekoaryah	endive (Am. chicory)
alcachofas	ahlkahchoafahss	artichoke
apio	ahpyoa	celery
arroz	ahrroth	rice
berenjena	bayraynkhaynah	aubergine (eggplant)
berza	bayrthah	cabbage
calabacín	kahlahbhatheen	courgette (zucchini)
cebolla	thayboalyah	onion
champiñones	chahmpeeñoanayss	button mushrooms
chirivías	cheereebheeahss	parsnips
coles de bruselas	koalayss day broossaylahss	Brussels sprouts
coliflor	koleeflor	cauliflower
espárragos	ayspahrrahgoass	asparagus
espinacas	ayspeenahkahss	spinach
garbanzos	gahrbahnthoass	chickpeas
guisantes	geessahntayss	peas
habas	ahbhahss	broad beans
hinojo	eenoakhoa	fennel
judías blancas	khoodheeahss blahnkahss	white beans
judías verdes	khoodheeahss behrdayss	green beans
lechuga	laychoogah	lettuce
lentejas	layntaykhahss	lentils
lombarda	loambahrdah	red cabbage
macedonia de legumbres	mahthaydhoaneeah day laygoombrayss	mixed vegetables
maíz	maheeth	sweet corn
patatas	pahtahtahss	potatoes
pepinillos	paypeeneelyoass	gherkins
pepino	paypeenoa	cucumber
pimientos morrones	peemyayntoass moarroanayss	sweet red peppers
puerros	pwayrroass	leeks
rábanos	rahbhahnoass	radishes
remolacha	raymoalahchah	beetroot
repollo	raypoalyoa	cabbage
setas	saytahss	mushrooms
tomates	toamahtayss	tomatoes
trufas	troofahss	truffles
zanahorias	thahnahoaryahss	carrots

Here's a savoury vegetable dish you're sure to like. It goes well with roast chicken or other roasted and grilled meats:

pisto
(peestoa)

a stew of green peppers, onions, tomatoes and courgettes (zucchini); in Catalonia it's called *samfaina,* and you might also see it referred to as *frito de verduras.*

Herbs and spices *Condimentos y especias*

What is it flavoured with?	¿Con qué está condimentado?	kon kay aystah kondeemayntahdhoa
Is it very spicy?	¿Tiene muchas especias?	tyaynay moochahss ayspaythyahss

ajo	ahkhoa	garlic
albahaca	ahlbahahkah	basil
alcaparra	ahlkahpahrrah	caper
anís	ahneess	aniseed
azafrán	ahthahfrahn	saffron
berro	bayrroa	cress
canela	kahnaylah	cinnamon
cebolleta	thaybhoalyaytah	chive
clavo	klahbhoa	clove
comino	koameenoa	caraway
eneldo	aynayldoa	dill
estragón	ehstrahgon	tarragon
guindilla	geendeelyah	chili pepper
hierbas finas	yayrbahss feenahss	mixture of herbs
hoja de laurel	oakhah day lahoorayl	bay leaf
jengibre	khaynkheebray	ginger
menta	mayntah	mint
mostaza	moastahthah	mustard
nuez moscada	nwayth moaskahdah	nutmeg
orégano	oaraygahnoa	oregano
perejil	payraykheel	parsley
perifollo	payreefoalyoa	chervil
pimentón	peemaynton	chili pepper
pimienta	peemyayntah	pepper
romero	roamayroa	rosemary
sal	sahl	salt
salvia	sahlbyah	sage
tomillo	toameelyoa	thyme
vainilla	bighneelyah	vanilla

Cheese *Queso*

Spanish restaurants seldom have a cheeseboard. Some well-known Spanish cheeses are listed below. Be sure to specify the cheese you'd like, otherwise you might be given imported cheese.

What sort of cheese do you have?	**¿Qué clases de queso tiene?**	kay **klah**ssayss day **kay**ssoa **tyay**nay
A piece of that one, please.	**Un trozo de ése, por favor.**	oon **troat**hoa day **ay**ssay por fa**bhor**

burgos
(**boor**goass)

A soft, creamy cheese named after the province from which it originates

cabrales
(kah**brah**layss)

A tangy, veined goat cheese; its flavour varies, depending upon the mountain region in which it was produced.

mahón
(ma**hon**)

A goat cheese from Menorca in the Balearic Islands

manchego
(mahn**chay**goa)

Produced from ewe's milk, this hard cheese from La Mancha can vary from milky white to golden yellow. The best *manchego* is said to come from Ciudad Real.

perilla
(peh**reel**yah)

A firm, bland cheese made from cow's milk; sometimes known as *teta*

roncal
(ron**kahl**)

A sharp ewe's milk cheese from northern Spain; hand-pressed, salted and smoked, with leathery rind

san simón
(sahn **see**mon)

Similar to *perilla*

villalón
(beelyah**lon**)

A curd cheese made from ewe's milk

blue	**tipo roquefort**	**tee**poa **ro**kehfoart
cream	**cremoso**	kray**moa**ssoa
hard	**duro**	**doo**roa
mild	**suave**	**swah**bhay
ripe	**añejo**	ah**ñay**khoa
soft	**blando**	**blahn**doa
strong	**fuerte**	**fwayr**tay

Fruit *Fruta*

Do you have fresh fruit?	**¿Tiene usted fruta fresca?**	tyaynay oostaydh frootah frehskah
I'd like a (fresh) fruit cocktail.	**Quisiera una ensalada de fruta (fresca).**	keessyayrah oonah aynsahlahdhah day frootah (frehskah)

albaricoques	ahlbahreekoakayss	apricots
almendras	ahlmayndrahss	almonds
arándanos	ahrahndahnoass	blueberries
avellanas	ahbhaylyahnahss	hazelnuts
brevas	braybhahss	blue figs
cacahuetes	kahkahwaytayss	peanuts
castañas	kahstahñahss	chestnuts
cerezas	thayraythahss	cherries
ciruelas	theerwaylahss	plums
ciruelas pasas	theerwaylahss pahssahss	prunes
coco	koakoa	coconut
dátiles	dahteelayss	dates
frambuesas	frahmbwayssahss	raspberries
fresas	frayssahss	strawberries
granadas	grahnahdhahss	pomegranates
grosellas negras	groassaylyahss naygrahss	blackcurrants
grosellas rojas	groassaylyahss roakhahss	redcurrants
higos	eegoass	figs
lima	leemah	lime
limón	leemon	lemon
mandarina	mahndahreenah	tangerine
manzana	mahnthahnah	apple
melocotón	mayloakoaton	peach
melón	maylon	melon
naranja	nahrahnkhah	orange
nueces	nwaythayss	walnuts
nueces variadas	nwaythayss bahryahdhahss	assorted nuts
pasas	pahssahss	raisins
pera	pehrah	pear
piña	peeñah	pineapple
plátano	plahtahnoa	banana
pomelo	poamayloa	grapefruit
ruibarbo	rweebhahrboa	rhubarb
sandía	sahndeeah	watermelon
uvas	oobhahss	grapes
blancas	blahnkahss	green
negras	naygrahss	blue
zarzamoras	thahrthahmoarahss	blackberries

Dessert *Postre*

I'd like a dessert, please.	**Quisiera un postre, por favor.**	keessyayrah oon poastray por fahbhor
Something light, please.	**Algo ligero, por favor.**	ahlgoa leekhayroa por fahbhor
Just a small portion.	**Una ración pequeña.**	oonah rahthyon paykayñah

If you aren't sure what to order, ask the waiter:

What do you have for dessert?	**¿Qué tiene de postre?**	kay tyaynay day poastray
What do you recommend?	**¿Qué me aconseja?**	kay may ahkoansehkhah
arroz con leche	ahrroth kon laychay	rice pudding
bizcocho	beethkoachoa	sponge cake
crema catalana	kraymah kahtahlahnah	caramel pudding
flan	flahn	caramel pudding
fritos	freetoass	fritters
galletas	gahlyaytahss	biscuits (cookies)
helado	aylahdhoa	ice-cream
de chocolate	day choakoalahtay	chocolate
de fresa	day frayssah	strawberry
de limón	day leemon	lemon
de moka	day moakah	mocha
de vainilla	day bighneelyah	vanilla
mantecado	mahntehkahdhoa	enriched ice-cream
mazapán	mahthahpahn	marzipan
melocotón en almíbar	mayloakoaton ayn ahlmeebhahr	peaches in syrup
membrillo	maymbreelyoa	quince paste
merengue	mayrayngay	meringue
nata batida	nahtah bahteedhah	whipped cream
pastas	pahstahss	biscuits (cookies)
pastel	pahstayl	cake
pastel de queso	pahstayl day kayssoa	cheesecake
tarta de almendras	tahrtah day ahlmayndrahss	almond tart
tarta de manzana	tahrtah day mahnthahnah	apple tart
tarta de moka	tahrtah day moakah	mocha cake
tarta helada	tahrtah aylahdhah	ice-cream cake
tarteletas	tahrtaylaytahss	small tarts
tortitas	torteetahss	waffles
turrón	toorron	nougat

Aperitifs *Aperitivos*

For most Spaniards, a before-dinner *vermut* (behr**moot**—vermouth) or *jerez* (kheh**rayss**—sherry) is just as important as our cocktail or highball. Vermouth is rarely drunk neat (straight) but usually on the rocks or with seltzer water. Some Spaniards, on the other hand, content themselves with a glass of the local wine. You'll probably be given a dish of olives or nuts to nibble on with your sherry or vermouth. Or in a bar specializing in *tapas* (see page 63), you can order various snacks.

Without question, the country's most renowned drink is its sherry. Like marsala, madeira and port wine, sherry has a bit of alcohol or brandy added to it—to "fortify" it—during the fermentation process.

Sherry was the first fortified wine to become popular in England. Back in Shakespeare's day it was called *sack* or *sherris sack*. *Sack* was derived from the Spanish *sacar* (to export) while the English wrote *Sherris* for the name of the town, *Jerez*, where sherry wine originated. Sherry can be divided into two groups:

fino (feenoa)	These are the pale, dry sherries which make good aperitifs. The Spaniards themselves are especially fond of *amontillado* and *manzanilla*. Some of the best *finos* are *Tío Pepe* and *La Ina*.
oloroso (oloarossoa)	These are the heavier, darker sherries which are sweetened before being bottled. They're fine after-dinner drinks. One exception is *amoroso* which is medium dry. Brown and cream sherries are full-bodied and slightly less fragrant than *finos*.

> **¡SALUD!**
> (sah**loodh**)
> YOUR HEALTH/CHEERS!

Wine   *Vino*

Though Spain is one of the world's principal producers of wine, the nation's *vino*—with the exception of sherry—is among the most unpredictable in terms of quality. Using outmoded techniques in both cultivating grapes and fermenting wine, the wine of a specific vineyard can vary considerably from one year to the next.

Some restaurants list their wine in a corner of the menu while others have them posted on a wall. As much of the country's wine doesn't travel well, don't expect an *hostería* to offer more than a few types of wine. Most of the wine must be drunk young so don't look too hard for vintage labels.

A government board permits some vintners to include *denominación de origen* on a bottle as an indication of the wine's quality. However, this designation is unreliable.

Uncontestably, Spain's best wine comes from Rioja, a region of Old Castile of which Logroño is the centre. Winemakers there add *garantía de origen* to wine they feel is of above average quality, and this term is a respected one. But other regions—notably Andalusia, Aragon, Catalonia, Navarre, New Castile, Toledo and Valdepeñas—produce quality wine, too. This is your opportunity to sample local wine, some of which is surprisingly good.

The Penedés region near Barcelona is a major source of the world's best selling white sparkling wine, unofficially called Spanish *champán*.

The general rule of thumb is that white wine goes well with fish and light meats while red wine is reserved for dark meats. A good rosé goes with almost anything. The chart on the following page will help you to choose your wine if you want to do some serious wine-tasting.

If you need help in choosing a wine, don't hesitate to ask the waiter. He'll often suggest a bottle of local renown, perhaps from the *patrón*'s own wine cellar.

Type of wine	Examples	Accompanies
sweet white wine	A *moscatel*	desserts, custards, cakes, rice puddings, biscuits (cookies)
light, dry white wine	Much local white wine falls into this category; much of the white wine of Rioja, like *Monopole*	fish, seafood, *tapas*, cold meat, boiled meat, egg dishes like *tortillas*
rosé	*López de Heredia, Marqués de Murrieta*	goes with almost anything but especially cold dishes, eggs, pork, lamb, *paella*
light-bodied red wine	Many local wines come into this group; much of the Rioja red wine classifies, including *Viña Pomal* or the Catalonian *Priorato Reserva especial*	roast chicken, turkey, veal, lamb, beef fillet, ham, liver, quail, pheasant, stews, steaks, *zarzuela, paella, tortillas*
full-bodied red wine	sometimes a red wine of Tarragone, Alicante or Rioja can be classed in this category	duck, goose, kidneys, most game, tangy cheese like *cabrales*—in short, any strong-flavoured preparations
sparkling wine	*Champán or Cordoniu*	goes well with desserts and custards; if it's really dry you might try some as an aperitif or with shellfish, nuts, dried fruit

May I please have the wine list?	¿Puedo ver la carta de vinos, por favor?	pwaydhoa behr lah kahrtah day beenoass por fahbhor
I'd like ... of ...	Quisiera ... de ...	keessyayrah ... day
a carafe	una garrafa	oonah gahrrahfah
a bottle	una botella	oonah boataylyah
half bottle	media botella	maydhyah boataylyah
a glass	un vaso	oon bahssoa
a small glass	un chato	oon chahtoa
a litre	un litro	oon leetroa
I want a bottle of white/red wine.	Quiero una botella de vino blanco/vino tinto.	kyayroa oonah boataylyah day beenoa blahnkoa/ beenoa teentoa

If you enjoyed the wine, you may want to say:

| Please bring me another ... | Tráigame otro/ otra ..., por favor. | trighgahmay oatroa/oatrah ... por fahbhor |
| Where does this wine come from? | ¿De dónde viene este vino? | day doanday byaynay aystay beenoa |

red	tinto	teentoa
white	blanco	blahnkoa
rosé	rosé	rosay
dry	seco	saykoa
full-bodied	de cuerpo	day kwehrpoa
light	liviano	leebhyahnoa
sparkling	espumoso	ayspoomoassoa
sweet	dulce	doolthay
very dry	muy seco	mwee saykoa

Sangria

Sangría (sahn**gree**ah) is an iced, hot-weather drink that combines red wine, brandy and mineral water, with fruit juice, sliced oranges and other fruit and sugar to taste. Beware: it can pack a punch, especially when laced with rough brandy, but you can always dilute *sangría* with soda water and plenty of ice.

Beer *Cerveza*

Spanish beer, generally served cool, is good and cheap. Try *Aguila especial* or *San Miguel especial*.

A beer, please.	**Una cerveza, por favor.**	oonah thayr**bhay**thah por fah**bhor**
light beer	**cerveza rubia**	thayr**bhay**thah roo**bhyah**
dark beer	**cerveza negra**	thayr**bhay**than **nay**grah
foreign beer	**cerveza extranjera**	thayr**bhay**thah aykstrahn-**khay**rah

Spirits and liqueurs *Licores*

If you'd like to sip a brandy after dinner, try a Spanish *coñac* like *Fundador* (foondah**dhor**) or *Carlos III* (**kahr**loass tehr**thay**roa). The Spaniards are also noted for their delicious liqueurs such as *Licor 43, Calisay,* or *Aromas de Montserrat.*

glass	**un vaso**	oon **bah**ssoa
bottle	**una botella**	oonah boa**tay**lyah
double (a double shot)	**doble**	**doa**blay
neat (straight)	**solo**	**soa**loa
on the rocks	**con hielo**	kon **yay**loa

I'd like a glass of ..., please.	**Quisiera un vaso de ..., por favor.**	kee**ssyay**rah oon **bah**ssoa day ... por fah**bhor**
Are there any local specialities?	**¿Tiene alguna especialidad local?**	**tyay**nay ahl**goo**nah ayspay-thyah**lee**dhadh loa**kahl**
Please bring me a ... of ...	**Tráigame un/una ... de ..., por favor.**	**trigh**gahmay oon/oonah ... day ... por fah**bhor**
aniseed liqueur	**anís**	ah**neess**
bourbon	**whisky americano**	**wee**skee ahmayree**kah**noa
brandy	**coñac**	koa**ñahk**
gin	**ginebra**	khee**nay**brah
gin-fizz	**ginebra con limón**	khee**nay**brah kon lee**mon**

gin and tonic	ginebra con tónica	kheenaybrah kon toaneekah
liqueur	licor	leekor
port	oporto	oaportoa
rum	ron	ron
rum coke	Cuba libre	koobhah leebray
Scotch	whisky escocés	weeskee ayskoathayss
sherry	jerez	khehrayss
vermouth	vermut	behrmoot
vodka	vodka	bodkah
whisky	whisky	weeskee
whisky and soda	whisky con soda	weeskee kon soadhah

Nonalcoholic drinks	*Bebidas sin alcohol*	
I'd like a/an ...	**Quisiera ...**	keessyayrah
(hot) chocolate	**un chocolate (caliente)**	oon choakoalahtay (kahlyayntay)
coffee	**un café**	oon kahfay
cup of coffee	**una taza de café**	oonah tahthah day kahfay
black coffee	**café solo**	kahfay soaloa
white coffee	**café con leche**	kahfay kon laychay
coffee with cream	**café con crema**	kahfay kon kraymah
espresso coffee	**café exprés**	kahfay ayksprayss
strong coffee	**un corto**	oon koartoa
caffein-free coffee	**café descafeinado**	kahfay dayskahfayeenahdhoa
fruit juice	**un jugo de fruta**	oon khoogoa day frootah
apple/grapefruit	**manzana/pomelo**	mahnthahnah/poamehloa
lemon/orange	**limón/naranja**	leemon/nahrahnkhah
pineapple/tomato	**piña/tomate**	peeñah/toamahtay
lemonade	**una limonada**	oonah leemoanahdhah
milk	**leche**	laychay
milkshake	**un batido**	oon bahteedhoa
mineral water	**agua mineral**	ahgwah meenayrahl
orangeade	**una naranjada**	oonah nahrahnkhahdhah
soda water	**una soda**	oonah soadhah
tea	**un té**	oon tay
with milk/lemon	**con leche/con limón**	kon laychay/kon leemon
iced tea	**un té helado**	oon tay aylahdhoa
tonic water	**una tónica**	oonah toaneekah
(iced) water	**agua (helada)**	ahgwah (aylahdhah)

Complaints *Reclamaciones*

That's not what I ordered.	**Esto no es lo que he pedido.**	aystoa noa ayss loa kay ay peh**dheed**hoa
I asked for ...	**He pedido ...**	ay peh**dheed**hoa
I asked for a small portion (for the child).	**He pedido una porción pequeña (para el niño).**	ay peh**dheed**hoa **oonah** por**thyon** pay**kayñah** (**pahrah** ayl nee**ñoa**)
There must be some mistake.	**Debe haber algún error.**	day**bhay** ah**bhayr** ahl**goon** ay**rroar**
May I change this?	**¿Puede cambiarme eso?**	**pway**dhay kahm**byahr**may **ayss**oa
The meat is ...	**Esta carne está ...**	**aystah kahrnay aystah**
overdone	**demasiado hecha**	daymah**ssyahd**hoa **ehchah**
underdone	**poco hecha**	**poakoa ehchah**
too rare	**demasiado cruda**	daymah**ssyahd**hoa **kroodhah**
too tough	**demasiado dura**	daymah**ssyahd**hoa **doorah**
This is too ...	**Esto está ...**	**aystoa aystah**
bitter/salty/sweet	**amargo/salado/dulce**	ah**mahr**goa/sah**lahd**hoa/**dool**thay
The food is cold.	**La comida está fría.**	lah koa**meed**hah **aystah free**ah
This isn't fresh.	**Esto no está fresco.**	**aystoa** noa **aystah frays**koa
What's taking you so long?	**¿Por qué se demora tanto?**	por kay say day**moar**ah **tahn**toa
Where are our drinks?	**¿Dónde están nuestras bebidas?**	**doan**day ays**tahn nways**trahss bay**bheed**hahss
There's a plate/glass missing.	**Falta un plato/vaso.**	**fahl**tah oon **plah**toa/**bahs**soa
The wine is too cold.	**El vino está demasiado frío.**	ayl **been**oa **aystah** daymah**ssyahd**hoa **free**oa
The wine is corked.	**El vino sabe al corcho.**	ayl **been**oa **sahb**hay ahl **kor**choa
This isn't clean.	**Esto no está limpio.**	**aystoa** noa **aystah leem**pyoa
Would you ask the head waiter to come over?	**¿Quiere usted decirle al jefe que venga?**	**kyay**ray oos**taydh** day**theer**lay ahl **kheh**fay kay **bayn**gah

The bill (check) *La cuenta*

The service charge (*el servicio*—ayl sehr**beet**hyoa) is generally included. On some set menus you'll notice that wine is included in the price *(vino incluido)*.

I'd like to pay.	**Quisiera pagar.**	keess**yay**rah pah**gahr**
We'd like to pay separately.	**Quisiéramos pagar separadamente.**	keess**yay**rahmoass pah**gahr** saypahrahdhah**mayn**tay
I think you made a mistake in this bill.	**Creo que se ha equivocado usted en esta cuenta.**	**kreh**oa kay say ah aykee-bhoa**kah**dhoa oos**taydh** ayn **ays**tah **kwayn**tah
What's this amount for?	**¿Para qué es esta cantidad?**	**pah**rah kay ayss **ays**tah kahntee**dhahdh**
Is service included?	**¿Está el servicio incluido?**	ays**tah** ayl sehr**beet**hyoa eenkloo**eedh**oa
Is the cover charge included?	**¿Está el cubierto incluido?**	ays**tah** ayl koo**byehr**toa eenkloo**eedh**oa
Is everything included?	**¿Está todo incluido?**	ays**tah** **toadh**oa eenkloo-**eedh**oa
Do you accept traveller's cheques?	**¿Acepta usted cheques de viajero?**	ahs**hayp**tah oos**taydh** chay-kayss day byah**khay**roa
Do you accept this credit card?	**¿Acepta esta tarjeta de crédito?**	ahs**hayp**tah **ays**tah tahr-**khay**tah day kray**dhee**toa
Thank you, this is for you.	**Gracias, esto es para usted.**	**grah**thyahss **ays**toa ayss **pah**rah oos**taydh**
That was a very good meal.	**Ha sido una comida excelente.**	ah **seedh**oa **oo**nah koa**meedh**ah aykthay-**layn**tay
We enjoyed it, thank you.	**Nos ha gustado, gracias.**	noss ah goos**tahdh**oa **grah**thyahss

---

SERVICIO INCLUIDO
SERVICE INCLUDED

TIPPING, see inside back-cover

Snacks – Picnic   *Tentempiés – Meriendas*

Tapas (**tah**pahss) are snacks, served with drinks in cafés and
tapa bars. The variety is enormous. A *tapa* can be anything
that tastes good and fits on a cocktail stick: smoked mountain
ham, spicy sausages, cheese, olives, sardines, mushrooms,
mussels, squid, octopus, meat balls, fried fish, plus sauces
and exotic-looking specialities of the house. *Una tapa* is
a mouthful, *una ración* is half a plateful, and *una porción* a
generous amount.

I'll have one of those, please.	**Déme uno de ésos, por favor.**	daymay oonoa day ayssoass por fahbhor
Give me two of these and one of those.	**Déme dos de éstos y uno de ésos, por favor.**	daymay doss day aystoass ee oonoa day ayssoass por fahbhor
to the left	**a la izquierda**	ah lah eethkyayrdah
to the right	**a la derecha**	ah lah dayraychah
above	**encima**	ayntheemah
below	**debajo**	daybhahkhoa
Please give me a/an/some ...	**Déme ... por favor.**	daymay ... por fahbhor
It's to take away.	**Es para llevar.**	ayss pahrah lyaybhahr
How much is that?	**¿Cuánto es?**	kwahntoa ayss

Here's a basic list of food and drinks that might come in
useful for a light meal or when shopping for a picnic.

apples	**manzanas**	mahnthahnahss
bananas	**unos plátanos**	oonoass plahtahnoass
biscuits (Br.)	**unas galletas**	oonahss gahlyaytahss
bread	**pan**	pahn
butter	**mantequilla**	mahntaykeelyah
cake	**unos bollos/ pasteles**	oonoass boalyoass/ pahstaylayss
candy	**unos caramelos**	oonoass kahrahmayloass
cheese	**queso**	kayssoa
chicken	**pollo**	poalyoa
half a roasted chicken	**medio pollo asado**	maydhyoa poalyoa ahssahdhoa
chips (Am.)	**patatas fritas/chips**	pahtahtahss freetahss
chips (Br.)	**patatas fritas**	pahtahtahss freetahss
chocolate	**chocolate**	choakoalahtay

coffee	café	kahfay
cold cuts	unos fiambres	oonoass fyahmbrayss
cookies	unas galletas	oonahss gahlyaytahss
crackers	unas galletas saladas	oonahss gahlyaytahss sahlahdhahss
cream	nata	nahtah
crisps (Br.)	patatas fritas/chips	pahtahtahss freetahss
cucumber	un pepino	oon paypeenoa
eggs	huevos	waybhoass
french fries	patatas fritas	pahtahtahss freetahss
fried eggs	huevos fritos	waybhoass freetoass
fried fish	pescado frito	payskahdhoa freetoa
gherkins	unos cohombrillos	oonoass kombreelyoass
grapes	unas uvas	oonahss oobhahss
ham	jamón	khahmon
ham and eggs	jamón y huevos	khahmon ee waybhoass
ham sandwich	un bocadillo de jamón	oon boakahdheelyoa day khahmon
ketchup	salsa de tomate	sahlsah day toamahtay
hamburger	una hamburguesa	oonah ahmboorgayssah
ice-cream	helado	aylahdhoa
lemons	unos limones	oonoass leemoanayss
lettuce	una lechuga	oonah laychoogah
melon	melón	maylon
milk	leche	laychay
mustard	mostaza	moastahthah
oranges	naranjas	nahrahnkhahss
pastry	pasteles	pahstaylayss
pâté	paté	pahtay
pepper	pimienta	peemyayntah
pickles	unos pepinillos	oonoass paypeeneelyoass
potatoes	unas patatas	oonahss pahtahtahss
rolls	unos panecillos	oonoass pahnaytheelyoass
salad	una ensalada	oonah aynsahlahdhah
salami	salchichón	sahlcheechon
salt	sal	sahl
sandwich	un bocadillo	oon boakahdheelyoa
sausages	unas salchichas	oonahss sahlcheechahss
spaghetti	espaguetis	ayspahgayteess
sugar	azúcar	ahthookahr
sweetener	un edulcorante	oon aydoolkoarahntay
sweets	unos caramelos	oonoass kahrahmayloass
tea	té	tay
tomatoes	unos tomates	oonoass toamahtayss
toast	unas tostadas	oonahss toastahdhahss
yoghurt	un yogur	oon yoagoor

Travelling around

Plane *Avión*

Is there a flight to Madrid?	**¿Hay algún vuelo a Madrid?**	igh ahl**goon** b**way**loa ah mah**dreedh**
Is it a nonstop flight?	**¿Es un vuelo sin escalas?**	ayss oon b**way**loa seen ays**kah**lahss
Do I have to change planes?	**¿Tengo que cambiar de avión?**	**tayn**goa kay kahmb**yahr** day ahb**hyon**
Can I make a connection to Alicante?	**¿Puedo hacer conexión con un vuelo a Alicante?**	p**way**dhoa ah**thayr** koanayk**syon** kon oon b**way**loa ah ahleek**ahn**tay
I'd like a ticket to London.	**Quisiera un billete para Londres.**	kees**say**rah oon beel**yay**tay **pah**rah **lon**drayss
What's the fare to París?	**¿Cuál es la tarifa a París?**	kwahl ayss lah tah**ree**fah ah pah**reess**
single (one-way)	**ida**	**ee**dhah
return (roundtrip)	**ida y vuelta**	**ee**dhah ee b**weh**ltah
What time does the plane take off?	**¿A qué hora despega el avión?**	ah kay **oa**rah days**pay**gah ayl ahb**hyon**
What time do I have to check in?	**¿A qué hora debo presentarme?**	ah kay **oa**rah **day**bhoa prayssaynt**ahr**may
Is there a bus to the airport?	**¿Hay un autobús que va al aeropuerto?**	igh oon owtoab**hooss** kay bah ahl ahehroap**wayr**toa
What's the flight number?	**¿Cuál es el número del vuelo?**	kwahl ayss ayl **noo**mayroa day b**way**loa
At what time do we arrive?	**¿A qué hora llegaremos?**	ah kay **oa**rah lyaygah**ray**moass
I'd like to … my reservation.	**Quisiera … mi reserva.**	kees**say**rah … mee rays**say**rbah
cancel	**anular**	ahnool**ahr**
change	**cambiar**	kahmb**yahr**
confirm	**confirmar**	konfeer**mahr**

LLEGADA	**SALIDA**
ARRIVAL	DEPARTURE

Train *Tren*

A nationalized company, the Red Nacional de los Ferro-carriles Españoles (R.E.N.F.E.—**rayn**fay) handles all rail services. While local trains are very slow, stopping at almost all stations, long-distance services, especially the *Talgo* and *Ter,* are fast and reasonably punctual. First-class coaches are comfortable; second-class, adequate. There is also a third class on some trains—not very comfortable, but cheap. Tickets can be purchased at travel agencies as well as at railway stations. Seat reservations are recommended.

Types of trains *Clases de trenes*

Talgo, Ter (**tahl**goa, tehr)	Express trains; first and second class with surcharge
Expreso, Rápido (ayks**prayss**oa, rah-**peed**hoa)	Direct trains; stop at all main towns
Omnibus, Tranvía, Automotor (**omneeb**hooss, trahn-**wee**ah, owtoamoa**toor**)	Local trains (frequent stops)

PRIMERA CLASE FIRST CLASS	SEGUNDA CLASE SECOND CLASS

Coche comedor (**koa**chay koamay**dhor**)	Dining-car
Coche cama (**koa**chay **kah**mah)	Sleeping-car; compartments with wash basins and 1, 2 or 3 berths.
Litera (lee**tay**rah)	Berths (with sheets, blankets and pillows)
Furgón de equipajes (foor**gon** day aykee-**pah**khayss)	Luggage van (baggage car); only registered luggage permitted

To the railway station *A la estación*

Where's the railway station?	¿Dónde está la estación de ferrocarril?	doanday aystah lah aystahthyon day fehrrokahrreel
Taxi, please!	¡Taxi! por favor.	tahksee por fahbhor
Take me to the railway station.	Lléveme a la estación de ferrocarril.	lyaybhaymay ah lah aystahthyon day fehrrokahrreel
What's the fare?	¿Cuál es la tarifa?	kwahl ayss lah tahreefah

| INFORMACION TURISTICA | TOURIST INFORMATION |
| CAMBIO DE MONEDA | CURRENCY EXCHANGE |

Where's ...? *¿Dónde está ...?*

Where is/are the ...?	¿Dónde está/ están ...?	doanday aystah/aystahn
booking office	la oficina de reservas	lah oafeetheenah day rayssayrbahss
buffet	el buffet	ayl boofay
currency-exchange office	la oficina de cambio de moneda	lah oafeetheenah day kahmbyoa day moanaydhah
information office	la oficina de información	lah oafeetheenah day eenformahthyon
left-luggage office (baggage check)	la oficina de equipaje	lah oafeetheenah day aykeepahkhay
lost property (lost and found) office	la oficina de objetos perdidos	lah oafeetheenah day obkhaytoass pehrdeedhoass
luggage lockers	la consigna automatica	lah konseegnah owtoamahteekah
newsstand	el quiosco de periódicos	ayl kyoskoa day payryodheekoass
platform 7	el andén 7	ayl ahndayn 7
restaurant	el restaurante	ayl raystowrahntay
ticket office	la taquilla	lah tahkeelyah
toilets	los servicios	loss sehrbeethyoass
waiting room	la sala de espera	lah sahlah day ayspayrah

TAXI, see page 21

Inquiries *Información*

What time does the ... train for Granada leave?	¿A qué hora sale el ... tren para Granada?	ah kay oarah sahlay ayl ... trayn pahrah grahnahdhah
first/last/next	primer/último/ próximo	preemayr/oolteemoa/ prokseemoa
Is it a direct train?	¿Es un tren directo?	ayss oon trayn deerehktoa
Is there a connection to ...?	¿Hay transbordo en ...?	igh trahnsbordoa ayn
Do I have to change trains?	¿Tengo que cambiar de tren?	tayngoa kay kahmbyahr day trayn
Is there sufficient time to change?	¿Hay tiempo suficiente para transbordar?	igh tyaympoa soofeethyayntay pahrah trahnsbordahr
Will the train leave on time?	¿Saldrá el tren a su hora?	sahldrah ayl trayn ah soo oarah
What time does the train arrive at Santander?	¿A qué lora llega el tren a Santander?	ah kay oarah lyaygah ayl trayn ah sahntahndayr
Is there a sleeping-car/dining-car on the train?	¿Hay coche cama/ coche restaurante en el tren?	igh koachay kahmah/ koachay raystowrahntay ayn ayl trayn
Does the train stop at Gerona?	¿Para el tren en Gerona?	pahrah ayl trayn ayn khayroanah
What platform does the train for Barcelona leave from?	¿De qué andén sale el tren para Barcelona?	day kay ahndayn sahlay ayl trayn pahrah bahrthayloanah
What platform does the train from ... arrive at?	¿A qué andén llega el tren de ...?	ah kay ahndayn lyaygah ayl trayn day
I'd like to buy a timetable.	Quisiera comprar una guía de ferrocarriles.	keessyayrah komprahr oonah geeah day fehrrokahrreelayss

ENTRADA	ENTRANCE
SALIDA	EXIT
A LOS ANDENES	TO THE PLATFORMS

Es un tren directo.	It's a through train.
Usted tiene que cambiar de tren en ...	You have to change at ...
Cambie de tren en ... y tome un tren de cercanías.	Change at ... and get a local train.
El andén ... está ...	Platform ... is ...
allí/arriba	over there/upstairs
a la izquierda/a la derecha	on the left/on the right
Hay un tren para Barcelona a las ...	There's a train to Barcelona at ...
Su tren sale del andén ...	Your train will leave from platform ...
Habrá una demora de ... minutos.	There'll be a delay of ... minutes.
Primera clase está al frente/ en medio/al final.	First class is in the front/ in the middle/at the end.

Tickets *Billetes*

I want a ticket to Bilbao.	**Quiero un billete para Bilbao.**	kyayroa oon beelyaytay pahrah beelbahoa
single (one-way)	**ida**	eedhah
return (roundtrip)	**ida y vuelta**	eedhah ee bwehltah
first class	**primera clase**	preemayrah klahssay
second class	**segunda clase**	saygoondah klahssay
half price	**media tarifa**	maydyah tahreefah
with surcharge for Talgo/Ter	**con suplemento para el Talgo/Ter**	kon sooplaymayntoa pahrah ayl tahlgoa/tehr

Reservation *Reserva*

I want to book a ...	**Quiero reservar ...**	kyayroa rayssayrbahr
seat by the window	**un asiento al lado de la ventana**	oon ahssyayntoa ahl lahdhoa day lah bayntahnah
smoking/ non-smoking	**fumadores/ no fumadores**	foomahdhorayss/ noa foomahdhorayss

berth	una litera	oonah leetayrah
upper	superior	soopayryor
middle	media	maydhyah
lower	inferior	eenfayryor
berth in the sleeping car	una litera en el coche cama	oonah leetayrah ayn ayl koachay kahmah
How much does it cost?	¿Cuánto cuesta?	kwahntoa kwaystah

All aboard   ¡Al tren!

Is this the right platform for the train to Paris?	¿Es éste el andén del tren para París?	ayss aystay ayl ahndayn dayl trayn pahrah pahreess
Is this the train to Madrid?	¿Es éste el tren para Madrid?	ayss aystay ayl trayn pahrah mahdreedh
Excuse me. May I get by?	Perdóneme. ¿Puedo pasar?	pehrdoanaymay. pwaydhoa pahssahr
Is this seat taken?	¿Está occupado este asiento?	aystah oakoopahdhoa aystay ahssyayntoa
Do you mind if I smoke?	¿Le importa si fumo?	lay eempoartah see foomoa

| FUMADORES | NO FUMADORES |
| SMOKER | NONSMOKER |

I think that's my seat.	Creo que ése es mi asiento.	krayoa kay ayssay ayss mee ahssyayntoa
Would you let me know before we get to Valencia?	¿Me avisaría antes de llegar a Valencia?	may ahbheessahreeah ahntayss day lyaygahr ah bahlaynthyah
What station is this?	¿Qué estación es ésta?	kay aystahthyon ayss aystah
How long does the train stop here?	¿Cuánto tiempo para el tren aquí?	kwahntoa tyaympoa pahrah ayl trayn ahkee
When do we get to Barcelona?	¿Cuándo llegamos a Barcelona?	kwahndoa lyaygahmoass ah bahrthayloanah

Sleeping *Durmiendo*

Are there any free compartments in the sleeping-car?	**¿Hay un departamento libre en el coche cama?**	igh oon daypahrtah-**maynto lee**bray ayn ayl koachay **kah**mah
Where's the sleeping-car?	**¿Dónde está el coche cama?**	doanday aystah ayl koachay **kah**mah
Where's my berth?	**¿Dónde está mi litera?**	doanday aystah mee lee**tay**rah
Would you make up our berths?	**¿Nos podrá hacer usted la litera?**	noss poadrah ahthayr oostaydh lah leetayrah
Would you call me at 7 o'clock?	**¿Me podrá llamar usted a las 7?**	may poadrah lyah**mahr** oostaydh ah lahss 7
Would you bring me some coffee in the morning?	**¿Me podrá traer usted café por la mañana?**	may poadrah trahehr oostaydh kahfay por lah mahñahnah

---

FACTURACION
REGISTERING (CHECKING) BAGGAGE

Baggage and porters *Equipaje y mozos*

Where's the left-luggage office (baggage check)?	**¿Dónde está la oficina de equipaje?**	doanday aystah lah oafee-theenah day aykeepahkhay
Where are the luggage lockers?	**¿Dónde está la consigna automática?**	doanday aystah la konseegnah owtoamahteekah
I'd like to leave my luggage, please.	**Quisiera dejar mi equipaje, por favor.**	keessyayrah daykhahr mee aykeepahkhay por fahbhor
I'd like to register (check) my luggage, please.	**Quisiera facturar mi equipaje, por favor.**	keessyayrah fahktoorahr mee aykeepahkhay por fahbhor
Where are the luggage trolleys (carts)?	**¿Dónde están los carritos de equipaje?**	doanday aystahn loss kahrreetoss day aykeepahkhay
Porter!	**¡Mozo!**	moathoa
Can you help me with my luggage?	**¿Puede usted ayudarme con mi equipaje?**	pwaydhay oostaydh ahyoodhahrmay kon mee aykeepahkhay

PORTERS, see also page 18

Coach (long-distance bus) *Autocar*

Travel by coach is good if you want to visit out-of-the-way places. There's no cross-country bus line. Most buses only serve towns and villages within a region or province, or they link the provincial capital with Madrid if there's no rail service.

Note: Most of the phrases on the previous pages can be used or adapted for bus travel.

Bus *Autobús*

In most buses, you pay as you enter. In some rural buses, you may find the driver also acting as the conductor. In major cities it may be worthwhile to get a pass or a booklet of tickets.

I'd like a pass/ booklets of tickets.	**Quisiera un pase/ taco de billetes.**	keessyayrah oon pahssay/ tahkoa day beelyaytayss
Where can I get a bus to the beach?	**¿Dónde puedo tomar un autobús para la playa?**	doanday pwaydhoa toamahr oon owtoabhooss pahrah lah plahyah
Which bus do I take for the university?	**¿Qué autobús debo tomar para la Universidad?**	kay owtoabhooss daybhoa toamahr pahrah lah ooneebhehrseedhahdh
Where's the ...?	**¿Dónde está ...?**	doanday aystah
bus stop	**la parada de autobuses**	lah pahrahdhah day owtoabhoossayss
terminus	**la terminal**	lah tehrmeenahl
When is the ... bus to the Prado?	**¿A qué hora sale el ... autobús para El Prado?**	ah kay oarah sahlay ayl ... owtoabhooss pahrah ayl prahdhoa
first/last/next	**primer/último/ próximo**	preemayr/oolteemoa/ prokseemoa
How often do the buses to the town centre run?	**¿Cada cuánto pasan los autobuses para el centro?**	kahdhah kwahntoa pahssahn loss owtoabhoossayss pahrah ayl thayntroa
How much is the fare to ...?	**¿Cuánto es la tarifa para ...?**	kwahntoa ayss lah tahreefah pahrah

How many bus stops are there to ...?	¿Cuántas paradas de autobús hay hasta ...?	kwahntahss pahrahdhahss day owtoabhooss igh ahstah
Do I have to change buses?	¿Tengo que cambiar de autobús?	tayngoa kay kahmbyahr day owtoabhooss
How long does the journey (trip) take?	¿Cuánto dura el viaje?	kwahntoa doorah ayl byahkhay
Will you tell me when to get off?	¿Me diría usted cuándo tengo que apearme?	may deereeah oostaydh kwahndoa tayngoa kay ahpayahrmay
I want to get off at the cathedral.	Quiero apearme en la Catedral.	kyayroa ahpayahrmay ayn lah kahtaydrahl
Please let me off at the next stop.	Por favor, pare en la próxima parada.	por fahbhor pahray ayn lah prokseemah pahrahdhah

---

PARADA DE AUTOBUS REGULAR BUS STOP
SOLO PARA A PETICION STOPS ON REQUEST

Underground (subway) *Estación de metro*

Madrid and Barcelona have extensive underground (subway) networks. The fare is the same irrespective of the distance. The underground is open from 5 a.m. to 11 p.m.

Where's the nearest underground station?	¿Dónde está la estación de metro más cercana?	doanday aystah lah aystahthyon day maytroa mahss thehrkahnah
Does this train go to ...?	¿Va este tren a ...?	bah aystay trayn ah
Where do I change for ...?	¿Dónde tengo que hacer transbordo para ...?	doanday tayngoa kay ahthayr trahnsbordao pahrah
Which line do I take?	¿Qué línea tengo que coger?	kay leenayah tayngoa kay koakhayr
Is the next station ...?	¿Es ... la próxima estación?	ayss ... lah prokseemah aystahthyon

Boat service *Barcos*

When does the next/ last boat for ... leave?	¿Cuándo sale el próximo/último barco para ...?	kwahndoa sahlay ayl prokseemoa/oolteemoa bahrkoa pahrah
Where's the embarkation point?	¿Dónde está el lugar de embarco?	doanday aystah ayl loogahr day aymbahrkoa
How long does the crossing take?	¿Cuánto dura la travesía?	kwahntoa doorah lah trahbaysseeah
At which ports do we stop?	¿En qué puertos nos detenemos?	ayn kay pwaytoass noass daytaynaymoass
I'd like to take a cruise.	Quisiera tomar un crucero.	keessyayrah toamahr oon kroothayroa
boat	el barco	ayl bahrkoa
cabin single/double	el camarote sencillo/doble	ayl kahmahroatay sayntheelyoa/doablay
cruise	el crucero	ayl kroothayroa
deck	la cubierta	lah koobhyayrtah
ferry	el transbordador	ayl trahnsboardahdhoar
hovercraft	el aerodeslizador	ayl ahayroadhaysleethahdhoar
hydrofoil	el hidroplano	ayl eedroaplahnoa
life belt/boat	el cinturón/bote salvavidas	ayl theentooron/boatay sahlbahbheedhahss
port	el puerto	ayl pwayrtoa
ship	la embarcación	lah aymbahrkahthyon

Other means of transport *Otros medios de transporte*

bicycle	la bicicleta	lah beetheeklaytah
cable car	el funicular	ayl fooneekoolahr
car	el coche	ayl koachay
helicopter	el helicóptero	ayl ayleekoptayroa
moped	el velomotor	ayl bayloamoatoar
motorbike	la motocicleta	lah moatoatheeklaytah
scooter	el escúter	ayl ayskootayr

Or perhaps you prefer:

to hitchhike	hacer auto-stop	ahthayr owtoa-stop
to ride	montar a caballo	moantahr ah kahbhahlyoa
to walk	caminar	kahmeenahr

Car *El coche*

Spain's expanding motorway (expressway) network is excellently engineered, but rather expensive tolls are charged. Main roads are adequate to very good. Unclassified country roads can be in a poor driving condition. Wearing of the seat belt *(el cinturón de seguridad)* is compulsory.

Filling station *Gasolinera*

Give me ... litres of petrol (gasoline).	Déme ... litros de gasolina.	daymay ... leetroass day gahssoaleenah
Full tank, please.	Llénelo, por favor.	lyaynayloa por fahbhor
super (premium)/ normal/unleaded petrol/diesel	super/normal/ gasolina sin plomo/diesel	soopayr/normahl/ gahssoaleenah seen ploamoa/deesayl
Please check the ...	Controle ...	kontrolay
battery	la batería	lah bahtayreeah
brake fluid	el líquido de frenos	ayl leekeedhoa day fraynoass
oil/water	el aceite/el agua	ayl ahthaytay/ayl ahgwah
Would you check the tyre pressure, please?	¿Puede controlar la presión de los neumáticos, por favor?	pwaydhay kontrolahr lah prayssyon day loass nayoomahteekoass por fahbhor
1.6 front, 1.8 rear.	1,6 delanteras, 1,8 traseras.	1 koamah 6 daylahntayrahss, 1 koamah 8 trahssayrahss
Please check the spare tyre, too.	Mire la rueda de repuesto también, por favor.	meeray lah rwaydhah day raypwaystoa tahmbyayn por fahbhor
Can you mend this puncture (fix this flat)?	¿Puede arreglar este pinchazo?	pwaydhay ahrrayglahr aystay peenchahthoa
Would you please change the ...?	¿Puede cambiar ..., por favor?	pwaydhay kahmbyahr ... por fahbhor
bulb	la bombilla	lah boambeelyah
fan belt	la correa del ventilador	lah korrayah dayl baynteelahdhor
spark(ing) plug	la bujía	lah bookheeah
tyre	el neumático	ayl nayoomahteekoa
wipers	los limpiaparabrisas	loass leempyahpahrahbreessahss

CAR HIRE, see page 20/CONVERSION CHARTS, see page 158

| Would you clean the windscreen (windshield)? | ¿Quiere limpiar el parabrisas? | kyayray leempyahr ayl pahrahbreessahss |
| Do you have a road map of this district? | ¿Tiene un mapa de carreteras de esta comarca? | tyaynay oon mahpah day kahrraytayrahss day aystah koamahrkah |

Asking the way—Street directions *Preguntas – Direcciones*

Can you tell me the way to ...?	¿Me puede decir cómo se va a ...?	may pwaydhay daytheer koamoa say bah ah
How do I get to ...?	¿Cómo se va a ...?	koamoa say bah ah
Where does this street lead to?	¿Adónde lleva esta calle?	ahdhoanday lyaybhah aystah kahlyay
Is the road good?	¿Está la carretera en buen estado?	aystah la kahrraytayrah ayn bwayn aystahdhoa
Is there a motorway (expressway)?	¿Hay una autopista?	igh oonah owtoapeesstah
Is there a road with little traffic?	¿Hay una carretera con poco tráfico?	igh oonah kahrraytayrah kon poakoa trahfeekoa
How long does it take by car/on foot?	¿Cuánto se tarda en coche/a pie?	kwahntoa say tahrdah ayn koachay/ah pyay
Are we on the right road for ...?	¿Es ésta la carretera hacia ...?	ayss aystah lah kahrraytayrah ahthyah
How far is the nex village?	¿Qué distancia hay hasta el próximo pueblo?	kay deestahnthyah igh ahstah ayl proaksseemoa pwaybloa
How far is it to ... from here?	¿Qué distancia hay desde aquí hasta ...?	kay deestahnthyah igh daysday ahkee ahstah
Can you tell me where ... is?	¿Puede decirme dónde está ...?	pwaydhay daytheermay doanday aystah
How do I get to this address?	¿Cómo puedo llegar a esta dirección?	koamoa pwaydhoa lyaygahr ah aystah deeraykthyon
Can I drive to the centre of town?	¿Puedo conducir hasta el centro de la ciudad?	pwaydhoa kondootheer ahstah ayl thayntroa day lah thyoodhahdh
Can you show me on the map where I am?	¿Puede enseñarme en el mapa dónde estoy?	pwaydhay aynsaynyahrmay ayn ayl mahpah doanday aystoy

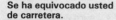

Se ha equivocado usted de carretera.	You're on the wrong road.
Siga todo derecho.	Go straight ahead.
norte/sur/este/oeste	north/south/east/west
Es hacia allí ...	It's down there ...
a la izquierda/derecha enfrente/atrás ... junto a/después de ...	on the left/right opposite/behind ... next to/after ...
Tome la carretera para ...	Take the road for ...
Tiene que regresar hasta ...	You have to go back to ...
Vaya al primer/segundo cruce.	Go to the first/second crossroads (intersection).
Doble a la izquierda en el semáforo.	Turn left at the traffic lights.
Doble a la derecha en la próxima esquina.	Turn right at the next corner.

Parking *Aparcamiento*

Where can I park?	¿Dónde puedo aparcar?	doanday pwaydhoa ahpahrkahr
Is there a car park nearby?	¿Hay un estaciona-miento cerca de aquí?	igh oon aystahthyonah-myayntoa thayrkah day ahkee
How long can I park here?	¿Cuánto tiempo puedo aparcar aquí?	kwahntoa tyaympoa pwaydhoa ahpahrkahr ahkee
What's the charge per hour?	¿Cuánto cuesta por hora?	kwahntoa kwaystah por oarah
Do you have some change for the parking meter?	¿Tiene suelto para el parquímetro?	tyaynay swayltoa pahrah ayl pahrkeemehtroa
Where can I get a parking disc?	¿Dónde puedo con-seguir un disco de aparcamiento?	doanday pwaydhoa konsaygeer oon deeskoa day ahpahrkahmyayntoa

Breakdown   *Averías*

Where's the nearest garage?	¿Dónde está el garaje más cercano?	doanday aystah ayl gahrahkhay mahss thehrkahnoa
What's the telephone number of the nearest garage?	¿Cuál es el número de teléfono del garaje más cercano?	kwahl ayss ayl noomayroa day taylayfoanoa dayl gahrahkhay mahss thehrkahnoa
My car won't start.	Mi coche no quiere arrancar.	mee koachay noa kyayray ahrrahnkahr
The battery is dead.	La batería está descargada.	lah bahtayreeah aystah dayskahrgahdhah
I've run out of petrol (gasoline).	Se ha terminado la gasolina.	say ah tayrmeenahdhoa lah gahssoaleenah
I have a flat tyre.	Tengo un pinchazo.	tayngoa oon peenchahthoa
The engine is overheating.	El motor está demasiado caliente.	ayl moator aystah daymahssyahdhoa kahlyayntay
There is something wrong with the ...	Hay algo estropeado en ...	igh ahlgoa aystroapayahdhoa ayn
brakes	los frenos	loass fraynoass
carburetor	el carburador	ayl kahrboorahdhoar
exhaust pipe	el tubo de escape	ayl tooboa day ayskahpay
radiator	el radiador	ayl rahdhyahdhoar
wheel	la rueda	lah rwaydhah
I've had a breakdown at ...	Tengo un coche estropeado en ...	tayngoa oon koachay aystroapayahdhoa ayn
Can you send a mechanic?	¿Puede usted mandar un mecánico?	pwaydhay oostaydh mahndahr oon maykahneekoa
Can you send a breakdown van (tow-truck)?	¿Puede usted mandar un coche grúa?	pwaydhay oostaydh mahndahr oon koachay grooah
How long will you be?	¿Cuánto tardarán?	kwahntoa tahrdahrahn

Accident—Police   *Accidentes – Policía*

Please call the police.	Llamen a la policía, por favor.	lyahmayn ah lah poaleetheeah por fahbhor
There's been an accident.	Ha habido un accidente.	ah ahbheedhoa oon ahktheedhayntay

It's about 2 km. from ...	**Está a unos 2 kilómetros de ...**	aystah ah oonoass 2 keeloamaytroass day
There are people injured.	**Hay gente herida.**	igh **khayn**tay ayreedhah
Call a doctor/an ambulance.	**Llamen a un doctor/una ambulancia.**	**lyah**mayn ah oon doak**tor**/oonah ahmboo**lahn**thyah
Here's my driving licence.	**Aquí está mi permiso de conducir.**	ahkee aystah mee payr-**mee**ssoa day kondoo**theer**
What's your name and address?	**¿Cuál es su nombre y dirección?**	kwahl ayss soo **nom**bray ee deerayk**thyon**
What's your insurance company?	**¿Cuál es su compañía de seguros?**	kwahl ayss soo kompah-**ñee**ah day say**goo**roass

Road signs *Señales de circulación*

ADUANA	Customs
¡ALTO!	Stop
ATENCION	Caution
AUTOPISTA (DE PEAJE)	Motorway/Turnpike (with toll)
CALZADA DETERIORADA	Bad road surface
CARRETERA CORTADA	No through road
CEDA EL PASO	Give way (yield)
CRUCE PELIGROSO	Dangerous crossroads
CUIDADO	Caution
CURVA PELIGROSA	Dangerous bend (curve)
DESPACIO	Drive slowly
DESVIACION	Diversion (detour)
DIRECCION UNICA	One-way street
ENCENDER LAS LUCES	Switch on headlights
ESCUELA	School
ESTACIONAMIENTO PROHIBIDO	No parking
ESTACIONAMIENTO REGLAMENTADO	Limited parking zone
FUERTE DECLIVE	Steep incline
OBRAS	Road works (men working)
PASO A NIVEL	Level (railroad) crossing
PASO PROHIBIDO	No entry
PEATONES	Pedestrians
PELIGRO	Danger
PROHIBIDO ADELANTAR	No overtaking (passing)
PUESTO DE SOCORRO	First-aid
SALIDA DE FABRICA	Factory exit

Sightseeing

Where's the tourist office/information centre?	¿Dónde está la oficina de turismo/la información?	doanday aystah lah oafeetheenah day tooreesmoa/lah eenformahthyon
What are the main points of interest?	¿Cuáles son los principales puntos de interés?	kwahlayss son loss preentheepahlayss poontoass day eentayrayss
We're here for only a few hours/a day.	Estamos aquí sólo unas pocas horas/un día.	aystahmoass ahkee soaloa oonahss poakahss oarahss/oon deeah
Can you recommend a ...?	¿Puede usted recomendarme ...?	pwaydhay oostaydh raykoamayndahrmay
sightseeing tour	un recorrido turístico	oon rehkorreedhoa tooreesteekoa
popular excursion	una excursión popular	oonah aykskoorsyon poapoolahr
What's the point of departure?	¿Cuál es el lugar de salida?	kwahl ayss ayl loogahr day sahleedhah
Will the coach pick us up at the hotel?	¿Nos recogerá el autocar en el hotel?	noss rehkoakhayrah ayl owtoakahr ayn ayl oatehl
How much does the tour cost?	¿Cuánto cuesta el recorrido?	kwahntoa kwaystah ayl rehkorreedhoa
What time does the tour start?	¿A qué hora empieza el recorrido?	ah kay oarah aympyaythah ayl rehkorreedhoa
Is lunch included?	¿Está incluido el almuerzo?	aystah eenklooeedhoa ayl ahlmwayrthoa
What time do we get back?	¿A qué hora volvemos?	ah kay oarah bolbaymoass
Do we have free time in ...?	¿Tenemos tiempo libre en ...?	taynaymoass tyaympoa leebray ayn
Is there an English-speaking guide?	¿Hay algún guía que hable inglés?	igh ahlgoon geeah kay ahblay eenglayss
I'd like to hire a private guide for ...	Quisiera un guía particular para ...	keessyayrah oon geeah pahrteekoolahr pahrah
half a day	medio día	maydhyoa deeah
a full day	todo el día	toadoa ayl deeah

TIME OF THE DAY, see page 153

Where is ...? *¿Dónde está ...?*

Where is/are the ...?	**¿Dónde está/ están ...?**	doanday aystah/aystahn
abbey	**la abadía**	lah ahbhadheeah
art gallery	**la galería de arte**	lah gahlayreeah day ahrtay
artist's quarter	**el barrio de los artistas**	ayl bahrreeoa day loss ahrteestahss
botanical gardens	**el jardín botánico**	ayl khahrdeen boatahneekoa
bullring	**la plaza de toros**	lah plahthah day toroass
castle	**el castillo**	ayl kahsteelyoa
cathedral	**la catedral**	lah kahtaydrahl
caves	**las cuevas**	lahss kwaybhahss
cemetery	**el cementerio**	ayl thaymayntayryoa
chapel	**la capilla**	lah kahpeelyah
church	**la iglesia**	lah eeglayssyah
city centre	**el centro de la ciudad**	ayl thayntroa day lah thyoodhahdh
concert hall	**la sala de conciertos**	lah sahlah day konthyehrtoass
convent	**el convento**	ayl konbayntoa
convention hall	**el palacio de convenciones**	ayl pahlahthyoa day konbaynthyonayss
court house	**el palacio de justicia**	ayl pahlahthyoa day khoosteethyah
downtown area	**el centro de la ciudad**	ayl thayntroa day lah thyoodhahdh
exhibition	**la exhibición**	lah ehkseebheethyon
factory	**la fábrica**	lah fahbreekah
fair	**la feria**	lah fayrryah
flea market	**el mercado de cosas viejas**	ayl mehrkahdhoa day kossahss byaykhahss
fortress	**la fortaleza/el alcázar**	lah fortahlaythah/ayl ahlkahthahr
fountain	**la fuente**	lah fwayntay
gardens	**los jardines públicos**	loss khahrdeenayss poobleekoss
harbour	**el puerto**	ayl pwayrtoa
library	**la biblioteca**	lah beeblyoataykah
market	**el mercado**	ayl mehrkahdhoa
monastery	**el monasterio**	ayl moanahstayryoa
monument	**el monumento**	ayl moanoomayntoa
museum	**el museo**	ayl moossayoa
old town	**la ciudad vieja**	lah thyoodhahdh byaykhah
palace	**el palacio**	ayl pahlahthyoa
park	**el parque**	ayl pahrkay

ASKING THE WAY, see page 76

parliament building	el edificio de las Cortes	ayl aydheefeethyoa day lahss kortayss
royal palace	el palacio real	ayl pahlahthyoa rayahl
ruins	las ruinas	lahss rweenahss
shopping area	la zona de tiendas	lah thoanah day tyayndahss
square	la plaza	lah plahthah
stadium	el estadio	ayl aystahdhyoa
statue	la estatua	lah aystahtwah
stock exchange	la bolsa	lah bolsah
tomb	la tumba	lah toombah
tower	la torre	lah torray
town hall	el ayuntamiento	ayl ahyoontahmyayntoa
town walls	las murallas	lahss moorahlyahss
university	la universidad	lah ooneebhehrseedhahdh
zoo	el zoológico	ayl thoalokheekoa

Admission *Entrada*

Is ... open on Sundays?	¿Está ... abierto los domingos?	aystah ... ahbhyayrtoa loss doameengoass
When does it open/close?	¿A qué hora abren/cierran?	ah kay oarah ahbrayn/thyayrrahn
How much is the entrance fee?	¿Cuánto vale la entrada?	kwahntoa bahlay lah ayntrahdhah
Is there any reduction for (the) ...?	¿Hay algún descuento para ...?	igh ahlgoon dayskwayntoa pahrah
disabled	incapacitados	eenkahpahtheetahdoass
groups	grupos	groopoass
pensioners	jubilados	khoobheelahdhoass
students	estudiantes	aystoodhyahntayss
Have you a guide-book (in English)?	¿Tiene usted una guía (en inglés)?	tyaynay oostaydh oonah geeah (ayn eenglayss)
Can I buy a catalogue?	¿Puedo comprar un catálogo?	pwaydhoa komprahr oon kahtahloagoa
Is it all right to take pictures?	¿Se pueden tomar fotografías?	say pwaydhayn toamahr foatoagrahfeeahss

| **ENTRADA LIBRE** | ADMISSION FREE |
| **PROHIBIDO TOMAR FOTOGRAFIAS** | NO CAMERAS ALLOWED |

Who—What—When? *¿Quién – Qué – Cuándo?*

What's that building?	**¿Qué es ese edificio?**	kay ayss **ay**ssay ayd**hee**fee**thy**oa
Who was the ...?	**¿Quién fue ...?**	kyayn fweh
architect	**el arquitecto**	ayl ahrkee**tehk**toa
artist	**el artista**	ayl ahr**tees**tah
painter	**el pintor**	ayl peentor
sculptor	**el escultor**	ayl ayskool**tor**
Who painted that picture?	**¿Quién pintó ese cuadro?**	kyayn peen**toa** **ay**ssay **kwah**droa
When did he live?	**¿En qué época vivió?**	ayn kay **ay**poakah bee**bhy**oa
When was it built?	**¿Cuándo se construyó?**	**kwahn**doa say konstroo**yoa**
Where's the house where ... lived?	**¿Dónde está la casa en que vivió ...?**	**doan**day ay**stah** lah **kah**ssah ayn kay bee**bhy**oa
We're interested in ...	**Nos interesa(n) ...**	noss eentay**rays**sah(n)
antiques	**las antigüedades**	lahss ahnteegwee-**dhah**dhayss
archaeology	**la arqueología**	lah ahrkayoaloa**khee**ah
art	**el arte**	ayl **ahr**tay
botany	**la botánica**	lah boa**tah**neekah
ceramics	**la cerámica**	lah thay**rah**meekah
coins	**las monedas**	lahss moa**nay**dhahss
fine arts	**las bellas artes**	lahss **bay**lyahss **ahr**tayss
furniture	**los muebles**	loss **mway**blayss
geology	**la geología**	lah khayoaloa**khee**ah
handicrafts	**la artesanía**	lah ahrtayssah**nee**ah
history	**la historia**	lah ee**stoar**yah
medicine	**la medicina**	lah maydee**thee**nah
music	**la música**	lah **moos**seekah
natural history	**la historia natural**	lah ee**stoar**yah nahtoo**rahl**
ornithology	**la ornitologia**	lah oarneetoaloa**khee**ah
painting	**la pintura**	lah peen**toor**ah
pottery	**la alfarería**	lah ahlfahray**ree**ah
religion	**la religión**	lah raylee**khyon**
sculpture	**la escultura**	lah ayskool**toor**ah
zoology	**la zoología**	lah thoaloa**khee**ah
Where's the ... department?	**¿Dónde está el departamento de ...?**	**doan**day ay**stah** ayl daypahrtah**mayn**toa day

It's ...	Es ...	ayss
amazing	**asombroso***	ahssoambroassoa
awful	**horrible**	orreeblay
beautiful	**hermoso**	ayrmoassoa
gloomy	**lúgubre**	loogoobray
impressive	**impresionante**	eemprayssyoanahntay
interesting	**interesante**	eentayrayssahntay
magnificent	**magnífico**	mahgneefeekoa
overwhelming	**abrumador**	ahbroomahdhor
strange	**extraño**	aykstrahñoa
superb	**soberbio**	soabhehrbyoa
terrible	**terrible**	tehrreeblay
terrifying	**aterrador**	ahtehrrahdhor
tremendous	**tremendo**	traymayndoa
ugly	**feo**	fehoa

Churches—Religious services   *Iglesias – Servicios religiosos*

Predominantly Roman Catholic, Spain is rich in cathedrals and churches worth visiting. Most are open to the public except, of course, during mass. If you're interested in taking pictures, you should obtain permission first. Shorts and backless dresses are definitely out when visiting churches.

Is there a/an ... near here?	**¿Hay una ... cerca de aquí?**	igh oonah ... therkah day ahkee
Catholic/Protestant church	**iglesia católica/ protestante**	eeglayssyah kahtoaleekah/ proataystahntay
synagogue	**sinagoga**	seenahgoagah
mosque	**mezquita**	maythkeetah
At what time is ...?	**¿A qué hora es ...?**	ah kay oarah ayss
mass	**la misa**	lah meessah
the service	**el servicio**	ayl sehrbeethyoa
Where can I find a ... who speaks English?	**¿Dónde puedo encontrar un ... que hable inglés?**	doanday pwaydhoa aynkontrahr oon ... kay ahblay eenglayss
priest/minister/ rabbi	**sacerdote/ministro/ rabino**	sahthehrdoatay/mee- neestroa/rahbheenoa
I'd like to visit the church.	**Quisiera visitar la iglesia.**	keessyayrah beesseetahr lah eeglayssyah

---

* For feminine and plural forms, see grammar section page 159 (adjectives).

Countryside *En el campo*

How high is that mountain?	**¿Qué altura tiene esa montaña?**	kay ahl**toorah tyay**nay **ay**ssah moan**tah**ñah
How far is it to ...?	**¿Qué distancia hay hasta ...?**	kay dees**tahn**thyah igh **ahs**tah
Can we walk?	**¿Podemos ir a pie?**	poa**day**moass eer ah pyay
Is there a scenic route to ...?	**¿Hay una carretera panorámica a ...?**	igh **oo**nah kahr**ray**tayrah pahnoh**rah**meekah ah
How do we get back to ...?	**¿Cómo regresamos a ...?**	**koa**moa raygray**ssah**moass ah
What's the name of that ...?	**¿Cómo se llama ...?**	**koa**moa say **lyah**mah
animal/bird/ flower/tree	**ese animal/pájaro/ esa flor/ese árbol**	**ay**ssay ahnee**mahl**/ **pah**khahroa/**ay**ssah floar/ **ay**ssay **ahr**boal

Landmarks *Puntos de referencia*

bridge	**el puente**	ayl **pway**ntay
building	**el edificio**	ayl ayd**hee**feethyoa
church	**la iglesia**	lah ee**glay**ssyah
cliff	**el acantilado**	ayl ahkahntee**lah**dhoa
farm	**la granja**	lah **grahn**khah
field	**el campo**	ayl **kahm**poa
footpath	**el sendero**	ayl sayn**day**roa
forest	**el bosque**	ayl **boas**kay
fortress	**la fortaleza**	lah fortah**lay**thah
garden	**el jardín**	ayl khahr**deen**
hill	**la colina**	lah koa**lee**nah
house	**la casa**	lah **kahs**sah
hut	**la cabaña**	lah kah**bhah**ñah
lake	**el lago**	ayl **lah** oa
meadow	**el prado**	ayl **prah**dhoa
river	**el río**	ayl **ree**oa
road	**la carretera**	lah kahr**ray**tayrah
sea	**el mar**	ayl mahr
valley	**el valle**	ayl **bah**lyay
village	**el pueblo**	ayl **pway**bloa
vineyard	**el viñedo**	ayl bee**ñay**dhoa
wall	**el muro**	ayl **moo**roa
waterfall	**la cascada**	lah kahs**kah**dhah
windmill	**el molino de viento**	ayl moa**lee**noa day **byayn**toa

ASKING THE WAY, see page 76

Relaxing

Cinema (Movies) — Theatre   *Cine – Teatro*

Most films are dubbed in Spanish. The first showing usually starts around 2 p.m. in cities, but at 4 elsewhere. Sometimes there are only two showings in the evening—at 7 and 10.30 or 11 p.m.; for these advance booking is advisable. Curtain time at the theatre is at 7 and 10.30 or 11 p.m. There are daily performances but a few theatres close one day a week.

You can find out what's playing from the newspapers and billboards or from magazines like ''This Week in ...''.

What's on at the cinema tonight?	¿Qué ponen en el cine esta noche?	kay **poa**nehn ayn ayl theenay **ays**tah **noa**chay
What's playing at the ... theatre?	¿Qué ponen en el teatro ...?	kay **poa**nehn ayn ayl tayahtroa
Can you recommend a ...?	¿Puede recomendarme ...?	**pway**dhay rehkoamayndahrmay
comedy	una comedia	oonah koamaydhyah
drama	un drama	oon **drah**mah
film	una película	oonah payleekoolah
musical	una comedia musical	oonah koamaydhyah moosseekahl
revue	una revista	oonah rehbheestah
thriller	una película de suspense	oonah payleekoolah day soospaynsay
western	una película del Oeste	oonah payleekoolah dayl oaaystay
What time does the first evening performance begin?	¿A qué hora empieza la primera función de noche?	ah kay **oa**rah aympyaythah lah preemayrah foonthyon day **noa**chay
Are there any seats for ...?	¿Quedan localidades para ...?	**kay**dhahn loakahleedhahdhayss pahrah
How much are the seats?	¿Cuánto valen las localidades?	**kwahn**toa bahlayn lahss loakahleedhahdhayss
I want to reserve 2 seats for the show on Friday evening.	Quiero reservar 2 localidades para la función del viernes por la noche.	**kyay**roa rayssayrbahr 2 loakahleedhahdhayss pahrah lah foonthyon dayl byayrnayss por lah **noa**chay

DAYS, see page 151

Can I have a seat for the matinée on Tuesday?	¿Me puede dar una localidad para la sesión de tarde del martes?	may **pwayd**hay dahr **oon**ah loakahlee**dhahd**h **pah**rah lah **sayss**yon day **tahr**day dayl **mahr**tayss
I want a seat in the stalls (orchestra).	Quiero una localidad de platea.	**kyayr**oa **oon**ah loakahlee**dhahd**h day plah**tay**ah
Not too far back.	No muy atrás.	noa mwee ah**trahss**
Somewhere in the middle.	En algún lugar en el medio.	ayn ahl**goon** loo**gar** ayn ayl **may**dhyoa
How much are the seats in the circle (mezzanine)?	¿Cuánto valen las localidades de anfiteatro?	**kwahn**toa **bah**layn lahss loakahlee**dhahd**hayss day ahnfeetay**ah**troa
May I please have a programme?	¿Me da un programa, por favor?	may dah oon proa**grah**mah por fah**bhor**

Lo siento, las localidades están agotadas.	I'm sorry, we're sold out.
Sólo quedan algunos asientos en el anfiteatro.	There are only a few seats left in the circle (mezzanine).
¿Puedo ver su entrada?	May I see your ticket?
Este es su sitio.	This is your seat.

Opera—Ballet—Concert *Opera – Ballet – Concierto*

Where's the opera house?	¿Dónde está el Teatro de la Opera?	**doan**day ay**stah** ayl tay**ah**troa day lah **oa**payrah
Where's the concert hall?	¿Dónde está la Sala de Conciertos?	**doan**day ay**stah** lah **sah**lah day kon**thyayr**toass
Can you recommend a ...?	¿Puede recomendarme ...?	**pway**dhay raykoamayn**dar**may
ballet	un ballet	oon bah**layt**
concert	un concierto	oon kon**thyayr**toa
opera	una ópera	**oon**ah **oa**payrah
operetta	una opereta	**oon**ah oapay**ray**tah
What's on at the opera tonight?	¿Qué ópera ponen esta noche?	kay **oa**payrah **poa**nehn ay**stah noa**chay

Diversiones

Who's singing/dancing?	¿Quién canta/baila?	kyayn **kahn**tah/**bigh**lah
What time does the programme start?	¿A qué hora empieza el programa?	ah kay **oa**rah aympy**ay**thah ayl proa**grah**mah
Which orchestra is playing?	¿Qué orquesta toca?	kay oar**kay**stah **toa**kah
What are they playing?	¿Qué tocan?	kay **toa**kahn
Who's the conductor?	¿Quién es el director?	kyayn ayss ayl deereh**ktor**

Nightclubs *Centros nocturnos*

Nightclubs—with dinner, dancing and a floor show—are found only in major cities and popular resorts. But you'll certainly want to experience the informal atmosphere of a *bodega* or *taberna*. Some of them are found in candlelit cellars or in bars where a tiny space has been set aside for entertainment. While sipping a sherry or Spanish brandy, you might watch fiery flamenco dancing or listen to melancholy guitar music.

Can you recommend a good nightclub?	¿Puede recomendarme un buen centro nocturno?	**pway**dhay raykoamayn-**dahr**may oon bwayn **thayn**troa noak**toor**noa
Is there a floor show?	¿Hay atracciones?	igh ahtrahk**thyo**nayss
What time does the floor show start?	¿A qué hora empiezan las atracciones?	ah kay **oa**rah aympy**ay**-thahn lahss ahtrahk**thyo**-nayss
Is evening attire necessary?	¿Se necesita traje de noche?	say naythays**see**tah **trah**khay day **noa**chay

Disco *Discoteca*

Where can we go dancing?	¿Dónde podemos ir a bailar?	**doan**day poa**dhay**moass eer ah bigh**lahr**
Is there a discotheque in town?	¿Hay alguna discoteca en la ciudad?	igh ahl**goo**nah deeskoatay-kah ayn lah thyoo**dhahdh**
May I have this dance?	¿Me permite este baile?	may payr**mee**tay **ay**stay **bigh**lay

Bullfight *La corrida*

The *corrida* (literally "running of the bulls") will either fascinate you or appal you. To a Spaniard, a bullfight is not a choice of life and death for the bull. It is simply an opportunity for it to die heroically.

In some ways the spectacle resembles a ballet. There are colourful moments when the procession *(paseo)* arrives. The entry of the bull into the arena is a moment of high suspense. The movements of cape and bullfighter are graceful and precise.

The *matador* and his team of assistants goad the bull so as to assess its reactions to the cape. A *picador* weakens the bull by piercing its neck muscles with a lance.

A *banderillero* then confronts the animal. At great peril, he thrusts three sets of barbed sticks between its shoulder blades. Throughout each stage of the performance, the Spanish crowd will be watching critically for the finer points—weighing the fearlessness of bull and man, and the *matador's* skill as he executes a series of dangerous passes, leading up to the final climax of the kill.

You may well find the whole performance cruel. Should death be a public spectacle? Disturbing, too, is the treatment of the *picador*'s horse. Although protected by padding, he catches the repeated fury of the bull's charge and horns. The horse takes this in silence, incidentally, because his vocal cords have been cut.

You'll be asked whether you want a seat in the sun or shade *(sol o sombra)*. Be sure to specify *sombra,* for the Spanish sun is hot. Rent a cushion for the hard concrete stands.

I'd like to see a bullfight.	**Quisiera ver una corrida.**	keessyayrah behr oonah korreedhah
I want a seat in the shade/in the sun.	**Quisiera una localidad de sombra/de sol.**	keessyayrah oonah loakah-leedhahdh day soambrah/day sol
I'd like to rent a cushion.	**Quisiera alquilar una almohadilla.**	keessyayrah ahlkeelahr oonah ahlmoaahdheelyah

Sports   *Deportes*

Football (soccer) and *pelota* are as popular in Spain as bull-fighting. *Pelota* is similar to handball but instead of a glove, the players wear a curved wicker basket *(cesta)*. The ball *(pelota)* is hard and covered with goatskin. It can be played off the back and side walls as well as the front. Caught in the *cesta,* and hurled at the wall with great force, it bounces with extraordinary speed. Usually played in the late after-noon or evening, *pelota* is well worth watching. In Latin America, the game is known as *jai alai* (the Basque word for the sport).

In spring and fall, there's good horse racing in Madrid, San Sebastián and Sevilla. Besides, facilities abound to go fishing—even deep-sea fishing—hunting, golfing, swimming, sailing, windsurfing or play tennis.

Though one wouldn't think of going to Spain to ski, you can don your ski togs from December to April in the Catalonian Pyrenees, near Madrid and in the Sierra Nevada near Granada.

Is there a football (soccer) match anywhere today?	**¿Hay algún partido de fútbol hoy?**	igh ahl**goon** pahr**teed**hoa day **foot**bol oy
Who's playing?	**¿Quiénes juegan?**	**kyay**nayss khway**gahn**
Can you get me 2 tickets?	**¿Puede conseguirme 2 entradas?**	**pway**dhay konsay**geer**may 2 ayn**trah**dhahss

basketball	**el baloncesto**	ayl bahloan**thays**toa
boxing	**el boxeo**	ayl boak**say**oa
cycling	**el ciclismo**	ayl thee**klees**moa
dog racing	**las carreras de galgos**	lahs kahr**rray**rahss day **gahl**goass
horse riding	**la equitación**	lah aykeetah**thyon**
skiing	**el esquí**	ayl ay**skee**
swimming	**la natación**	lah nahtah**thyon**
volleyball	**el balonvolea**	ayl bahloanboa**lay**ah

I'd like to see a pelota match.	**Quisiera ver un partido de pelota.**	keessyayrah behr oon pahrteedhoa day payloatah
Where's the nearest golf course?	**¿Dónde está el campo de golf más cercano?**	doanday aystah ayl kahmpoa day goalf mahss thehrkahnoa
Can we hire (rent) clubs?	**¿Podemos alquilar los palos?**	poadhaymoass ahlkeelahr loss pahloass
Where are the tennis courts?	**¿Dónde están las pistas de tenis?**	doanday aystahn lahss peestahss day tayneess
Can I hire rackets?	**¿Puedo alquilar raquetas?**	pwaydhoa ahlkeelahr rahkaytahss
What's the charge per ...?	**¿Cuánto cuesta por ...?**	kwahntoa kwaystah por
day/round/hour	**día/juego/hora**	deeah/khwaygoa/oarah
Where's the nearest race course (track)?	**¿Dónde está la pista de carreras más cercana?**	doanday aystah lah peestah day kahrrayrahss mahss thehrkahnah
What's the admission charge?	**¿Cuánto vale la entrada?**	kwahntoa bahlay lah ayntrahdhah
Is there a swimming pool here?	**¿Hay una piscina aquí?**	igh oonah peestheenah ahkee
Is it open-air/ indoors?	**¿Está al aire libre/ Es cubierta?**	aystah ahl ighray lebray/ ayss koobhyayrtah
Can one swim in the lake/river?	**¿Se puede nadar en el lago/río?**	say pwaydhay nahdhahr ayn ayl lahgoa/reeoa
Is there a sandy beach?	**¿Hay una playa de arena?**	igh oonah plahyah day ahraynah
Is there any good fishing/hunting around here?	**¿Hay un buen lugar para pescar/cazar en los alrededores?**	igh oon bwayn loogahr pahrah payskahr/kahthahr ayn loass ahlraydhaydhoa-rayss
Do I need a permit?	**¿Se requiere per-miso?**	say raykyayray payrmee-ssoa
Where can I get one?	**¿Dónde puedo con-seguir uno?**	doanday pwaydhoa konsay-geer oonoa
What are the skiing conditions like at ...?	**¿Cómo están las condiciones para esquiar en ...?**	koamoa aystahn lahss kondeethyonayss pahrah ayskyahr ayn
Are there ski lifts?	**¿Hay telesquís?**	igh taylayskeess

On the beach *En la playa*

Is it safe for swimming?	¿Se puede nadar sin peligro?	say pwaydhay nahdhahr seen pehleegroa
Is there a lifeguard?	¿Hay vigilante?	igh beekheelahntay
There are some big waves.	Hay algunas olas muy grandes.	igh ahlgoonahss oalahss mwee grahndayss
Are there any dangerous currents?	¿Hay alguna corriente peligrosa?	igh ahlgoonah korryayntay pehleegroassah
Is it safe for children?	¿Es seguro para los niños?	ayss sehgooroa pahrah loos neeñoass
What time is high/ low tide?	¿A qué hora es la marea alta/baja?	ah kay oarah ayss lah mahrehah ahltah/bahkhah
What's the temperature of the water?	¿Cuál es la temperatura del agua?	kwahl ayss lah taympayrahtoorah dayl ahgwah
I want to hire a/an/ some ...	Quiero alquilar ...	kyayroa ahlkeelahr
air mattress (raft)	un colchón neumático	oon koalchon nayoomahteekoa
bathing hut (cabana)	una cabina	oonah kahbheenah
deck-chair	una silla de lona	oonah seelyah day loanah
skin-diving equipment	un equipo para natación submarina	oon aykeepoa pahrah nahtahthyon soobmahreenah
sunshade (umbrella)	una sombrilla	oonah soambreelyah
surfboard	una plancha de deslizamiento	oonah plahnchah day daysleethahmyayntoa
water-skis	unos esquís acuáticos	oonoass ayskeess ahkwahteekoass
Where can I rent a ...?	¿Dónde puedo alquilar ...?	doanday pwaydhoa ahlkeelahr
canoe	una canoa	oonah kahnoaah
motorboat	una motora	oonah moatoarah
rowing-boat	una barca	oonah bahrkah
sailing-boat	un velero	oon baylehroa
What's the charge per hour?	¿Cuánto cobran por hora?	kwahntoa koabrahn por oarah

PLAYA PARTICULAR	PRIVATE BEACH
PROHIBIDO BAÑARSE	NO SWIMMING

Making friends

Introductions *Presentaciones*

How do you do? (Pleased to meet you.)	**Encantado(a)* de conocerle.**	aynkahntahdhoa(ah) day koanoathayrlay
How are you?	**¿Cómo está usted?**	koamoa aystah oostaydh
Fine, thanks. And you?	**Bien, gracias. ¿Y usted?**	byayn grahthyahss. ee oostaydh
May I introduce ...	**Quiero presentarle a ...**	kyayroa prayssayntahrlay ah
My name's ...	**Me llamo ...**	may lyahmoa
What's your name?	**¿Cómo se llama?**	koamoa say lyahmah
Glad to know you.	**Tanto gusto.**	tahntoa goostoa

Follow-up *Continuación ...*

How long have you been here?	**¿Cuánto tiempo lleva usted aquí?**	kwahntoa tyaympoa lyaybhah oostaydh ahkee
We've been here a week.	**Llevamos aquí una semana.**	lyaybhahmoass ahkee oonah saymahnah
Is this your first visit?	**¿Es la primera vez que viene?**	ayss lah preemayrah behth kay byaynay
No, we came here last year.	**No, vinimos el año pasado.**	noa beeneemoass ayl ahñoa pahssahdhoa
Are you enjoying your stay?	**¿Está disfrutando de su estancia?**	aystah deesfrootahndoa day soo aystahnthyah
Yes, I like ... very much.	**Sí, me gusta mucho ...**	see may goostah moochoa
Where do you come from?	**¿De dónde es usted?**	day doanday ayss oostaydh
I'm from ...	**Soy de ...**	soy day
Where are you staying?	**¿Dónde se hospeda?**	doanday say ospehdhah

*A woman would say *encantada*

COUNTRIES, see page 146

Are you on your own?	¿Ha venido usted solo/sola?	ah bayneedhoa oostaydh soaloa/soalah
I'm with my ...	Estoy con ...	aystoy kon
husband	mi marido	mee mahreedhoa
wife	mi mujer	mee mookhehr
family	mi familia	mee fahmeelyah
parents	mis padres	meess pahdrayss
boyfriend	mi amigo	mee ahmeegoa
girlfriend	mi amiga	mee ahmeegah

father/mother	el padre/la madre	ayl pahdray/lah mahdray
son/daughter	el hijo/la hija	ayl eekhoa/lah eekhah
brother/sister	el hermano/ la hermana	ayl ayrmahnoa/ lah ayrmahnah
uncle/aunt	el tío/la tía	ayl teeoa/lah teeah
nephew/niece	el sobrino/la sobrina	ayl soabreenoa/ lah soabreenah
cousin	el primo/la prima	ayl preemoa/lah preemah

Are you married/ single?	¿Está casado(a)/ soltero(a)*?	aystah kahssahdhoa(ah) soaltayroa(ah)
Do you have children?	¿Tiene niños?	tyaynay neeñoass
What's your occupation?	¿Cuál es su ocupación?	kwahl ays soo oakoopahthyon
I'm a student.	Soy estudiante.	soy aystoodhyahntay
I'm here on a business trip.	Estoy aquí en viaje de negocios.	aystoy ahkee ayn byah- khay day naygoathyoass
We hope to see you again soon.	Esperamos verle pronto por aquí.	ayspayrahmoass bayrlay proantoa por ahkee
See you later/See you tomorrow.	Hasta luego/Hasta mañana.	ahstah lwaygoa/ahstah mahñahnah

The weather *El tiempo*

| What a lovely day! | ¡Qué día tan bueno! | kay deeah tahn bwaynoa |
| What awful weather! | ¡Qué tiempo más malo! | kay tyaympoa mahss mahloa |

---

* If addressing a woman *casada/soltera*

Is it usually as cold/warm as this?	¿Hace normalmente este frío/calor?	ahthay noarmahlmayntay aystay freeoa/kahlor
Do you think it'll ... tomorrow?	¿Cree usted que ... mañana?	krayeh oostaydh kay ... mahñahnah
rain/snow	lloverá/nevará	lyoabhayrah/naybhahrah
clear up/be sunny	hará mejor/hará sol	ahrah mehkhor/ahrah sol
be windy/cloudy	hará viento/estará nublado	ahrah byayntoa/aystahrah nooblahdhoa

Invitations *Invitaciones*

Would you like to have dinner with us on ...?	¿Quiere acompañarnos a cenar en ...?	kyayray ahkoampahñahrnoass ah thaynahr ayn
May I invite you for lunch?	¿Puedo invitarlo/la a almorzar?	pwaydhoa eenbeetahrloa/lah ah ahlmoarthahr
Can you come over for a drink this evening?	¿Puede usted venir a tomar una copa esta noche?	pwaydhay oostaydh bayneer ah toamahr oonah koapah aystah noachay
That's very kind of you.	Es usted muy amable.	ayss oostaydh mwee ahmahblay
What time shall we come?	¿A qué hora vamos?	ah kay oarah bahmoass
May I bring a friend?	¿Puedo llevar a un amigo/una amiga?	pwaydhoa lyaybhar ah oon ahmeegoa/oonah ahmeegah
I'm afraid we've got to leave now.	Me temo que debemos marcharnos ahora.	may taymoa kay daybhaymoass mahrchahrnoass ahoarah
Next time you must come to visit us.	Otro día tienen que venir ustedes a vernos.	oatroa deeah tyaynayn kay bayneer oostaydhayss ah bayrnoass
Thanks for the evening. It was great.	Muchas gracias por la velada. Ha sido estupenda.	moochahss grahthyahss por lah baylahdhah. ah seedhoa aystoopayndah

Dating *Citas*

| Would you like a cigarette? | ¿Quiere usted un cigarrillo? | kyayray oostaydh oon theegahrreelyoa |
| Do you have a light, please? | ¿Tiene usted lumbre, por favor? | tyaynay oostaydh loombray por fahbhor |

DAYS, see page 151

Can I get you a drink?	¿Quiere usted beber algo?	kyayray oostaydh baybhayr ahlgoa
Are you waiting for someone?	¿Está usted esperando a alguien?	aystah oostaydh ayspay-rahndoa ah ahlgyayn
Do you mind if I sit down here?	¿Le importa si me siento aquí?	lay eempoartah see may syayntoa ahkee
Are you free this evening?	¿Está usted libre esta tarde?	aystah oostaydh leebray aystah tahrday
Would you like to go out with me tonight?	¿Quisiera usted salir conmigo esta noche?	keessyayrah oostaydh sahleer konmeegoa aystah noachay
Would you like to go dancing?	¿Quisiera usted ir a bailar?	keessyayrah oostaydh eer ah bighlahr
Shall we go to the cinema (movies)?	¿Quiere que vayamos al cine?	kyayray kay bahyahmoass ahl theenay
Would you like to go for a drive?	¿Quiere usted dar un paseo en coche?	kyayray oostaydh dahr oon pahssayoa ayn koachay
Where shall we meet?	¿Dónde nos encontramos?	doanday noss aynkontrahmoass
What's your address/telephone number?	¿Cuál es su dirección/número de teléfono?	kwahl ayss soo deeraykthyon/noomayroa day taylayfoanoa
I'll call for you at 8 o'clock.	Iré a recogerla a las 8.	eeray ah rehkohkhayrlah ah lahss 8
May I take you home?	¿Puedo acompañarla hasta su casa?	pwaydhoa ahkoampahñahr-lah ahstah soo kahssah
Can I see you again tomorrow?	¿Puedo verla mañana?	pwaydhoa bayrlah mahñahnah

... and you might answer:

I'd love to, thank you.	Me encantaría, gracias.	may aynkahntahreeah grahthyahss
I've enjoyed myself.	Lo he pasado muy bien.	loa ay pahssahdhoa mwee byayn
Thank you, but I'am busy.	Gracias, pero estoy ocupado(a).	grathyahss payroa aystoy oakoopahdhoa(ah)
No, thank you, I'd rather not.	No gracias, mejor no.	noa grathyahss maykhoar noa

Shopping guide

This shopping guide is designed to help you find what you want with ease, accuracy and speed. It features:

1. A list of all major shops, stores and services (p. 98)
2. Some general expressions required when shopping to allow you to be specific and selective (p. 100)
3. Full details of the shops and services most likely to concern you, grouped under the headings below.

		Page
Bookshop/ Stationer's	books, magazines, newspapers, stationery	104
Camping equipment	all items required for camping	106
Chemist's (drugstore)	medicine, first-aid, cosmetics, toilet articles	108
Clothing	shoes, clothes, accessories	112
Electrical appliances	radios, cassette-recorders, shavers	119
Grocery	some general expressions, weights, measures and packaging	120
Jeweller's/ Watchmaker's	jewellery, watches, watch repairs	121
Optician	glasses, lenses, binoculars	123
Photography	cameras, films, developing accessories	124
Tobacconist's	smoker's supplies	126
Miscellaneous	souvenirs, records, cassettes, toys	127

LAUNDRY, see page 29/HAIRDRESSER'S, see page 30

Shops and services *Comercios y servicios*

Shopping hours: 9.30 a.m. to 1.30 p.m. and 4 to 8 p.m. Monday to Friday, 9.30 a.m. to 2 p.m. on Saturdays; department stores are generally open from 10 a.m. to 8 p.m. without a break, Monday to Saturday.

Where's the nearest ...?	¿Dónde está ... más cercano/cercana?	doanday aystah ... mahss thayrkahnoa/thayrkahnah
antique shop	la tienda de antigüedades	lah tyayndah day ahnteegwaydhahdhayss
art gallery	la galería de arte	lah gahlayreeah day ahrtay
baker's	la panadería	lah pahnahdhayreeah
bank	el banco	ayl bahnkoa
barber's	la barbería	lah bahrbayreeah
beauty salon	el salón de belleza	ayl sahlon day baylyaythah
bookshop	la librería	lah leebrayreeah
butcher's	la carnicería	lah kahrneethayreeah
cake shop	la pastelería	lah pahstaylayreeah
camera shop	la tienda de fotografía	lah tyayndah day foatoagrahfeeah
candy store	la bombonería	lah boamboanayreeah
chemist's	la farmacia	lah fahrmahthyah
confectioner's	la confitería	lah konfeethayreeah
dairy	la lechería	lah laychayreeah
delicatessen	la mantequería	lah mahntaykayreeah
dentist	el dentista	ayl daynteestah
department store	los grandes almacenes	loss grahndayss ahlmahthaynayss
doctor	el médico	ayl maydeekoa
drugstore	la farmacia	lah fahrmahthyah
dry cleaner's	la tintorería	lah teentoarayreeah
electrician	el electricista	ayl aylayktreetheestah
fishmonger's	la pescadería	lah payskahdhayreeah
flower shop	la florería	lah floarayreeah
fruit stand	la frutería	lah frootayreeah
furrier's	la peletería	lah paylaytayreeah
greengrocer's	la verdulería	lah bayrdoolayreeah
grocery	la tienda de comestibles	lah tyayndah day koamaysteeblayss
hairdresser's (ladies)	la peluquería	lah paylookayreeah
hardware store	la ferretería	lah fehrraytayreeah
health food shop	la tienda de alimentos dietéticos	lah tyayndah day ahleemayntoass dyaytayteekoass
hospital	el hospital	ayl oaspeetahl
ironmonger's	la ferretería	lah fehrraytayreeah

jeweller's	la joyería	lah khoyayreeah
launderette	la launderama	lah lahoondayrahmah
laundry	la lavandería	lah lahbhahndayreeah
leather goods store	la tienda de artí-culos de cuero	lah **tyayn**dah day ahrtee-kooloass day **kway**roa
library	la biblioteca	lah beeblyo**tay**kah
market	el mercado	ayl mehr**kah**dhoa
newsstand	el quiosco de periódicos	ayl **kyos**koa day payryodheekoass
optician	el óptico	ayl **op**teekoa
pastry shop	la pastelería	lah pahstaylayreeah
photographer	el fotógrafo	ayl foa**to**agrahfoa
police station	la comisaría	lah koameessahreeah
post office	la oficina de correos	lah oafee**thee**nah day korre**hoass**
shirt-maker's	la camisería	lah kahmeessehreeah
shoemaker's (repairs)	el zapatero	ayl thahpah**tay**roa
shoe shop	la zapatería	lah thahpahtayreeah
shopping centre	el centro comercial	ayl **thayn**troa koamayr**thyahl**
souvenir shop	la tienda de objetos de regalo	lay **tyayn**dah day oabkhay-toass day ray**gah**loa
sporting goods shop	la tienda de artícu-los de deportes	lah **tyayn**dah day ahrtee-kooloass day day**por**tayss
stationer's	la papelería	lah pahpaylayreeah
supermarket	el supermercado	ayl soopaymayr**kah**dhoa
sweet shop	la bombonería	lah boamboanayreeah
tailor's	el sastre	ayl **sahs**tray
telephone office	la oficina de teléfonos	lah oafee**thee**nah day taylayfoanoass
tobacconist's	el estanco/los tabacos	ayl ehstahnkoa/loss tahbhahkoass
toy shop	la juguetería	lah khoogaytayreeah
travel agency	la agencia de viajes	lah ahkhaynthyah day byahkhayss
vegetable store	la verdulería	lah bayrdoolayreeah
veterinarian	el veterinario	ayl baytayreenahryoa
watchmaker's	la relojería	lah rehlokhayreeah
wine merchant's	la tienda de vinos/la bodega	lah **tyayn**dah day bee-noass/lah boadhaygah

ENTRADA	ENTRANCE
SALIDA	EXIT
SALIDA DE EMERGENCIA	EMERGENCY EXIT

Where? ¿Dónde?

Where's a good ...?	¿Dónde hay un buen/una buena ...?	doanday igh oon bwayn/oonah bwaynah
Where can I find a ...?	¿Dónde puedo encontrar un/una ...?	doanday pwaydhoa aynkoantrahr oon/oonah
Where do they sell ...?	¿Dónde venden ...?	doanday bayndayn
Where's the main shopping area?	¿Dónde está la zona de tiendas más importante?	doanday aystah lah thoanah day tyayndahss mahss eempoartahntay
Is it far from here?	¿Está muy lejos de aquí?	aystah mwee lehkhoass day ahkee
How do I get there?	¿Cómo puedo llegar allí?	koamoa pwaydhoa lyaygahr ahlyee

Service Servicio

Can you help me?	¿Puede usted atenderme?	pwaydhay oostaydh ahtayndayrmay
I'm just looking.	Estoy sólo mirando.	aystoy soaloa meerahndoa
I want ...	Quiero ...	kyayroa
Do you have any ...?	¿Tiene usted ...?	tyaynay oostaydh
Where is the ... department?	¿Dónde está el departamento de ...?	doanday aystah ayl daypahrtahmayntoa day
Where's the lift (elevator)/escalator?	¿Dónde está el ascensor/la escalera mecánica?	doanday aystah ayl ahsthaynsoar/lah ayskahlayrah maykahneekah
Where do I pay?	¿Dónde pago?	doanday pahgoa

That one Ese

Can you show me ...?	¿Puede usted enseñarme ...?	pwaydhay oostaydh aynsayñahrmay
that/those	ése/ésos	ayssay/ayssoass
the one in the window/in the display case	el del escaparate/de la vitrina	ayl dayl ehskahpahrahtay/day lah beetreenah
It's over there.	Está allí.	aystah ahlyee

Preference *Preferencias*

Can you show me some more?	**¿Puede usted enseñarme algo más?**	pwaydhay oostaydh aynsayñahrmay ahlgoa mahss
Haven't you anything ...?	**¿No tiene usted algo ...?**	noa tyaynay oostaydh ahlgoa
cheaper/better	**más barato/mejor**	mahss bahrahtoa/mehkhor
larger/smaller	**más grande/más pequeño**	mahss grahnday/mahss paykayñoa
more/less colourful	**más/menos colorido**	mahss/maynoass koaloareedhoa

big	**grande** *	grahnday
cheap	**barato**	bahrahtoa
dark	**oscuro**	oskooroa
good	**bueno**	bwaynoa
heavy	**pesado**	payssahdhoa
large	**grande**	grahnday
light (weight)	**ligero**	leekhayroa
light (colour)	**claro**	klahroa
rectangular	**rectangular**	rehktahngoolahr
round	**redondo**	raydhondoa
small	**pequeño**	paykayñoa
square	**cuadrado**	kwahdrahdhoa

How much? *¿Cuánto cuesta?*

How much is this?	**¿Cuánto cuesta esto?**	kwahntoa kwaystah aystoa
I don't understand.	**No entiendo.**	noa ayntyayndoa
Please write it down.	**Escríbamelo, por favor.**	ayskreebhahmayloa por fahbhor
I don't want anything too expensive.	**No quiero algo muy caro.**	noa kayroa ahlgoa mwee kahroa
I don't want to spend more than ...	**No quiero gastar más de ...**	noa kyayroa gahstahr mahss day ...

REBAJAS   SALE

---

* For feminine and plural forms, see grammar section page 159 (adjectives).

COLOURS, see page 113

Decision *Decisión*

It's not quite what I want.	**No es realmente lo que quiero.**	noa ayss rehahlmayntay loa kay kyayroa
No, I don't like it.	**No, no me gusta.**	noa noa may goostah
I'll take it.	**Me lo llevo.**	may loa lyaybhoa

Anything else? *¿Algo más?*

No, thanks, that's all.	**No gracias, eso es todo.**	noa grahthyahss ayssoa ayss toadhoa
Yes, I want ...	**Sí, quiero ...**	see kyayroa

Ordering *Encargar*

Can you order it for me?	**¿Puede usted encargarlo para mí?**	pwaydhay oostaydh aynkahrgahrloa pahrah mee
How long will it take?	**¿Cuánto tardará?**	kwahntoa tahrdahrah

Delivery *Enviar*

Deliver it to the ... Hotel.	**Envíelo al hotel ...**	aynbeeayloa ahl oatehl
Please send it to this address.	**Por favor, mándelo a estas señas.**	por fahbhor mahndayloa ah aystahss sayñahss
Do I have to pay the sales tax?	**¿Tengo que pagar el impuesto?**	tayngoa kay pahgahr ayl eempwaysstoa
Will I have any difficulty with the customs?	**¿Tendré alguna dificultad con la aduana?**	tayndray ahlgoonah deefeekooltahdh kon lah ahdwahnah

Paying *Pagar*

How much is it?	**¿Cuánto es?**	kwahntoa ayss
Can I pay by traveller's cheque?	**¿Puedo pagar con cheque de viajero?**	pwaydhoa pahgahr kon chaykay day byahkhayroa
Do you accept dollars/pounds/credit cards?	**¿Acepta usted dólares/libras/tarjetas de crédito?**	ahthayptah oostaydh doalahrayss/leebrahss/tahrkhaytahss day kraydheetoa

Haven't you made a mistake in the bill?	¿No se ha equivocado usted en la cuenta?	noa say ah aykeebhoakahdhoa oostaydh ayn lah kwayntah
Will you please wrap it?	¿Me hace el favor de envolverlo?	may ahthay ayl fahbhor day aynboalbehrloa
May I have a bag, please?	¿Puede darme una bolsa, por favor?	pwayday dahrmay oonah boalsah por fahbhor

Dissatisfied *Descontento*

Can you please exchange this?	¿Podría usted cambiarme esto, por favor?	poadreeah oostaydh kahmbyahrmay aystoa por fahbhor
I want to return this.	Quiero devolver esto.	kyayroa daybholbehr aystoa
I'd like a refund. Here's the receipt.	Quisiera que me devolviesen el dinero. Aquí está el recibo.	keessyayrah kay may daybholbyayssayn ayl deenayroa. ahkee aystah ayl raytheebha

¿En qué puedo ayudarle?	Can I help you?
¿Qué desea?	What would you like?
¿Qué ... desea?	What ... would you like?
color/forma calidad/cantidad	colour/shape quality/quantity
Lo siento, no lo tenemos.	I'm sorry, we haven't any.
Se nos ha agotado.	We're out of stock.
¿Quiere que se lo encarguemos?	Shall we order it for you?
¿Lo llevará consigo o se lo enviamos?	Will you take it with you or shall we send it?
¿Algo más?	Anything else?
Son ... pesetas, por favor.	That's ... pesetas, please.
La caja está allí.	The cashier's over there.

Bookshop—Stationer's   *Librería – Papelería*

In Spain, bookshops and stationer's are usually separate shops, though the latter will often sell paperbacks. Newspapers and magazines are sold at newsstands.

Where's the nearest ...?	¿Dónde está ... más cercano/cercana?	doanday aystah ... mahss thehrkahnoa/thehrkahnah
bookshop	la librería	lah leebrayreeah
stationer's	la papelería	lah pahpaylayreeah
newsstand	el quiosco de periódicos	ayl kyoskoa day payryo-dheekoass
Where can I buy an English newspaper?	¿Dónde puedo comprar un periódico inglés?	doanday pwaydhoa komprahr oon payryo-dheekoa eenglayss
Where's the guide-book section?	¿Dónde está la sección de libros-guía?	doanday aystah lah sayk-thyon day leebroass geeah
Where do you keep the English/second-hand books?	¿Dónde están los libros ingleses/de segunda mano?	doanday aystahn loss leebroass eenglayssayss/ day saygoondoa mahnoa
Where can I make photocopies?	¿Dónde puedo hacer fotocopias?	doanday pwaydhoa ahthayr foatoakoapyahss
I want to buy a/an/some ...	Quiero ...	kyayroa
address book	un librito de direcciones	oon leebreetoa day deerehkthyonayss
ball-point pen	un bolígrafo	oon boaleegrahfoa
book	un libro	oon leebroa
calendar	un calendario	oon kahlayndahryoa
carbon paper	papel carbón	pahpehl kahrbon
cellophane tape	cinta adhesiva	theentah ahdaysseebhah
crayons	unos lápices de color	oonoas lahpeethayss day koaloar
dictionary Spanish-English	un diccionario Español-Inglés	oon deekthyoanahryoa ayspahñoal-eenglayss
drawing paper	papel de dibujo	pahpehl day deebhookhoa
drawing pins	chinchetas	cheenchaytahss
envelopes	unos sobres	oonoas soabrayss
eraser	una goma de borrar	oonah goamah day borrahr
exercise book	un cuaderno	oon kwahdhernoa
felt-tip pen	un rotulador	oon roatoolahdhoar
file	una carpeta	oonah kahrpaytah
fountain pen	una pluma estilo-gráfica	oonah ploomah aysteeloa-grahfeekah

glue	**cola de pegar**	koalah day pay**gahr**
grammar book	**un libro de gra-mática**	con lee**broa** day grah-**mah**teekah
guidebook	**una guía**	oonah **gee**ah
ink	**tinta**	**teen**tah
black/red/blue	**negra/roja/azul**	**nay**grah/**roa**khah/ah**thool**
(adhesive) labels	**unas etiquetas (adhesivas)**	oonahss aytee**kay**tahss (ahday**ssee**bhahss)
magazine	**una revista**	oonah ray**bhees**tah
map	**un mapa**	oon **mah**pah
of the town	**de la ciudad**	day lay thyoo**dhahd**h
road map of ...	**de carreteras de ...**	day kahrray**tay**rahss day
newspaper	**un periódico**	oon payr**yod**heekoa
American/English	**americano/inglés**	ahmayree**kah**noa/een**glayss**
notebook	**un cuaderno**	oon kwah**dhehr**noa
note paper	**papel de cartas**	pah**pehl** day **kahr**tahss
paperback	**una rústica**	oonah **roos**teekah
paper napkins	**unas servilletas de papel**	oonahss sayrbeel**yay**tahss day pah**pehl**
paintbox	**una caja de pinturas**	oonah **kahkhah** day peen**toorahss**
paste	**engrudo**	ayn**grood**hoa
pen	**una pluma**	oonah **ploo**mah
pencil	**un lápiz**	oon **lah**peeth
pencil sharpener	**un sacapuntas**	oon sahkah**poon**tahss
playing cards	**unas naipes**	oonahss **nigh**payss
pocket calculator	**una calculadora de bolsillo**	oonah kahlkoolah**dhoarah** day boal**seel**yoa
post cards	**unas tarjetas postales**	oonahss tahr**khay**tahss poas**tah**layss
refill (for a pen)	**un recambio (para pluma)**	oon ray**kahm**byoa (**pah**rah **ploo**mah)
rubber	**una goma de borrar**	oonah **goa**mah day boar**rahr**
ruler	**una regla**	oonah **reh**glah
sketching block	**un bloc de dibujo**	oon bloak day dee**bhoo**khoa
staples	**unas grapas**	oonahss **grah**pahss
string	**una cuerda**	oonah **kwayr**dah
thumbtacks	**chinchetas**	cheen**chay**tahss
tissue paper	**papel de seda**	pah**pehl** day **say**dhah
tracing paper	**papel transparente**	pah**pehl** trahnspah**rayn**tay
typewriter ribbon	**una cinta para máquina**	oonah **theen**tah **pah**rah **mah**keenah
typing paper	**papel de máquina**	pah**pehl** day **mah**keenah
wrapping paper	**papel de envolver**	pah**pehl** day aynboal**behr**
writing pad	**un bloc de papel**	oon bloak day pah**pehl**

Camping equipment *Equipo de camping*

I'd like a/an/some ...	Quisiera ...	keessyayrah
bottle-opener	un abridor de botellas	oon ahbreedhor day boataylyahss
bucket	un cubo	oon koobhoa
butane gas	gas butano	gahss bootahnoa
campbed	una cama de campaña	oonah kahmah day kahmpahñah
can opener	un abrelatas	oon ahbraylahtahss
candles	unas velas	oonahss baylahss
chair	una silla	oonah seelyah
folding chair	silla plegable	seelyah playgahblay
charcoal	carbón	kahrbon
clothes pegs	unas perchas	oonahss payrchahss
compass	una brújula	oonah brookhoolah
cool box	una nevera portátil	oonah naybhayrah poartahteel
corkscrew	un sacacorchos	oon sahkahkoarchoass
crockery	una vajilla	oonah bahkheelyah
cutlery	unos cubiertos	oonoass koobhyayrtoass
deckchair	una silla de lona	oonah seelyah day loanah
dishwashing detergent	detergente para la vajilla	daytayrkhayntay pahrah lah bahkheelyah
first-aid kit	un botiquín	oon boateekeen
fishing tackle	un aparejo de pesca	oon ahpahrehkhoa day payskah
flashlight	una linterna	oonah leentehrnah
food box	una fiambrera	oonah fyahmbrayrah
frying pan	una sartén	oonah sahrtayn
groundsheet	una alfombra (de hule)	oonah ahlfoambrah (day oolay)
hammer	un martillo	oon mahrteelyoa
ice pack	un elemento congelable	oon aylaymayntoa koankhaylahblay
kerosene	petróleo	paytroalehoa
lamp	una lámpara	oonah lahmpahrah
matches	unas cerillas	oonahss thayreelyahss
mattress	un colchón	oon koalchon
methylated spirits	alcohol de quemar	ahlkoaol day kaymahr
mosquito net	una red para mosquitos	oonah raydh pahrah moaskeetoass
paraffin	petróleo	paytroalehoa
penknife	un cortaplumas	oon koartahploomahss
picnic basket	una bolsa para merienda	oonah boalsah pahrah mayryayndah

plastic bags	unas bolsas de plástico	oonahss boalsahss day plahsteekoa
rope	una cuerda	oonah kwayrdah
rucksack	una mochila	oonah moacheelah
saucepan	un cazo	oon kahthoa
scissors	unas tijeras	oonahss teekhayrahss
screwdriver	un destornillador	oon daystoarneelyahdhor
sleeping bag	un saco de dormir	oon sahkoa day doarmeer
stew pot	una cacerola	oonah kahthayroalah
table	una mesa	oonah mayssah
folding table	mesa plegable	mayssah playgahblay
tent	una tienda de campaña	oonah tyayndah day kahmpahñah
tent peg	una estaca	oonah ehstahkah
tent pole	un mástil	oon mahsteel
tinfoil	papel de estaño	pahpehl day aystahñoa
tin opener	un abrelatas	oon ahbraylahtahss
tool kit	una caja de herramientas	oonah kahkhah day ehrrahmyayntahss
torch	una linterna	oonah leentehrnah
vacuum flask	un termo	oon tayrmoa
washing powder	jabón en polvo	khahbhoan ayn poalboa
washing-up liquid	detergente para la vajilla	daytayrkhayntay pahrah lah bahkheelyah
water flask	una cantimplora	oonah kahnteemploarah
wood alcohol	alcohol de quemar	ahlkoaol day kaymahr

Crockery *Vajilla*

cups	unas tazas	oonahss tahthahss
mugs	unas tazas altas sin plato	oonahss tahthahss ahltahss seen plahtoa
plates	unos platos	oonoass plahtoass
saucers	unos platillos	oonoass plahteelyoass

Cutlery *Cubiertos*

forks	unos tenedores	oonoass taynaydhoarayss
knives	unos cuchillos	oonoass koocheelyoass
spoons	unas cucharas	oonahss koochahrahss
teaspoons	unas cucharillas	oonahss koochahreelyahss
(made of) plastic	(de) plástico	(day) plahsteekoa
(made of) stainless steel	(de) acero inoxidable	(day) ahthayroa eenoakseedhahblay

Chemist's (drugstore) *Farmacia*

A Spanish chemist's normally doesn't stock the range of items that you'll find in England or in the U.S. For example, he doesn't sell photographic equipment or books. And for perfume, make-up, etc., you must go to a *perfumería* (payrfoomay**ree**ah).

This section has been divided into two parts:

1. Pharmaceutical—medicine, first-aid, etc.
2. Toiletry—toilet articles, cosmetics

Where's the nearest (all-night) chemist's?	**¿Dónde está la farmacia (de guardia) más cercana?**	doanday aystah lah fahr-mahthyah (day gwahrdyah) mahss thehrkahnah
What time does the chemist's open/close?	**¿A qué hora abren/cierran la farmacia?**	ah kay oarah ahbrayn/thyerrahn lah fahrmahthyah

1—Pharmaceutical *Productos farmacéuticos*

I want something for ...	**Quiero algo para ...**	kyayroa ahlgoa pahrah
a cold/a cough	**un resfriado/una tos**	oon raysfryahdhoa/oonah toss
hay fever	**la fiebre del heno**	lah fyehbray dayl aynoa
a hangover	**la resaca**	lah rayssahkah
insect bites	**las picaduras de insecto**	lahss peekahdhoorahss day eensayktoa
sunburn	**las quemaduras del sol**	lahss kaymahdhoorahss dayl sol
travel sickness	**el mareo**	ayl mahrehoa
an upset stomach	**las molestias de estómago**	lahss moalaystyahss day aystoamahgoa
How many do I take?	**¿Cuántos(as) debo tomar?**	kwanhtoass(ahss) daybhoa toamahr
Can you make up this prescription for me?	**¿Puede usted prepararme esta receta?**	pwaydhay oostaydh pray-pahrahrmay aystah raythaytah
Shall I wait?	**¿Espero?**	ayspayroa
Can I get it without a prescription?	**¿Puede dármelo sin receta?**	pwaydhay dahrmayloa seen raythaytah

DOCTOR, see page 137

Can I have a/an/ some ...?	¿Puede darme ...?	pwaydhay dahrmay
antiseptic cream	una crema anti-séptica	oonah kraymah ahntee-ssaypteekah
aspirins	unas aspirinas	oonahss ahspeereenahss
bandage	una venda	oonah bayndah
elastic bandage	vendas elásticas	bayndahss aylahsteekahss
Band Aids	esparadrapo	ehspahrahdrahpoa
contraceptives	unos anticoncep-tivos	oonoass ahnteekoanthayp-teebhoass
corn plasters	unos callicidas	oonoass kahlyeethee-dhahss
cotton wool (ab-sorbent cotton)	algodón	ahlgoadon
cough drops	unas gotas para la tos	oonahss goatahss pahrah lah toss
disinfectant	un desinfectante	oon daysseenfehktahntay
ear drops	gotas para los oídos	goatahss pahrah loss oaeedhoass
Elastoplast	esparadrapo	ehspahrahdrahpoa
eye drops	unas gotas para los ojos	oonahss goatahss pahrah loss okhoass
gauze	gasa	gahssah
insect repellent/ spray	un repelente/spray para insectos	oon raypaylayntay/aysprehy pahrah eensehktoass
iodine	yodo	yoadhoa
laxative	un laxante	oon lahksahntay
mouthwash	unos gargarismos	oonoass gahrgahreesmoass
sanitary towels (napkins)	unas compresas	oonahss komprayssahss
sleeping pills	un somnífero	oon soamneefayroa
suppositories	unos supositorios	oonoass soopoasseetoaryoass
surgical dressing	unas hilas	oonahss eelahss
... tablets	unas tabletas para ...	oonahs tahblaytahss pahrah
tampons	unos tampones higiénicos	oonoass tahmpoanayss eekhyayneekoass
thermometer	un termómetro	oon tayrmoamaytroa
throat lozenges	unas pastillas para la garganta	oonahss pahsteelyahss pahrah lah gahrgahntah
tranquillizer	un sedante	oon saydhahntay

¡VENENO!	POISON!
SOLO PARA USO EXTERNO	FOR EXTERNAL USE ONLY

2 — Toiletry   *Artículos de tocador*

I'd like a/an/some ...	Quisiera ...	keessyayrah
acne cream	una crema para el acné	oonah **kray**mah **pah**rah ayl ahk**nay**
after-shave lotion	una loción para después del afeitado	oonah loathyon **pah**rah dayss**pwayss** dayl ahfay-**tah**dhoa
astringent	un astringente	oon ahstreen**khayn**tay
bath salts	sales de baño	**sah**layss day **bah**ñoa
cologne	agua de colonia	**ah**gwah day koaloa**nyah**
cream	una crema	oonah **kray**mah
cleansing cream	limpiadora	leempyahd**hoa**rah
cold cream	nutritiva	nootree**teeb**hah
foundation cream	maquillaje	mahkeely**ahk**hay
moisturizing cream	hidratante	eedrah**tahn**tay
night cream	de noche	day **noa**chay
cuticle remover	un quitacutículas	oon keetahkoo**tee**koolahss
deodorant	un desodorante	oon dayssoadhoa**rahn**tay
emery boards	unas limas de papel	oonahss **lee**mahss day pah**pehl**
eye liner	un perfilador de ojos	oon pehrfeelah**dhor** day **okh**oss
eye pencil	un lápiz de ojos	oon **lah**peeth day **okh**oss
eye shadow	una sombra de ojos	oonah **soam**brah day **okh**oss
face powder	polvos de la cara	**poal**boass day lah **kah**rah
foot cream	una crema para los pies	oonah **kray**mah **pah**rah loss **pyayss**
hand cream/lotion	una crema/loción para las manos	oonah **kray**mah/loa**thyon** **pah**rah lahss **mah**noass
lipsalve	cacao para los labios	kah**kah**oa **pah**rah loss **lahb**hyoass
lipstick	un lápiz de labios	oon **lah**peeth day **lahb**hyoass
make-up remover pads	unas toallitas de maquillaje	oonahss toaahly**ee**tahss day mahkeely**ahk**hay
mascara	pintura de pestañas	peen**toor**ah day peh**stah**ñahss
nail clippers	alicates de uñas	ahlee**kah**tayss day **oo**ñahss
nail file	una lima de uñas	oonah **lee**mah day **oo**ñahss
nail polish	un esmalte de uñas	oon ehs**mahl**tay day **oo**ñahss
nail polish remover	acetona quita-esmalte de uñas	ahthay**toa**nah keetahehs-**mahl**tay day **oo**ñahss
nail scissors	tijeras de uñas	tee**khayr**ahss day **oo**ñahss
perfume	perfume	pehr**foo**may

powder	polvos	poalboass
razor	una máquina (navaja) de afeitar	oonah mahkeenah (nah-bhahkhah) day ahfaytahr
razor blades	unas hojas de afeitar	oonahss oakhahss day ahfaytahr
rouge (blusher)	colorete	koaloaraytay
safety pins	unos imperdibles	oonoass eempehrdeeblayss
shaving cream	crema de afeitar	kraymah day afaytahr
soap	jabón	khahbhon
sponge	una esponja	oonah ehsponkhah
sun-tan cream	una crema solar	oonah kraymah soalahr
talcum powder	polvos de talco	poalboass day tahlkoa
tissues	unos pañuelos de papel	oonoass pahñwayloass day pahpehl
toilet paper	papel higiénico	pahpehl eekhyayneekoa
toothbrush	un cepillo de dientes	oon thaypeelyoa day dyayntayss
toothpaste	pasta de dientes	pahstah day dyayntayss
tweezers	unas pinzas	oonahss peenthahss

For your hair   *Para su cabello*

colour shampoo	un champú colorante	oon champoo koaloarahntay
comb	un peine	oon paynay
dye	una tintura	oonah teentoorah
hairbrush	un cepillo para el pelo	oon thaypeelyoa pahrah ayl pehloa
hairgrips (bobby pins)	unas horquillas de pinza	oonahss orkeelyahss day peenthah
hair lotion	un loción capilar	oonah loathyon kahpeelahr
hair spray	una laca para el pelo	oonah lahkah pahrah ayl payloa
hairpins	unas horquillas	oonahss oarkeelyahss
rollers	unos rulos	oonoass rooloass
setting lotion	un fijador	oon feekhahdhoar
(dry) shampoo	un champú (seco)	oon chahmpoo (saykoa)
for dry/greasy (oily) hair	para cabellos secos/grasos	pahrah kahbhaylyoass saykoass/grahssoass
tint	un tinte	oon teentay

For the baby   *Para el bebé*

baby food	alimento para bebé	ahleemayntoa pahrah baybhay
bib	un babero	oon bahbhayroa
dummy (pacifier)	un chupete	oon choopaytay
feeding bottle	un biberón	oon beebhayroan
nappies (diapers)	pañales	pahñahlayss
teat (nipple)	una tetina	oonah tayteenah

Clothing *Prendas de vestir*

If you want to buy something specific, prepare yourself in advance. Look at the list of clothing on page 117. Get some idea of the colour, material and size you want. They're all listed on the next few pages.

I'd like ...	**Quisiera ...**	keessyayrah
I want ... for a 10 year-old boy/girl.	**Quiero ... para un niño/una niña de 10 años.**	kyayroa ... pahrah oon neeñoa/oonah neeñah day 10 ahñoass
I want something like this.	**Quiero algo como esto.**	kyayroa ahlgoa koamoa aystoa
I like the one in the window.	**Me gusta el que está en el escaparate.**	may goostah ayl kay aystah ayn ayl eskahpah-rahtay
How much is that per metre?	**¿Cuánto cuesta el metro?**	kwahntoa kwaystah ayl maytroa

1 centimetre (cm.) =	0.39 in.	1 inch =	2.54 cm.
1 metre (m.)	= 39.37 in.	1 foot =	30.5 cm.
10 metres (m.)	= 32.81 ft.	1 yard =	0.91 m.

Colour *Color*

I want something in ...	**Quiero algo en ...**	kyayroa ahlgoa ayn
I want a darker/lighter shade.	**Quiero un tono más oscuro/claro.**	kyayroa oon toanoa mahss oaskooroa/klahroa
I want something to match this.	**Quiero algo que haga juego con esto.**	kyayroa ahlgoa kay ahgah khwaygoa kon aystoa
I don't like the colour.	**No me gusta el color.**	noa may goostah ayl koaloar

liso
(leesoa)

rayas
(rahyahss)

lunares
(loonahrayss)

cuadros
(kwahdroass)

estampado
(ehstahmpahdhoa)

beige	**beige** *	"behzh"
black	**negro**	nehgroa
blue	**azul**	ahthool
brown	**marrón**	mahrron
cream	**crema**	kraymah
golden	**dorado**	doarahdhoa
green	**verde**	behrday
grey	**gris**	greess
mauve	**malva**	mahlbah
orange	**naranja**	nahrahnkhah
pink	**rosa**	rossah
purple	**purpúreo**	poorpoorehoa
red	**rojo**	roakhoa
scarlet	**escarlata**	ayskahrlahtah
silver	**plateado**	plahtayahdhoa
turquoise	**turquesa**	toorkayssah
white	**blanco**	blahnkoa
yellow	**amarillo**	ahmahreelyoa
light ...	**... claro**	klahroa
dark ...	**... oscuro**	oaskooroa

Material   *Tejidos*

Do you have anything in ...?	**¿Tiene usted algo en ...?**	tyaynay oostaydh ahlgoa ayn
I want a cotton blouse.	**Quisiera una blusa de algodón.**	keessyayrah oonah bloo-sah day ahlgoadon
Is that handmade/made here?	**¿Está hecho a mano/aquí?**	aystah aychoa ah mah-noa/ahkee
Is it ...?	**¿Es ...?**	ayss
pure cotton/wool	**puro algodón/pura lana**	pooroa ahlgoadhon/poorah lahnah
colour fast	**color fijo**	koaloar feekhoa
machine/hand washable	**lavable en máquina/a mano**	lahbhahblay ayn mah-keenah/ah mahnoa
Can it be dry-cleaned?	**¿Puede limpiarse en seco?**	pwaydhay leempyahrsay ayn saykoa
Will it shrink?	**¿Encogerá?**	aynkoakhayrah

---

* For feminine and plural forms, see grammar section page 159 (adjectives).

I want something thinner.	**Quiero algo más tenue.**	kyayroa ahlgoa mahss taynooay
Do you have any better quality?	**¿Tiene usted una calidad mejor?**	tyaynah oostaydh oonah kahleedhadh mehkhor
What's it made of?	**¿De qué está hecho?**	day kay aystah aychoa

cambric	**batista**	bahteestah
camel hair	**pelo de camello**	pehloa day kahmaylyoa
chiffon	**gasa**	gahssah
corduroy	**pana**	pahnah
cotton	**algodón**	ahlgoadon
crepe	**crepé**	kraypay
denim	**algodón asargado**	ahlgoadon ahssahrgahdhoa
felt	**fieltro**	fyayltroa
flannel	**franela**	frahnaylah
gabardine	**gabardina**	gahbahrdeenah
lace	**encaje**	aynkahkhay
leather	**cuero**	kwayroa
linen	**hilo**	eeloa
pique	**piqué**	peekay
poplin	**popelín**	poapayleen
satin	**raso**	rahssoa
serge	**estameña**	aystahmaynah
silk	**seda**	saydhah
suede	**ante**	ahntay
taffeta	**tafetán**	tahfaytahn
terrycloth	**tela de toalla**	taylah day toaahlyah
tulle	**tul**	tool
tweed	**cheviot**	chaybhyoat
velvet	**terciopelo**	tehrthyoapehloa
wool	**lana**	lahnah
worsted	**estambre**	aystahmbray
artificial	**artificial**	ahrteefeethyahl
synthetic	**sintético**	seentayteekoa

Size *Talla*

My size is 38.	**Mi talla es la 38.**	mee tahlyah ayss lah 38
Could you measure me?	**¿Puede usted medirme?**	pwaydhay oostaydh maydheermay
I don't know Spanish sizes.	**No conozco las tallas españolas.**	noa koanoathkoa lahss tahlyahss ayspahñolahss

This is your size *Esta es su talla*

Sizes can vary somewhat from country to country and from
one manufacturer to another, so be sure to try on shoes and
clothing before you buy.

Women *Señoras*

Dresses/Suits					
American	8	10	12	14	16	18
British	10	12	14	16	18	20
Continental	36	38	40	42	44	46

Stockings							Shoes			
American		8	8½	9	9½	10	10½	6	7	8	9
British	}							4½	5½	6½	7½
Continental	0	1	2	3	4	5	37	39	40	41

Men *Caballeros*

Suits/Overcoats							Shirts			
American	}	36	38	40	42	44	46	15	16	17	18
British											
Continental	46	48	50	52	54	56	38	41	43	45

Shoes									
American	}	5	6	7	8	8½	9	9½	10	11
British										
Continental	38	39	41	42	43	43	44	44	45

A good fit? *Una buena caída*

Can I try it on?	**¿Puedo probár-melo?**	pwaydhoa probhahr-mayloa
Where's the fitting room?	**¿Dónde está el probador?**	doanday aystah ayl probhahdhor
Is there a mirror?	**¿Tiene usted un espejo?**	tyaynay oostaydh oon ayspaykhoa
It fits very well.	**Me queda muy bien.**	may kaydhah mwee byayn

NUMBERS, see page 147

It doesn't fit.	**No me queda bien.**	noa may **kay**dhah byayn
It's too ...	**Es demasiado ...**	ayss daymah**ssyah**dhoa
short/long	**corto/largo**	**koar**toa/**lahr**goa
tight/loose	**ajustado/ancho**	ahk**hoos**tahdoa/**ahn**choa
How long will it take to alter?	**¿Cuánto tardarán en arreglarlo?**	**kwahn**toa tahrdah**rahn** ayn ahrray**glahr**loa

Shoes   *Zapatos*

I'd like a pair of ...	**Quisiera un par de ...**	kee**ssyay**rah oon pahr day
(rain) boots	**botas (par la lluvia)**	**boa**tahss pahrah lah **lyoob**hyah
plimsolls (sneakers)	**zapatos de lona**	thah**pah**toass day **loa**nah
sandals	**sandalias**	sahn**dah**lyahss
shoes	**zapatos**	thah**pah**toass
flat/with a heel	**planos/con tacón**	**plah**noass/kon tah**kon**
leather/suede	**de cuero/de ante**	day **kway**roa/day **ahn**tay
slippers	**zapatillas**	thahpah**teel**yahss
These are too ...	**Estos son demasiado ...**	**ays**toass son daymah**ssyah**dhoa
narrow/wide	**estrechos/anchos**	ays**tray**choass/**ahn**choass
large/small	**grandes/pequeños**	**grahn**dayss/**pay**kayñoass
Do you have a smaller/larger size?	**¿Tiene una talla más pequeña/grande?**	**tyay**nay **oo**nah **tahl**yah mahss/**pay**kayñah/**grahn**day
Do you have the same in brown/black?	**¿Tiene usted lo mismo en marrón/negro?**	**tyay**nay oos**taydh** loa **mees**moa ayn mah**rron**/**neh**groa
I need some shoe polish/shoelaces.	**Necesito crema/cordones para zapatos.**	naythays**see**toa **kray**mah/koar**doa**nayss **pah**rah thah**pah**toass

Shoes worn out? Here's the key to getting them fixed again:

Can you repair these shoes?	**¿Puede usted reparar estos zapatos?**	**pway**dhay oos**taydh** raypah**rahr** **ays**toass thah**pah**toass
I want new soles and heels.	**Quiero nuevas suelas y tacones.**	**kyay**roa **nway**bhahss **sway**lahss ee tah**koa**nayss
When will they be ready?	**¿Cuándo estarán listos?**	**kwahn**doa aystah**rahn** **lees**toass

COLOURS, see page 113

Clothes and accessories   *Ropa y accessorios*

I'd like a/an/some ...	Quisiera ...	keessyayrah
bathing cap	un gorro de baño	oon gorroa day bahñoa
bathing suit	un traje de baño	oon trahkhay day bahñoa
bathrobe	un albornoz	oon ahlboarnoth
blazer	un blázer	oon blahther
blouse	una blusa	oonah bloossah
bow tie	una corbata de lazo	oonah korbahtah day lahthoa
bra	un sostén	oon soastayn
braces	unos tirantes	oonoass teerahntayss
briefs	unos calzoncillos	oonoass kahlthontheelyoass
cap	una gorra	oonah gorrah
cardigan	una chaqueta de punto	oonah chakaytah day poontoa
coat (woman's)	un abrigo	oon ahbreegoa
coat (man's)	un gabán	oon gahbhahn
dinner jacket	un smoking	oon smoakeeng
dress	un vestido	oon baysteedhoa
dressing gown	una bata	oonah bahtah
evening dress (woman's)	un traje de noche	oon trahkhay day noachay
garter belt	un portaligas	oon poartahleegahss
garters	unas ligas	oonahss leegahss
girdle	una faja	oonah fahkhah
gloves	unos guantes	oonoass gwahntayss
handbag	un bolso de mano	oon boalsoa day mahnoa
handkerchief	un pañuelo	oon pahñwayloa
hat	un sombrero	oon soambrayroa
jacket	una chaqueta	oonah chahkaytah
jeans	unos tejanos	oonoass tehkhahnoass
jersey	un jersey	oon khayrsay
nightdress	un camisón	oon kahmeesson
panties	unas bragas	oonahss brahgahss
pants (Am.)	unos pantalones	oonoass pahntahloanayss
panty girdle	una faja braga	oonah fahkhah brahgah
panty hose	unos leotardos	oonoass layoatahrdoass
pullover	un pullover	oon pooloabhehr
roll-neck (turtle-neck)/round-neck/V-neck	cuello vuelto/redondo/en forma de V	kwaylyoa bwehltoa/raydoandoa/ayn foarmah day bayeh
with long/short sleeves	con mangas largas/cortas	kon mahngahss lahrgahss/koartahss
without sleeves	sin mangas	seen mahngahss

pyjamas	un pijama	oon peekhahmah
raincoat	un impermeable	oon eempehrmayahblay
scarf	una bufanda	oonah boofahndah
shirt	una camisa	oonah kahmeessah
shorts	unos pantalones cortos	oonoass pahntahloanayss koartoass
skirt	una falda	oonah fahldah
slip	una combinación	oonah koambeenahthyon
socks	unos calcetines	oonoass kahlthayteenayss.
stockings	unas medias	oonahss maydhyahss
suit (man's)	un traje	oon trahkhay
suit (woman's)	un vestido	oon baysteedhoa
suspenders	unos tirantes	oonoass teerahntayss
sweater	un suéter	oon swaytehr
sweatshirt	un suéter de tela de punto	oon swaytehr day taylah day poontoa
swimming trunks	un bañador	oon bahähdoar
swimsuit	un traje de baño	oon trahkhay day bahñoa
T-shirt	una camiseta	oonah kahmeessaytah
tie	una corbata	oonah korbahtah
tights	unos leotardos	oonoass layoatahrdoass
tracksuit	un chandal de entrenamiento	oon chahndahl day ehntraynahmyayntoa
trousers	unos pantalones	oonoass pahntahloanayss
tuxedo	un smoking	oon smoakeeng
twin set	un conjunto de lana	oon koankhoontoa day lahnah
umbrella	un paraguas	oon pahrahgwahss
underpants	unos calzoncillos	oonoass kahlthontheelyoass
undershirt	una camiseta	oonah kahmeessaytah
vest (Am.)	un chaleco	oon chahlaykoa
vest (Br.)	una camiseta	oonah kahmeessaytah
waistcoat	un chaleco	oon chahlaykoa

belt	un cinturón	oon theentooron
buckle	una hebilla	oonah aybheelyah
button	un botón	oon boaton
collar	un cuello	oon kwaylyoa
elastic	un elástico	oon aylahsteekoa
pocket	un bolsillo	oon boalseelyoa
press stud (snap fastener)	un broche de presión	oon broachay day prayssyon
zip (zipper)	una cremallera	oonah kraymahlyayrah

Electrical appliances   *Aparatos eléctricos*

Today 220-volt A.C. 50 cycles is becoming standard, but older installations of 125 volts can still be found. So check the voltage before you plug your appliance in. Don't forget to take along a plug adaptor: two-pin (prong) continental plugs are used in Spain.

What's the voltage?	**¿Cuál es el voltaje?**	kwahl ayss ayl boaltahkhay
This is broken. Can you repair it?	**Esto está roto. ¿Puede usted arreglarlo?**	aystoa aystah roatoa. pwaydhay oostaydh ahrrayglahrloa
I'd like (to hire) a video cassette/ video recorder.	**Quisiera (alquilar) una video-cassette/ video-grabadora.**	keessyayrah (ahlkeelahr) oonah beedhayoa-kahssayttay/beedhayoa-grahbhahdhoarah
Can you show me how it works?	**¿Puede mostrarme cómo funciona?**	pwaydhay moastrahrmay koamoa foonthyonah
I'd like a/an/some ...	**Quisiera ...**	keessyayrah
adaptor	**un adaptador**	oon ahdhahptahdhor
amplifier	**un amplificador**	oon ahmpleefeekahdhor
battery	**una pila**	oonah peelah
bulb	**una bombilla**	oonah boambeelyah
electric toothbrush	**un cepillo de dientes eléctrico**	oon thaypeelyoa day dyayntayss aylayktreekoa
hair dryer	**un secador de pelo**	oon saykahdhor day pehloa
headphones	**un casco con auriculares**	oon kahskoa kon owreekoolahrayss
(travelling) iron	**una plancha (de viaje)**	oonah plahnchah day byahkhay
lamp	**una lámpara**	oonah lahmpahrah
plug	**una clavija de enchufe**	oonah klahbheekhah day aynchoofay
portable ...	**... portátil**	... portahteel
radio	**una radio**	oonah rahdhyoa
car radio	** una radio para coche**	oonah rahdhyoa pahrah koachay
record player	**un tocadiscos**	oon toakahdheeskoass
shaver	**una máquina de afeitar eléctrica**	oonah mahkeenah day ahfaytahr aylayktreekah
speakers	**unos altavoces**	oonoass ahltahbhoathayss
(cassette) tape recorder	**un magnetófono (cassette)**	oon mahgnaytofoanoa (kahssayttay)
transformer	**un transformador**	oon trahnsformahdhor

Grocery *Tienda de comestibles*

I want some bread, please.	**Quiero pan, por favor.**	kyayroa pahn por fabhor
What sort of cheese do you have?	**¿Qué clases de queso tiene?**	kay klahssayss day kayssoa tyaynay
A piece of ...	**Un trozo ...**	oon troathoa
that one	**de ése**	day ayssay
the one on the shelf	**del que está en el estante**	dayl kay aystah ayn ayl aystahntay
I'd like one of these and two of those.	**Quisiera uno de éstos y dos de ésos.**	keessyayrah oonoa day aystoass ee oonoa day ayssoass
May I help myself?	**¿Puedo servirme yo mismo?**	pwaydhoa sehrbeermay yoa meesmoa
I'd like ...	**Quisiera ...**	keessyayrah
a kilo of apples	**un kilo de manzanas**	oon keeloa day mahnthahnahss
half a kilo of tomatoes	**medio kilo de tomates**	maydhyoa keeloa day toamahtayss
100 g of butter	**100 gr. de mantequilla**	100 grahmoass day mahntaykeelyah
a litre of milk	**un litro de leche**	oon leetroa day laychay
4 slices of ham	**4 rebanadas de jamón**	4 raybhahnahdhahss day khahmon
a packet of tea	**un paquete de té**	oon pahkaytay day tay
a jar of honey	**un tarro de miel**	oon tahrroa day myehl
a tin (can) of pears	**una lata de peras**	oonah lahtah day pehrahss
a tube of mustard	**un tubo de mostaza**	oon toobhoa day moastahthah

---

1 kilogram or kilo (kg.) = 1000 grams (g.)

| 100 g. = 3.5 oz. | ½ kg. = 1.1 lbs. |
| 200 g. = 7.0 oz. | 1 kg. = 2.2 lbs. |

1 oz. = 28.35 g.
1 lb. = 453.60 g.

---

1 litre (l.) = 0.88 imp. quarts = 1.06 U.S. quarts

| 1 imp. quart = 1.14 l. | 1 U.S. quart = 0.95 l. |
| 1 imp. gallon = 4.55 l. | 1 U.S. gallon = 3.8 l. |

FOOD, see also page 63

Jeweller's—Watchmaker's *Joyería – Relojería*

I'd like a small present for ...	Quisiera un regalito para ...	keesyayrah oon raygahleetoa pahrah
Is this real silver?	¿Es esto de plata auténtica?	ayss aystoa day plahtah owtaynteekah
Do you have anything in gold?	¿Tiene usted algo de oro?	tyaynay oostaydh ahlgoa day oaroa
How many carats is this?	¿De cuántos quilates es esto?	day kwahntoass keelahtayss ayss aystoa
Can you repair this watch?	¿Puede arreglar este reloj?	pwaydhay ahrrayglahr aystay rehlokh
I'd like a/an/some ...	Quisiera ...	keessyayrah

alarm clock	un despertador	oon dayspayrtahdhor
bangle	una esclava	oonah aysklahbhah
battery	una pila	oonah peelah
bracelet	una pulsera	oonah poolsayrah
charm bracelet	pulsera de fetiches	poolsayrah day fayteechayss
brooch	un broche	oon brochay
chain	una cadena	oonah kahdhaynah
charm	un amuleto	oon ahmoolaytoa
cigarette case	una pitillera	oonah peeteelyayrah
cigarette lighter	un encendedor	oon aynthayndaydhor
clip	un clip	oon kleep
clock	un reloj	oon rehlokh
cross	una cruz	oonah krooth
cuff links	unos gemelos	oonoass khaymayloass
cutlery	unos cubiertos	oonoass koobhyehrtoass
earrings	unos pendientes	oonoass payndyayntayss
jewel box	un joyero	oon khoyayroa
mechanical pencil	un lapicero	oon lahpeethayroa
necklace	un collar	oon koalyahr
pendant	un medallón	oon maydhahlyon
pin	un alfiler	oon ahlfeelehr
pocket watch	un reloj de bolsillo	oon rehlokh day boalseelyoa
powder compact	una polvera	oonah poalbayrah
propelling pencil	un lapicero	oon lahpeethayroa
ring	una sortija	oonah sorteekhah
engagement ring	sortija de pedida	sorteekhah day paydheedhah
signet ring	sortija de sello	sorteekhah day saylyoa
wedding ring	un anillo de boda	oon ahneelyoa day boadhah

rosary	un rosario de cuentas	oon roassahryoa day kwayntahss
silverware	unos objetos de plata	oonoass obkhaytoass day plahtah
tie clip	un sujetador de corbata	oon sookhaytahdhor day korbahtah
tie pin	un alfiler de corbata	oon ahlfeelehr day korbahtah
watch (wristwatch)	un reloj (de pulsera)	oon rehlokh (day poolsayrah)
automatic	automático	aotoamahteekoa
with a second hand	con segundero manecilla	kon saygoondayroa mahnaytheelyah
with quartz movement	con mecanismo de cuarzo	kon maykahneesmoa day kwahrthoa
watchstrap (watchband)	una correa de reloj	oonah korrehah day rehlokh

amber	ámbar	ahmbahr
amethyst	amatista	ahmahteestah
copper	cobre	koabray
coral	coral	korahl
crystal	cristal	kreestahl
cut glass	cristal tallado	kreestahl tahlyahdhoa
diamond	diamante	dyahmahntay
emerald	esmeralda	aysmayrahldah
enamel	esmalte	aysmahltay
gold	oro	oaroa
gold plate	lámina de oro	lahmeenah day oaroa
ivory	marfil	mahrfeel
jade	jade	khahdheh
onyx	ónix	oneekss
pearl	perla	pehrlah
pewter	peltre	pehltray
platinum	platino	plahteenoa
ruby	rubí	roobhee
sapphire	zafiro	thahfeeroa
silver	plata	plahtah
silver plate	plata chapada	plahtah chahpahdhah
stainless steel	acero inoxidable	ahthayroa eenokseedhahblay
topaz	topacio	topahthyoa
turquoise	turquesa	toorkayssah

Optician   *El óptico*

Where can I find an optician?	¿Dónde puedo encontrar un óptico?	doanday pwaydhoa aynkoantrahr oon oapteekoa
I've broken my glasses.	Se me han roto las gafas.	say may ahn roatoa lahss gahfahss
Can you repair them for me?	¿Me las puede usted arreglar?	may lahss pwaydhay oostaydh ahrrayglahr
When will they be ready?	¿Cuándo estarán listas?	kwahndhoa aystahrahn leestahss
Can you change the lenses?	¿Puede cambiar los lentes?	pwaydhay kahmbyahr loss layntayss
I want tinted lenses.	Quiero cristales ahumados.	kyayroa kreestahlayss owmahdhoass
I'd like to have my eyes checked.	Quisiera que me controlara los ojos.	keessyayrah kay may koantroalahrah loass oakhoass
I'm short-sighted/long-sighted.	Soy miope/présbite.	soy myoapay/praysbeetay
I want some contact lenses.	Quiero lentes de contacto.	kyayroa layntayss day kontahktoa
I've lost a contact lens.	He perdido un lente de contacto.	ay payrdheedhoa oon layntay day koantahktoa
I have hard/soft lenses.	Tengo lentes duros/suaves.	tayngoa layntays dooroas/swahbhayss
Do you have some solution for contact lenses?	¿Tiene una solución para lentes de contacto?	tyaynay oonah soaloothyon pahrah layntayss day koantahktoa
May I look in a mirror?	¿Puedo verme en un espejo?	pwaydhoa bayrmay ayn oon ayspaykhoa
I'd like a spectacle case.	Quisiera un estuche para gafas.	keessyayrah oon aystoochay pahrah gahfahss
I'd like to buy a pair of binoculars.	Quisiera comprar unos binoculares.	keessyayrah komprahr oonoass beenoakoolahrayss
I'd like to buy a pair of sunglasses.	Quisiera comprar unas gafas de sol.	keessyayrah komprahr oonahss gahfass day sol
How much do I owe you?	¿Cuánto le debo?	kwahntoa lay daybhoa

NUMBERS, see page 147

Photography *Fotografía*

I want a camera.	**Quisiera una cámara.**	keessyayrah oonah kahmahrah
automatic/inexpensive/simple	**automática/barata/sencilla**	owtoamahteekah/bahrahtah/sayntheelyah
Show me a cine (movie) camera, please.	**Enséñeme una cámara de filmar, por favor.**	aynsayñaymay oonah kahmahrah day feelmahr por fahbhor
I'd like to have some passport photos taken.	**Quisiera que me haga unas fotos para pasaporte.**	keessyayrah kay may ahgah oonahss footoass pahrah pahssahpoartay

Film *Rollos/Películas*

I'd like a film for this camera.	**Quisiera un rollo para esta cámara.**	keessyayrah oon roalyoa pahrah aystah kahmahrah
black and white	**en blanco y negro**	ayn blahnkoa ee naygroa
colour	**en color**	ayn koaloar
colour negative	**negativo de color**	naygahteebhoa day koaloar
colour slide	**diapositivas**	dyahposseteebhahss
cartridge	**un cartucho**	oon kahrtoochoa
disc film	**un disco-película**	oon deeskoa payleekoolah
roll film	**un carrete/rollo**	oon kahrraytay/roalyoa
cine (movie) film	**una película**	oonah payleekoolah
super eight	**super ocho**	soopehr oachoa
video tape	**una cinta video**	oonah theentah beedhayoa
24/36 exposures	**24/36 exposiciones**	baynteekwahtroa/trayntah ee sayss aykspoasseethyonayss
this ASA/DIN number	**este número de ASA/DIN**	aystay noomayroa day ahssah/deen
this size	**de este tamaño**	day aystay tahmahñoa
artificial light/daylight type	**para luz artificial/del día**	pahrah looth ahrteefeethyahl/dayl deeah
fast (high-speed)	**rápido**	rahpeedhoa
fine grain	**de grano fino**	day grahnoa feenoa

Processing *Revelado*

How much do you charge for developing/printing?	**¿Qué cobra por el revelado/la impresión?**	kay koabrah por ayl raybhaylahdhoa/lah eemprayssyon

NUMBERS, see page 147

I want ... prints of each negative.	Quiero ... copias de cada negativo.	kyayroa ... koapyahss day kahdhah naygahteebhoa
with a mat/glossy finish	con acabado mate/ de brillo	kon ahkahbhahdhoa mahtay/day breelyoa
Will you please enlarge this?	¿Haría usted una ampliación de ésta, por favor?	ahreeah oostaydh oonah ahmplyahthyon day aystah por fahbhor
When will the photos be ready?	¿Cuándo estarán listas las fotos?	kwahndoa aystahrahn leestahss lahss foatoas

Accessories and repairs   *Accesorios y reparaciones*

I want a/an ...	Quisiera ...	keessyayrah
battery	una pila	oonah peelah
cable release	un cable del dispa- rador	oon kahblay dayl dees- pahrahdhoar
camera case	una funda	oonah foondah
(electronic) flash	un flash (electrónico)	oon flash (aylayktroa- neekoa)
filter	un filtro	oon feeltroa
for black and white	para blanco y negro	pahrah blahnkoa ee naygroa
for colour	para color	pahrah koaloar
lens	un objetivo	oon obkhayteebhoa
telephoto lens	de acercamiento	day ahthayrkahmyayntoa
wide-angle lens	gran angular	grahn ahngoolahr
lens cap	un capuchón para el objetivo	oon kapoochon pahrah ayl obkhayteebhoa
This camera doesn't work. Can you repair it?	Esta cámara está estropeada. ¿Puede usted repararla?	aystah kahmahrah aystah aystroapehahdhah. pwaydhay oostaydh raypahrahrlah
The film is jammed.	La película está atrancada.	lah payleekoolah aystah ahtrahnkahdhah
There's something wrong with the ...	Hay algo que va mal en ...	igh ahlgoa kay bah mahl ayn
exposure counter	la escala de expo- sición	lah ayskahlah day aykspoasseethyon
film winder	el enrollador	ayl aynroalyahdhor
light meter	el exposímetro	ayl aykspoasseemehtroa
rangefinder	el telémetro	ayl taylaymaytroa
shutter	el obturador	ayl obtoorahdhor

Tobacconist's   *Tabacos*

Most Spanish cigarettes are made of strong, black tobacco.
Nearly all major foreign brands are available in Spain at two
to three times the price of local cigarettes.

A packet/carton of cigarettes, please.	**Una cajetilla/un cartón de cigarrillos, por favor.**	oonah kahkhay**teel**yah/oon kahr**ton** day theegahr-**reel**yoass por fah**bhor**
I'd like a box of ...	**Quisiera una caja de ...**	kees**syay**rah oonah **kah**khah day
May I have a/an/ some ..., please?	**¿Puede darme ..., por favor?**	**pway**day **dahr**may por fah**bhor**
candy	**unos caramelos**	oonoass kahrah**may**loass
chewing gum	**un chicle**	oon **chee**klay
chocolate	**un chocolate**	oon choakoa**lah**tay
cigarettes	**unos cigarrillos**	oonoass theegahr**reel**yoass
American	**americanos**	ahmayreekah**no**ass
English	**ingleses**	eeng**lay**ssayss
menthol	**mentolados**	mayntoa**lahd**hoass
mild/strong	**suaves/fuertes**	**swahb**hayss/**fwehr**tayss
cigarette lighter	**un encendedor**	oon aynthaynday**dhor**
cigarette paper	**papel para cigarrillos**	pah**pehl** pahrah theegahr**reel**yoass
cigars	**unos puros**	oonoass **poo**roass
flints	**unas piedras de mechero**	oonahss **pyay**drahss day may**chay**roa
lighter fluid/gas	**gasolina/gas para encendedor**	gahssoa**lee**nah/gahss pahrah aynthaynday**dhor**
matches	**unas cerillas**	oonahss thay**reel**yahss
pipe	**una pipa**	oonah **pee**pah
pipe cleaners	**unas limpiapipas**	oonahss leempyah**pee**pahss
pipe tobacco	**tabaco para pipa**	tah**bhah**koa pahrah **pee**pah
pipe tool	**utensilios para pipa**	ootayn**seel**yoass pahrah **pee**pah
post cards	**unas tarjetas postales**	oonahss tahr**khay**tahss poas**tah**layss
snuff	**rapé**	rah**pay**
stamps	**unos sellos**	oonoass **sayl**yoass
sweets	**unos caramelos**	oonoass kahrah**may**loass
wick	**una mecha**	oonah **may**chah

filter tipped	**con filtro**	kon **feel**troa
without filter	**sin filtro**	seen **feel**troa

Miscellaneous *Diversos*

Souvenirs *Recuerdos*

Spain's souvenir industry churns out everything from personalized bull-fighting posters to plastic castanets. Kitsch aside, you will also find a selection of fine hand-crafted articles: shawls, embroidered linen, lace-work, painted fans, hand-woven shopping baskets, wicker-work and carved wood.

You may come across special outlets for handicrafts *(artesanía),* some of them government sponsored.

bullfight poster	**el cartel de toros**	ayl kahr**tayl** day **to**aroass
bullfighter's cap	**la montera**	lah moan**tay**rah
castanets	**las castañuelas**	lahss kahstah**ñway**lahss
copperware	**objetos de cobre**	oabkhaytoass day **ko**abray
doll	**la muñeca**	lah moo**ñay**kah
earrings	**los pendientes**	loss payn**dyayn**tayss
earthenware	**la loza de barro**	lah **lo**athah day **bahr**roa
embossed leather	**el cuero repujado**	ayl **kway**roa raypook**hah**dhoa
embroidery	**el bordado**	ayl boar**dah**dhoa (day
fan	**el abanico**	ayl ahbahh**nee**koa
guitar	**la guitarra**	lah gee**tahr**rah
jewellery	**las joyas**	lahss **kho**yahss
lace	**los encajes**	loss ayn**kah**khayss
mantilla	**la mantilla**	lah mahn**tee**lyah
pitcher	**el botijo**	ayl boa**tee**khoa
poncho	**el poncho**	ayl **pon**choa
rosary	**el rosario**	ayl roa**ssah**ryoa
tambourine	**la pandereta**	lah pahnday**ray**tah
wineskin	**la bota**	lah **boa**tah
woodcarving	**la talla en madera**	lah **tah**lyah ayn mah**dhay**rah

Records — Cassettes *Discos – Cassettes*

I'd like a …	**Quisiera …**	kee**ssyay**rah
cassette	**una cassette**	oonah kahs**sayt**tay
compact disc	**un disco compacto**	oon **dees**koa koam**pahk**toa
record	**un disco**	oon **dees**koa
video cassette	**una video-cassette**	oonah beedhayoa-kah-**ssayt**tay

Can I listen to this record?	¿Puedo escuchar este disco?	pwaydhoa aysskoochahr aystay deeskoa

L.P. (33 rmp)	33 revoluciones	trayntah ee trayss raybhoaloothyonayss
E.P. (45 rmp)	maxi 45	maxi kwahrayntah ee theenkoa
single	45 revoluciones	kwahrayntah ee theenkoa raybhoaloothyonayss

chamber music	música de cámara	moosseekah day kahmahrah
classical music	música clásica	moosseekah klahsseekah
folk music	música folklórica	moosseekah folkloareekah
instrumental music	música instrumental	moosseekah eenstroomayntahl
light music	música ligera	moosseekah leekhayrah
orchestral music	música de orquesta	moosseekah day orkaystah
pop music	música pop	moosseekah pop

Toys *Juguetes*

I'd like a toy for a boy/a 5-year-old-girl.	Quisiera un juguete para un niño/una niña de 5 años.	keessyayrah oon khoogaytay pahrah oon neeñoa/oonah neeñah day 5 ahñoass
I'd like a/an/some ...	Quisiera ...	keessyayrah
beach ball	una pelota de playa	oonah payloatah day plahyah
bucket and spade (pail and shovel)	un cubo y una pala	oon koobhoa ee oonah pahlah
building blocks	unos cubos de construcción	oonoass koobhoass day koanstrookthyon
card game	un juego de cartas	oon khwaygoa day kahrtahss
chess set	un ajedrez	oon ahkhaydrayth
dice	unos dados	oonoass dahdhoass
electronic game	un juego electrónico	oon khwaygoa aylayktroaneekoa
flippers	unas aletas para nadar	oonahss ahlaytahss pahrah nahdhahr
roller skates	unos patines de ruedas	oonoass pahteenayss day rwaydhahss
snorkel	unos espantasuegras	oonoass ayspahntahswaygrahss

Your money: banks—currency

The normal banking hours in Spain are from 9 a.m. to 2 p.m. Monday to Friday (Saturday 9 a.m. to 1 p.m.). Outside normal banking hours, many travel agencies, major hotels and other businesses displaying a *cambio* sign will change foreign currency into pesetas. Always take your passport with you for identification when you go to change money.

Credit cards   *Tarjetas de crédito*

All the internationally recognized credit cards are accepted by hotels, restaurants and businesses in Spain.

Traveller's cheques   *Cheques de viajero*

In tourist areas, shops and all banks, hotels and travel agencies accept traveller's cheques, though you are likely to get a better rate of exchange at a national or regional bank. You'll have no problem settling bills or paying for purchases with Eurocheques.

Monetary unit   *La unidad monetaria*

The basic unit of currency is the *peseta* (pay**ssay**tah), abbreviated *pta*. There are coins of 1, 2, 5, 10, 25, 50 and 100 pesetas and banknotes of 100, 200, 500, 1,000, 2,000 and 5,000 pesetas.

Where's the nearest bank?	**¿Dónde está el banco más cercano?**	doanday aystah ayl bahnkoa mahss thehrkahnoa
Where's the nearest currency exchange office?	**¿Dónde está la oficina de cambio más cercana?**	doanday aystah lah oafeetheenah day kahmbyoa mahss thehrkahnah
What time does the bank open/close?	**¿A qué hora abren/ cierran el banco?**	ah kay oarah ahbrayn/ thyayrrahn ayl bahnkoa
Where can I cash a traveller's cheque (check)?	**¿Dónde puedo cobrar un cheque de viajero?**	doanday pwaydhoa koabrahr oon chaykay day byahkhayroa

At the bank   *En el banco*

I want to change some dollars/pounds.	**Quiero cambiar unos dólares/unas libras esterlinas.**	kyayroa kahmbyahr oonoass doalahrayss/oonahss leebrahss aystayrleenahss
I want to cash a traveller's cheque.	**Quiero cobrar un cheque de viajero.**	kyayroa koabrahr oon chaykay day byahkhayroa
Here's my passport.	**Aquí está mi pasaporte.**	ahkee aystah mee passahportay
What's the exchange rate?	**¿A cómo está el cambio?**	ah koamoa aystah ayl kahmbyoa
How much of commission do you charge?	**¿Qué comisión cargan?**	kay koameessyon kahrgahn
Can you cash a personal cheque?	**¿Puede hacer efectivo un cheque personal?**	pwaydhay ahthayr ayfaykteebhoa oon chaykay pehrsoanahl
How long will it take to clear?	**¿Cuánto tardará en tramitarlo?**	kwahntoa tahrdahrah ayn trahmeetahrloa
Can you telex my bank in London?	**¿Puede mandar un télex a mi banco en Londres?**	pwaydhay mahndahr oon taylayks ah mee bahnkoa ayn londrayss
I have a/an/some ...	**Tengo ...**	tayngoa
credit card	**una tarjeta de crédito**	oonah tahrkhaytah day kraydeetoa
Eurocheques	**unos eurocheques**	oonoass ayooroachaykayss
introduction from ...	**un formulario de presentación de ...**	oon foarmoolahryoa day prayssayntahthyon day
letter of credit	**una carta de crédito**	oonah kahrtah day kraydeetoa
I'm expecting some money from Chicago. Has it arrived yet?	**Espero una transferencia de Chicago. ¿Ha llegado ya?**	ayspayroa oonah trahnsfayraynthyah day cheekahgoa ah lyaygahdhoa yah
Please give me ... notes (bills) and some small change.	**Por favor, déme ... billetes y algo en moneda.**	por fahbhor daymay ... beelyaytayss ee ahlgoa ayn moanaydhah
Give me ... large notes and the rest in small notes.	**Déme ... en los billetes de más valor que tenga y el resto en billetes de menor valor.**	daymay ... ayn loss beelyaytayss day mahss bahlor kay tayngah ee ayl raystoa ayn beelyaytayss day maynor bahlor

NUMBERS, see page 146

Depositing *Depósitos*

I want to credit this to my account.	**Quiero acreditar esto a mi cuenta.**	kyayroa ahkraydheetahr aystoa ah mee kwayntah
I want to credit this to Mr ... 's account.	**Quiero acreditar esto a la cuenta del Señor ...**	kyayroa ahkraydheetahr aystoa ah lah kwayntah dayl sayñor
I want to open an account/withdraw ... pesetas.	**Quiero abrir una cuenta/retirar ... pesetas.**	kyayroa ahbreer oonah kwayntah/rayteerahr ... payssaytahss

Business terms *Expresiones de negocios*

My name is ...	**Me llamo ...**	may lyahmoa
Here's my card.	**Aquí está mi tarjeta.**	ahkee aystah mee tahrkhaytah
I have an appointment with ...	**Tengo una cita con ...**	tayngoa oonah theetah kon
Can you give me an estimate of the cost?	**¿Puede darme una estimación del precio?**	pwaydhay dahrmay oonah aysteemahthyon dayl praythyoa
What's the rate of inflation?	**¿Cuál es la tasa de inflación?**	kwahl ayss lah tahssah day eenflathyon
Can you provide me with an interpreter/a secretary?	**¿Puede conseguirme un intérprete/una secretaria?**	pwaydhay konsaygeermay oon eentayrpraytay/oonah saykraytahryah

amount	**la suma**	lah soomah
balance	**el balance**	ayl bahlahnthay
capital	**el capital**	ayl kahpeetahl
cheque book	**la chequera**	lah chaykayrah
interest	**el interés**	ayl eentayrayss
investment	**la inversión**	lah eenbayrsyon
invoice	**la factura**	lah fahktoorah
loss	**la pérdida**	lah payrdeedhah
mortgage	**la hipoteca**	lah eepoataykah
payment	**el pago**	ayl pahgoa
profit	**la ganancia**	lah gahnahnthyah
purchase	**la compra**	lah koamprah
sale	**la venta**	lah bayntah
transfer	**la transferencia**	lah trahnsfayraynthyah
value	**el valor**	ayl bahloar

At the post office

Post offices are for mail and telegrams only; normally you can't make telephone calls from them. Hours vary slightly from town to town, but routine postal business is generally transacted from 9 a.m. to 1 or 1.30 p.m. and 4 to 6 or 7 p.m., Monday to Saturday except for Saturday afternoons.

Stamps are also on sale at tobacconists' *(tabacos)* and often at hotels. Letter boxes (mailboxes) are yellow with a red insignia.

Where's the nearest post office?	¿Dónde está la oficina de correos más cercana?	doanday aystah lah oafee-theenah day korrehoass mahss thehrkahnah
What time does the post office open/close?	¿A qué hora abren/cierran correos?	ah kay oarah ahbrayn/thyayrrahn korrehoass
Which window do I go to for stamps?	¿A qué ventanilla debo ir para comprar sellos?	ah kay bayntahneelyah daybhoa eer pahrah koamprahr saylyoass
At which counter can I cash an international money order?	¿En qué mostrador puedo hacer efectivo un giro postal internacional?	ayn kay moastrahdhor pwaydhoa ahthayr ayfayk-teebhoa oon kheeroa postahl eentehrnahthyonahl
I want some stamps, please.	Quiero unos sellos, por favor.	kyayroa oonoass saylyoass por fahbhor
A stamp for this letter/postcard, please.	Un sello para esta carta/tarjeta, por favor.	oon saylyoa pahrah aystah kahrtah/tahrkhaytah por fahbhor
What's the postage for a letter/postcard to London?	¿Cuál es el franqueo para una carta/tarjeta para Londres?	kwahl ayss ayl frahnkayoa pahrah oonah kahrtah/tahrkhaytah pahrah londrayss
Do all letters go airmail?	¿Van todas las cartas por correo aéreo?	bahn toadhahss lahss kahrtahss por korrehoa ahayrehoa
I want to send this parcel.	Quiero mandar este paquete.	kyayroa mahndahr aystay pahkaytay

Do I need to fill in a customs declaration?	¿Es necesario que cumplimente una declaración para la aduana?	ayss naythayssahryoa kay koompleemayntay oonah dayklahrahthyon pahrah lah ahdwahnah
Where's the letter box (mailbox)?	¿Dónde está el buzón?	doanday aystah ayl boothon
I want to send this ...	Quiero mandar esto ...	kyayroa mahndahr aystoa
airmail	por correo aéreo	por korrehoa ahayrehoa
express (special delivery)	urgente	oorkhayntay
registered mail	por correo certificado	por korrehoa thayrteefee-kahdhoa
Where's the poste restante (general delivery)?	¿Dónde está la Lista de Correos?	doanday aystah lah leestah day korrehoass
Is there any mail for me? My name is ...	¿Hay correo para mí? Me llamo ...	igh korrehoa pahrah mee. may lyahmoa

SELLOS	STAMPS
PAQUETES	PARCELS
GIROS POSTALES	MONEY ORDERS

Telegrams *Telegramas*

In Spain telegrams are dispatched by the post office.

I want to send a telegram/telex.	Quiero mandar un telegrama/télex.	kyayroa mahndahr oon taylaygrahmah/taylayks
May I please have a form?	¿Me da un impreso, por favor?	may dah oon eemprayssoa por fahbhor
How much is it per word?	¿Cuánto cuesta por palabra?	kwahntoa kwaystah por pahlahbrah
How long will a cable to Boston take?	¿Cuánto tardará un telegrama a Boston?	kwahntoa tahrdahrah oon taylaygrahmah ah boston
I'd like to reverse the charges.	Quisiera que fuera por cobro revertido.	keessyayrah kay fwayrah por koabroa raybhayrtee-dhoa

Telephoning *Teléfonos*

Local and international calls can be made from call boxes (phone booths). Area codes for different countries are displayed in booths. In main towns, long-distance calls can also be placed from telephone offices (usually distinct from post offices).

Where's the telephone?	¿Dónde está el teléfono?	doanday aystah ayl taylayfoanoa
Where's the nearest call box (phone booth)?	¿Dónde está la cabina de teléfonos más cercana?	doanday aystah lah kahbheenah day taylayfoanoass mahss thehrkahnah
May I use your phone?	¿Puedo usar su teléfono?	pwaydhoa oossahr soo taylayfoanoa
Do you have a telephone directory for Valladolid?	¿Tiene usted una guía de teléfonos de Valladolid?	tyaynay oostaydh oonah geeah day taylayfoanoass day bahlyahdhoaleedh
Can you help me get this number?	¿Me puede usted obtener este número?	may pwaydhay oostaydh obtehnayr aystay noomayroa
Can I dial direct?	¿Puedo marcar directamente?	pwaydhoa mahrkahr deerayktahmayntay
What's the dialing (area) code for ...?	¿Cuál es el indicativo para ...?	kwahl ayss ayl eendeekahteebhoa pahrah
How do I get the (international) operator?	¿Cómo puedo conseguir la telefonista (internacional)?	koamoa pwaydhoa konsaygeer lah taylayfoaneestah (eentayrnahthyoanahl)

Operator *La telefonista*

Do you speak English?	¿Habla usted inglés?	ahblah oostaydh eenglayss
Good morning, I want Madrid 123 45 67.	Buenos días, quiero hablar con Madrid, número 123 45 67.	bwaynoass deeahss kyayroa ahblahr kon mahdreedh noomayroa 123 45 67
I want to place a personal (person-to-person) call.	Quiero una llamada personal.	kyayroa oonah lyahmahdhah pehrsoanahl

| I want to reverse the charges. | **Quiero que sea con cobro revertido.** | kyayroa kay sehah kon koabroa raybhayrteedhoa |
| Will you tell me the cost of the call afterwards? | **¿Puede decirme el coste de la llamada después?** | pwaydhay daytheermay ayl koastay day lah lyah-mahdhah dayspwayss |

Telephone alphabet

A	**Antonio**	antoanyoa	N	**Navarra**	nahbhahrrah
B	**Barcelona**	bahrthehloanah	Ñ	**Ñoño**	ñoañoa
C	**Carmen**	kahrmayn	O	**Oviedo**	oabhyaydhoa
CH	**Chocolate**	choakoalahtay	P	**París**	pahreess
D	**Dolores**	doaloarayss	Q	**Querido**	kayreedhoa
E	**Enrique**	aynreekay	R	**Ramón**	rahmon
F	**Francia**	frahnthyah	S	**Sábado**	sahbhahdhoa
G	**Gerona**	khehroanah	T	**Tarragona**	tahrrahgoanah
H	**Historia**	eestoaryah	U	**Ulises**	ooleessayss
I	**Inés**	eenayss	V	**Valencia**	bahlaynthyah
J	**José**	khoassay	W	**Washington**	wahsheenton
K	**Kilo**	keeloa	X	**Xiquena**	kseekaynah
L	**Lorenzo**	loaraynthoa	Y	**Yegua**	yehgwah
LL	**Llobregat**	lyoabraygaht	Z	**Zaragoza**	thahrahgothah
M	**Madrid**	mahdreedh			

Speaking *Hablando*

Hello. This is ... speaking.	**Oiga. Aquí habla con ...**	oygah. ahkee ahblah kon
I want to speak to ...	**Quiero hablar con ...**	kyayroa ahblahr kon
I want extension ...	**Quisiera la extensión ...?**	keessyayrah lah aykstayn-ssyon
Is this ...?	**¿Es ...?**	ayss
Speak louder/more slowly, please.	**Hable más fuerte/ más despacio, por favor.**	ahblay mahss fwayrtay/ mahss dayspahthyoa por fabhor

Bad luck *Mala suerte*

| Would you please try again later? | **¿Querría intentarlo de nuevo más tarde?** | kehrreeah eentayntahrloa day nwaybhoa mahss tahrday |

| Operator, you gave me the wrong number. | **Señorita, me ha dado el número equivocado.** | sayñoareetah may ah dahdhoa ayl noomayroa aykeebhoakahdhoa |
| Operator, we were cut off. | **Señorita, se nos ha cortado la línea.** | sayñoareetah say noas ah koartahdhoa lah leenayah |

Not there   *Está ausente*

When will he/she be back?	**¿Cuándo estará de vuelta?**	kwahndoa aystahrah day bwayltah
Will you tell him/her I called? My name is ...	**Dígale que lo/la he llamado. Mi nombre es ...**	degahlay kay loa/lah ay lyahmahdhoa. mee noambray ayss
Would you ask him/her to call me?	**¿Querría pedirle que me llame?**	kehrreeah pehdheerlay kay may lyahmay
Would you please take a message?	**¿Por favor, quiere tomar un recado?**	por fahbhor kyayray toamahr oon raykahdhoa

Charges   *Tarifas*

| What was the cost of that call? | **¿Cuál ha sido el coste de esa llamada?** | kwahl ah seedhoa ayl koastay day ayssah lyahmahdhah |
| I want to pay for the call. | **Quiero pagar la llamada.** | kyayroa pahgahr lah lyahmahdhah |

Hay una llamada para usted.	There's a telephone call for you.
¿A qué número llama?	What number are you calling?
Comunica.	The line's engaged.
No contestan.	There's no answer.
Tiene el número equivocado.	You've got the wrong number.
No está ahora.	He's/She's out at the moment.
Un momento.	Just a moment.
Espere, por favor.	Hold on, please.

Doctor

To be at ease, make sure your health insurance policy covers any illness or accident while on holiday. If not, ask your insurance representative, automobile association or travel agent for details of special health insurance.

General *Locuciones básicas*

Can you get me a doctor?	**¿Puede llamar a un médico?**	pwaydhay lyahmahr ah oon mehdheekoa
Is there a doctor here?	**¿Hay un médico aquí?**	igh oon mehdheekoa ahkee
I need a doctor—quickly.	**Necesito un médico—rápidamente.**	naythayseetoa oon mehdheekoa rahpeedhahmayntay
Where can I find a doctor who speaks English?	**¿Dónde puedo encontrar un médico que hable inglés?**	doanday pwaydhoa aynkontrahr oon mehdheekoa kay ahblay eenglayss
Where's the surgery (doctor's office)?	**¿Dónde es la consulta?**	doanday ayss lah koansooltah
What are the surgery (office) hours?	**¿Cuáles son las horas de consulta?**	kwahlayss son lahss oarahss day koansooltah
Could the doctor come to see me here?	**¿Podría venir el médico a reconocerme?**	poadreeah bayneer ayl mehdheekoa ah raykoanoathayrmay
What time can the doctor come?	**¿A qué hora puede venir el doctor?**	ah kay oarah pwaydhay bayneer ayl doaktoar
Can you recommend a/an ...?	**¿Me puede recomendar a un ...?**	may pwaydhay raykoamayndahr ah oon
general practitioner	**generalista**	khaynayrahleestah
children's doctor	**pediatra**	paydhyahtrah
eye specialist	**oculista**	oakooleestah
gynaecologist	**ginecólogo**	kheenaykoaloagoa
Can I have an appointment ...?	**¿Me puede dar una cita ...?**	may pwaydhay dahr oonah theetah
right now	**inmediatamente**	eenmaydhyahtahmayntay
tomorrow	**mañana**	mahñahnah
as soon as possible	**tan pronto como sea posible**	tahn proantoa koamoa sayah poasseeblay

CHEMIST'S, see page 108

Parts of the body *Partes del cuerpo*

arm	**el brazo**	ayl **brah**thoa
artery	**la arteria**	lah ahr**tay**ryah
back	**la espalda**	lah ays**pahl**dah
bladder	**la vesícula**	lah bays**see**koolah
bone	**el hueso**	ayl **way**ssoa
bowels	**los intestinos**	loass eentays**tee**noass
breast	**el seno**	ayl **say**noa
chest	**el pecho**	ayl **pay**choa
ear	**la oreja**	lah oa**ray**khah
eye	**el ojo**	ayl **oak**hoa
face	**la cara**	lah **kah**rah
finger	**el dedo**	ayl **dayd**hoa
foot	**el pie**	ayl **pyay**
gland	**la glándula**	lah **glahn**doolah
hand	**la mano**	lah **mah**noa
head	**la cabeza**	lah kah**bhay**thah
heart	**el corazón**	ayl koa**rah**thon
jaw	**la mandíbula**	lah mahn**dee**bhoolah
joint	**la articulación**	lah ahrteekoolah**thyon**
kidney	**el riñón**	ayl ree**ñon**
knee	**la rodilla**	lah roa**dhee**lyah
leg	**la pierna**	lah **pyehr**nah
lip	**el labio**	ayl **lahb**hyoa
liver	**el hígado**	ayl **ee**gahdhoa
lung	**el pulmón**	ayl **pool**mon
mouth	**la boca**	lah **boak**ah
muscle	**el músculo**	ayl **moos**kooloa
neck	**el cuello**	ayl **kway**lyoa
nerve	**el nervio**	ayl **nehr**byoa
nervous system	**el sistema nervioso**	ayl **see**staymah **nehr**byoassoa
nose	**la nariz**	lah nah**reeth**
rib	**la costilla**	lah koas**tee**lyah
shoulder	**la espalda**	lah ays**pahl**dah
skin	**la piel**	lah **pyayl**
spine	**la espina dorsal**	lah ays**pee**nah doar**sahl**
stomach	**el estómago**	ayl ays**toam**ahgoa
tendon	**el tendón**	ayl **tayn**don
thigh	**el muslo**	ayl **moos**loa
throat	**la garganta**	lah gahr**gahn**tah
thumb	**el pulgar**	ayl **pool**gahr
toe	**el dedo del pie**	ayl **dayd**hoa dayl **pyay**
tongue	**la lengua**	lah **layn**gwah
tonsils	**las amígdalas**	lahss ah**meeg**dahlahss
vein	**la vena**	lah **bay**nah

Accident—Injury   *Accidente – Herida*

There has been an accident.	**Ha habido un accidente.**	ah ahbheedhoa oon aktheedaynttay
My child has had a fall.	**Se ha caído el niño/la niña.**	say ah kaheedhoa ayl neeñoa/lah neeñah
He/She has hurt his/her head.	**Se ha dado un golpe en la cabeza.**	say ah dahdhoa oon goalpay ayn lah kahbhaythah
He's/She's unconscious.	**Está inconsciente.**	aystah eenkoansthyaynttay
He's/She's bleeding heavily.	**Está sangrando mucho.**	aystah sahngrahndoa moochoa
He's/She's (seriously) injured.	**Tiene una herida (muy seria).**	tyaynay oonah ayreedhah (mwee sayryah)
His/Her arm is broken.	**Su brazo está roto.**	soo brahthoa aystah roatoa
His/Her ankle is swollen.	**Su tobillo está hinchado.**	soo toabheelyoa aystah eenchahdhoa
I've cut myself.	**Me he cortado.**	may ay koartahdhoa
I've pulled a muscle.	**Tengo un músculo distendido.**	tayngoa oon mooskooloa deestayndeedhoa
I've got something in my eye.	**Me ha entrado algo en el ojo.**	may ah ayntrahdhoa ahlgoa ayn ayl oakhoa
I've got a/an ...	**Tengo ...**	tayngoa
blister	**una ampolla**	oonah ahmpoalyah
boil	**un forúnculo**	oon foaroonkooloa
bruise	**un cardenal**	oon kahrdaynahl
burn	**una quemadura**	oonah kaymahdhoorah
cut	**una cortadura**	oonah koartahdhoorah
graze	**un arañazo**	oon ahrahñahthoa
insect bite	**una picadura de insecto**	oonah peekahdhoorah day eensehktoa
lump	**un chichón**	oon cheechoan
rash	**un sarpullido**	oon sahrpoolyeedhoa
sting	**una picadura**	oonah peekahdhoorah
swelling	**una hinchazón**	oonah eenchahthon
wound	**una herida**	oonah ayreedhah
Could you have a look at it?	**¿Podría mirarlo?**	poadreeah meerahrloa
I can't move my ... It hurts.	**No puedo mover el/la ... Me duele.**	noa pwaydhoa moabher ayl/lah ... may dwaylay

Médico

No se mueva.	Don't move.
¿Dónde le duele?	Where does it hurt?
¿Qué clase de dolor es?	What kind of pain is it?
apagado/agudo palpitante/constante intermitente	dull/sharp throbbing/constant on and off
Está roto/torcido/ dislocado/desgarrado.	It's broken/sprained/ dislocated/torn.
Quiero que le hagan una radiografía.	I want you to have an X-ray taken.
Lo van a enyesar.	You'll get a plaster.
Está infectado.	It's infected.
¿Lo han vacunado contra el tétanos?	Have you been vaccinated against tetanus?
Le daré un antiséptico/ un analgésico.	I'll give you an antiseptic/ a painkiller.
Quiero que venga a verme dentro de … días.	I'd like you to come back in … days.

Illness *Enfermedad*

I'm not feeling well.	**No me siento bien.**	noa may **syayn**toa byayn
I'm ill.	**Estoy enfermo(a).**	aystoy ayn**fehr**moa(ah)
I feel …	**Me siento …**	may **syayn**toa
dizzy	**mareado(a)**	mahrayahdhoa(ah)
nauseous	**con náuseas**	kon **now**ssayahss
shivery	**con escalofríos**	kon ayskahloafreeoass
I've got a fever.	**Tengo fiebre.**	**tayn**goa **fyeh**bray
My temperature is 38 degrees.	**Tengo 38 grados de temperatura.**	**tayn**goa 38 **grah**dhoass day taympayrah**too**rah
I've been vomiting.	**He tenido vómitos.**	ay tay**nee**dhoa **boa**meetoass
I'm constipated.	**Estoy estreñido(a).**	aystoy aystreh**ñee**dhoa(ah)
I've got diarrhoea.	**Tengo diarrea.**	**tayn**goa dyah**rray**ah
My … hurts.	**Me duele …**	may **dway**lay

NUMBERS, see page 147

I've got (a/an) ...	Tengo ...	tayngoa
asthma	asma	ahsmah
backache	dolor de espalda	doaloar day ayspahldah
cold	un resfriado	oon raysfryahdhoa
cough	tos	toass
cramps	calambres	kahlahmbrayss
earache	dolor de oídos	doalor day oaeedhoass
headache	dolor de cabeza	doalor day kahbhaythah
indigestion	una indigestión	oonah eendeekhaystyon
nosebleed	una hemorragia nasal	oonah aymoarrahkhyah nahssahl
palpitations	palpitaciones	pahlpeetahthyonayss
rheumatism	reumatismo	rayoomahteesmoa
sore throat	anginas	ahnkheenahss
stiff neck	tortícolis	torteekoaleess
stomach ache	dolor de estómago	doalor day aystoamahgoa
sunstroke	una insolación	oonah eensoalahthyon

I have difficulties breathing.	Tengo dificultades respiratorias.	tayngoa deefeekooltahdhayss rayspeerahtoaryahss
I have a pain in my chest.	Tengo un dolor en el pecho.	tayngoa oon doalor ayn ayl paychoa
I had a heart attack ... years ago.	Tuve un ataque al corazón hace ... años.	toobhay oon ahtahkay ahl koarahthon ahthay ... ahñoass
My blood pressure is too high/too low.	Mi presión sanguínea es demasiado alta/baja.	mee prayssyon sahngeenayah ayss daymahssyahdhoa ahltah/bahkhah
I'm allergic to ...	Soy alérgico(a) a ...	soy ahlehrkheekoa(ah) ah
I'm a diabetic.	Soy diabético(a).	soy dyahbhayteekoa(ah)

Women's section *Asuntos de la mujer*

I have period pains.	Tengo dolores menstruales.	tayngoa doaloarayss maynstrooahlayss
I have a vaginal infection.	Tengo una infección vaginal.	tayngoa oonah eenfaykthyon bahkheenahl
I'm on the pill.	Tomo la píldora.	toamoa lah peeldoarah
I haven't had my period for 2 months.	Hace dos meses que no tengo reglas.	ahthay doass mayssayss kay noa tayngoa rayglahss
I'm (3 months) pregnant.	Hace (3 meses) que estoy embarazada.	ahthay (3 mayssayss) kay aystoy aymbahrahthahdhah

DOCTOR

 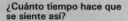

¿Cuánto tiempo hace que se siente así?	How long have you been feeling like this?
¿Es la primera vez que ha tenido esto?	Is this the first time you've had this?
Le voy a tomar la presión/la temperatura.	I'll take your blood pressure/temperature.
Súbase la manga, por favor.	Roll up your sleeve, please.
Desvístase (hasta la cintura), por favor.	Please undress (down to the waist).
Acuéstese ahí, por favor.	Please lie down over there.
Abra la boca.	Open your mouth.
Respire profundo.	Breathe deeply.
Tosa, por favor.	Cough, please.
¿Dónde le duele?	Where do you feel the pain?
Tiene (un/una) ...	You've got (a/an) ...
apendicitis	appendicitis
cistitis	cystitis
enfermedad venérea	venereal disease
gastritis	gastritis
gripe	flu
ictericia	jaundice
inflamación de ...	inflammation of ...
intoxicación	food poisoning
neumonía	pneumonia
sarampión	measles
Le pondré una inyección.	I'll give you an injection.
Necesito una muestra de sangre/heces/orina.	I want a specimen of your blood/stools/urine.
Debe quedarse en cama durante ... días.	You must stay in bed for ... days.
Quiero que consulte a un especialista.	I want you to see a specialist.
Quiero que vaya al hospital para un reconocimiento general.	I want you to go to the hospital for a general check-up.
Tendrán que operarlo.	You'll have to have an operation.

Médico

Prescription—Treatment *Prescripción – Tratamiento*

This is my usual medicine.	**Esta es la medicina que tomo normalmente.**	aystah ayss lah maydheethee-nah kay **toa**moa noarmahl-**mayn**tay
Can you give me a prescription for this?	**¿Puede darme una receta para esto?**	pwaydhay **dahr**may oonah raythaytah **pah**rah **ays**toa
Can you prescribe an antidepressant/ some sleeping pills?	**¿Puede recetarme un antidepresivo/ un somnífero?**	pwaydhay raythay**tahr**may oon ahnteedaypray**ssee**bhoa oon soam**nee**fayroa
I'm allergic to anti-biotics/penicilline.	**Soy alérgico(a) a los antibióticos/ la penicilina.**	soy ah**lehr**kheekoa(ah) ah loass ahntee**bhyoa**teekoass/ lah paynee**thee**leenah
I don't want any-thing too strong.	**No quiero nada demasiado fuerte.**	noa **kyay**roa **nah**dhah day-mah**ssyah**dhoa **fwayr**tay
How many times a day should I take it?	**¿Cuántas veces al día tengo que tomarlo?**	**kwahn**tahss **bay**thayss ahl **dee**ah **tayn**goa kay toa**mahr**loa

---

¿Qué tratamiento está siguiendo?	What treatment are you having?
¿Qué medicina está tomando?	What medicine are you taking?
¿Qué dosis utiliza normal-mente?	What's your normal dose?
En inyección u oral?	Injection or oral?
Tome .. cucharillas de esta medicina ... cucharillas de esta medicina ...	Take ... teaspoons of this medicine ...
Tome una píldora con un vaso de agua ...	Take one pill with a glass of water ...
cada ... horas	every ... hours
... veces por día	... times a day
antes/después de cada comida	before/after each meal
por la mañana/por la noche	in the morning/at night
en caso de dolor	in case of pain
durante ... días	for ... days

CHEMIST'S, see p. 108

Fee *Honorarios*

How much do I owe you?	¿Cuánto le debo?	kwahntoa lay daybhoa
May I have a receipt for my health insurance?	¿Puede darme un recibo para mi seguro?	pwaydhay dahrmay oon raytheebhoa pahrah mee saygooroa
Can I have a medical certificate?	¿Me puede dar un certificado médico?	may pwaydhay dahr oon thayrteefeekahdhoa maydheekoa
Would you fill in this health insurance form, please?	¿Quiere llenar esta hoja de seguro, por favor?	kyayray lyaynahr aystah oakhah day saygooroa por fahbhor

Hospital *Hospital*

What are the visiting hours?	¿Cuáles son las horas de visita?	kwahlayss son lahss oarahss day beeseetah
When can I get up?	¿Cuándo puedo levantarme?	kwahndoa pwaydhoa laybhahntahrmay
When will the doctor come?	¿Cuándo viene el médico?	kwahndoa byaynay ayl maydheekoa
I can't eat/sleep.	No puedo comer/dormir.	noa pwaydhoa koamayr/dormeer
I'm in pain.	Me duele.	may dwaylay
Can I have a painkiller?	¿Me puede dar un analgésico?	may pwaydhay dahr oon ahnahlkhaysseekoa

doctor/surgeon	el médico/cirujano	ayl maydheekoa/theerookhahnoa
nurse	la enfermera	lah aynfayrmayrah
patient	el/la paciente	ayl/lah pahthyayntay
anaesthetic	el anestésico	ayl ahnaystaysseekoa
blood transfusion	la transfusión de sangre	lah trahnsfoossyon day sahngray
injection	la inyección	lah eenyaykthyon
operation	la operación	lah oapayrahthyon
bed	la cama	lah kahmah
bedpan	la silleta	lah seelyaytah
thermometer	el termómetro	ayl tayrmoamaytroa

Dentist *Dentista*

Can you recommend a good dentist?	¿Puede recomendarme un buen dentista?	pwaydhay raykoamayn-dahrmay oon bwayn daynteestah
Can I make an (urgent) appointment to see Dr ...?	¿Puedo pedir cita (urgente) para ver al Doctor ...?	pwaydhoa paydheer theetah (oorkhayntay) pahrah behr ahl doaktor
Can't you possibly make it earlier than that?	¿No sería posible antes?	noa sayreeah poasseeblay ahntayss
I have a broken tooth.	Me he roto un diente.	may ay roatoa oon dyayntay
I have a toothache.	Tengo dolor de muelas.	tayngoa doalor day mwaylahss
I have an abscess.	Tengo un flemón.	tayngoa oon flaymon
This tooth hurts.	Me duele este diente.	may dwaylay aystay dyayntay
at the top	arriba	ahrreebhah
at the bottom	abajo	ahbhahkhoa
in the front	delante	daylahntay
at the back	detrás	daytrahss
Can you fix it temporarily?	¿Puede usted arreglarlo temporalmente?	pwaydhay oostaydh ahrrayglahrloa taympoarahlmayntay
I don't want it extracted.	No quiero que me la saque.	noa kyayroa kay may lah sahkay
Could you give me an anaesthetic?	¿Puede ponerme anestesia local?	pwaydhay poanayrmay ahnaystayssyah loakahl
I've lost a filling.	He perdido un empaste.	ay pehrdeedhoa oon aympahstay
The gum is very sore/bleeding.	La encía está muy inflamada/sangra.	lah ayntheeah aystah mwee eenflahmahdhah/sahngrah
I've broken this denture.	Se me ha roto la dentadura.	say may ah roatoa lah dayntahdhoorah
Can you repair this denture?	¿Puede usted arreglar esta dentadura?	pwaydhay oostaydh ahrrayglahr aystah dayntahdhoorah
When will it be ready?	¿Cuándo estará lista?	kwahndoa aystahrah leestah

Reference section

Where do you come from? *¿De dónde viene usted?*

Africa	**Africa**	ahfreekah
Asia	**Asia**	ahssyah
Australia	**Australia**	owstrahlyah
Europe	**Europa**	ayooroapah
North/South/ Central America	**América del Norte/ del Sur/Central**	ahmayreekah dayl nortay/ dayl soor/thayntrahl
Algeria	**Argelia**	ahrkhaylyah
Austria	**Austria**	owstryah
Belgium	**Bélgica**	baylkheekah
Canada	**Canadá**	kahnahdhah
China	**China**	cheenah
Denmark	**Dinamarca**	deenahmahrka
England	**Inglaterra**	eenglahtayrrah
Finland	**Finlandia**	feenlahndyah
France	**Francia**	frahnthyah
Germany	**Alemania**	ahlaymahnyah
Gibraltar	**Gibraltar**	kheebrahltahr
Great Britain	**Gran Bretaña**	grahn braytahñah
Greece	**Grecia**	graythyah
India	**India**	eendyah
Ireland	**Irlanda**	eerlahndah
Israel	**Israel**	eesrahayl
Italy	**Italia**	eetahlyah
Japan	**Japón**	khahpon
Luxembourg	**Luxemburgo**	looksaymboorgoa
Morocco	**Marruecos**	mahrrwaykoass
Netherlands	**Países Bajos**	paheessayss bahkhoass
New Zealand	**Nueva Zelandia**	nwaybhah thaylahndyah
Norway	**Noruega**	noarwaygah
Portugal	**Portugal**	portoogahl
Scotland	**Escocia**	ayskoathyah
South Africa	**Africa del Sur**	ahfreekah dayl soor
Soviet Union	**Unión Soviética**	oonyon soabhyayteekah
Spain	**España**	ayspahñah
Sweden	**Suecia**	swaythyah
Switzerland	**Suiza**	sweethah
Tunisia	**Túnez**	toonayth
Turkey	**Turquía**	toorkeeah
United States	**Estados Unidos**	aystahdhoass ooneedhoass
Wales	**País de Gales**	paheess day gahlayss
Yugoslavia	**Yugoslavia**	yogoaslahbhyah

Numbers *Números*

0	cero	thayroa
1	uno	oonoa
2	dos	doss
3	tres	trayss
4	cuatro	kwahtroa
5	cinco	theenkoa
6	seis	sayss
7	siete	syaytay
8	ocho	oachoa
9	nueve	nwaybhay
10	diez	dyayth
11	once	onthay
12	doce	doathay
13	trece	traythay
14	catorce	kahtorthay
15	quince	keenthay
16	dieciséis	dyaytheessayss
17	diecisiete	dyaytheessyaytay
18	dieciocho	dyaytheeoachoa
19	diecinueve	dyaytheenwaybhay
20	veinte	bayntay
21	veintiuno	baynteeoonoa
22	veintidós	baynteedoss
23	veintitrés	baynteetrayss
24	veinticuatro	baynteekwahtroa
25	veinticinco	baynteetheenkoa
26	veintiséis	baynteessayss
27	veintisiete	baynteessyaytay
28	veintiocho	baynteeoachoa
29	veintinueve	baynteenwaybhay
30	treinta	trayntah
31	treinta y uno	trayntah ee oonoa
32	treinta y dos	trayntah ee doss
33	treinta y tres	trayntah ee trayss
40	cuarenta	kwahrayntah
50	cincuenta	theenkwayntah
60	sesenta	sayssayntah
70	setenta	saytayntah
80	ochenta	oachayntah
90	noventa	noabhayntah
100	cien/ciento*	thyayn/thyayntoa
101	ciento uno	thyayntoa oonoa
102	ciento dos	thyayntoa doss

* *cien* is used before nouns and adjectives.

110	**ciento diez**	**thyaynt**oa dyayth
120	**ciento veinte**	**thyaynt**oa **bayn**tay
200	**doscientos**	dos**thyaynt**oass
300	**trescientos**	trays**thyaynt**oass
400	**cuatrocientos**	kwahtroa**thyaynt**oass
500	**quinientos**	keenyayntoass
600	**seiscientos**	says**thyaynt**oass
700	**setecientos**	saytay**thyaynt**oass
800	**ochocientos**	oachoa**thyaynt**oass
900	**novecientos**	noabhay**thyaynt**oass
1,000	**mil**	meel
1,100	**mil cien**	meel thyayn
2,000	**dos mil**	dos meel
10,000	**diez mil**	dyayth meel
100,000	**cien mil**	thyayn meel
1,000,000	**un millón**	oon meel**yon**

1981	**mil novecientos**	meel noabhay**thyaynt**oass
	ochenta y uno	oa**chayn**tah ee **oo**noa
1992	**mil novecientos**	meel noabhay**thyant**oass
	noventa y dos	noabhayntah ee doss
2003	**dos mil tres**	dos meel trayss

first	**primero**	pree**mayr**oa
second	**segundo**	say**goon**doa
third	**tercero**	tehr**thayr**oa
fourth	**cuarto**	**kwahr**toa
fifth	**quinto**	**keen**toa
sixth	**sexto**	**sayks**toa
seventh	**séptimo**	**sayp**teemoa
eighth	**octavo**	oak**tah**bhoa
ninth	**noveno**	noabhaynoa
tenth	**décimo**	**day**theemoa

once	**una vez**	**oo**nah behth
twice	**dos veces**	doss **bay**thayss
three times	**tres veces**	trayss **bay**thayss

a half	**una mitad**	**oo**nah mee**tahdh**
half a ...	**medio ...**	**may**dhyoa
half of ...	**la mitad de ...**	lah mee**tahdh** day
half (adj.)	**medio**	**may**dhyoa
a quarter	**un cuarto**	oon **kwahr**toa
one third	**un tercio**	oon **tehr**thyoa
a dozen	**una docena**	**oo**nah do**thay**nah
3.4%	**3,4 por ciento**	trayss **koa**mah cuatro por **thyaynt**oa

Year and age   *Año y edad*

year	**el año**	ayl ahñoa
leap year	**el año bisiesto**	ayl ahñoa beessyaystoa
decade	**la década**	lah daykahdah
century	**el siglo**	ayl seegloa

this year	**este año**	aystay ahñoa
last year	**el año pasado**	ayl ahñoa pahssahdhoa
next year	**el año próximo**	ayl ahñoa proakseemoa
each year	**cada año**	kahdhah ahñoa

| Which year? | **¿Qué año?** | kay ahñoa |

two years ago	**hace dos años**	ahthay doss ahñoass
in one year	**dentro de un año**	dayntroa day oon ahñoa
in the eighties	**en los años ochenta**	ayn loass ahñoass oachayntah
from the fifties	**desde los años cincuenta**	daysday loass ahñoass theenkwayntah

the 16th century	**el siglo XVI**	ayl seegloa dyaytheessayss
from the 19th century	**desde el siglo XIX**	daysday ayl seegloa dyaytheenwaybhay
in the 20th century	**en el siglo XX**	ayn ayl seegloa bayntay

old/young	**viejo/joven**	byaykhoa/khoabhehn
old/new	**viejo/nuevo**	byaykhoa/nwaybhoa
recent	**reciente**	raythyayntay

How old are you?	**¿Cuántos años tiene?**	kwahntoass ahñoass tyaynay
I'm 30 years old.	**Tengo 30 años.**	tayngoa 30 ahñoass
What's his/her age?	**¿Cuál es su edad?**	kwahl ays soo aydhahdh
He/She was born in 1977.	**Nació en 1977.**	nahthyoa ayn 1977
Children under 16 are not admitted.	**No se admiten niños menores de 16 años.**	noa say ahdmeetayn neeñoass maynoarayss day 16 ahñoass

Seasons   *Estaciones*

spring	**la primavera**	lah preemahbhayrah
summer	**el verano**	ayl bayrahnoa
autumn	**el otoño**	ayl otoañoa
winter	**el invierno**	ayl eenbyayrnoa

| in spring | **en primavera** | ayn preemahbhayrah |
| during the summer | **durante el verano** | doorahntay ayl bayrahnoa |

| high season | **alta estación** | ahltah aystahthyon |
| low season | **baja estación** | bahkhah aystahthyon |

Months *Meses*

January	**enero***	aynayroa
February	**febrero**	fehbrehroa
March	**marzo**	mahrthoa
April	**abril**	ahbreel
May	**mayo**	mahyoa
June	**junio**	khoonyoa
July	**julio**	khoolyoa
August	**agosto**	ahgoastoa
September	**septiembre**	sehptyaymbray
October	**octubre**	oktoobray
November	**noviembre**	noabhyaymbray
December	**diciembre**	deethyaymbray
after June	**después de junio**	dayspwayss day khoonyoa
before July	**antes de julio**	ahntays day khoolyoa
during the month of August	**durante el mes de agosto**	doorahntay ayl mayss day ahgoastoa
in September	**en septiembre**	ayn sehptyaymbray
until November	**hasta noviembre**	ahstah noabhyaymbray
since December	**desde diciembre**	daysday deethyaymbray
last month	**el mes pasado**	ayl mayss pahssahdhoa
next month	**el mes próximo**	ayl mayss prokseemoa
the month before	**el mes anterior**	ayl mayss ahntehryor
the month after	**el mes siguiente**	ayl mayss seegyayntay
the beginning of January	**a principios de enero**	ah preentheepyoass day aynayroa
the middle of February	**a mediados de febrero**	ah maydhyahdhoass day fehbrehroa
the end of March	**a finales de marzo**	ah feenahlayss day mahrthoa

Dates *Fechas*

What's the date today?	**¿En qué fecha estamos?**	ayn kay **fay**chah ay**stah**moass
When's your birthday?	**¿Cuándo es su cumpleaños?**	**kwahn**doa ayss soo koomplayah**ñoass**
July 1	**el primero de julio**	ayl pree**may**roa day **khool**yoa
March 10	**el diez de marzo**	ayl dyayth day **mahr**thoa

---

* The names of months aren't capitalized in Spanish.

Days *Días de la semana*

What day is it today?	¿Qué día es hoy?	kay **deeah** ayss oy
Sunday	domingo*	doa**meen**goa
Monday	lunes	**loo**nayss
Tuesday	martes	**mahr**tayss
Wednesday	miércoles	**myayr**koalayss
Thursday	jueves	**khway**bhayss
Friday	viernes	**byayr**nayss
Saturday	sábado	**sahb**hadhoa
in the morning	por la mañana	por lah mah**ñah**nah
during the day	durante el día	doo**rahn**tay ayl **dee**ah
in the afternoon	por la tarde	por lah **tahr**day
in the evening	por la tarde	por lah **tahr**day
at night	por la noche	por lah **noa**chay
at dawn	al amanecer	ahl ahmah**nay**thayr
at dusk	al anochecer	ahl ahnoa**chay**thayr
yesterday	ayer	ah**yehr**
today	hoy	oy
tomorrow	mañana	mah**ñah**nah
the day before	el día anterior	ayl **deeah** ahn**teh**ryor
the next day	el día siguiente	ayl **deeah** see**gyayn**tay
two days ago	hace dos días	**ahthay** doss **deeahss**
in three days' time	en tres días	ayn **trayss** **deeahss**
last week	la semana pasada	lah **saymahnah** pah**ssahdhah**
next week	la semana próxima	lah **saymahnah** **prokseemah**
in two weeks	por una quincena	por **oonah** keen**thehnah**
birthday	el cumpleaños	ayl koom**playah**ñoass
day	el día	ayl **deeah**
day off	el día libre	ayl **deeah** **leebray**
holiday	el día festivo	ayl **deeah** **faysteebhoa**
holidays	las vacaciones	lahss bahkah**thyo**nayss
school holidays	las vacaciones del colegio	lahss bahkah**thyo**nayss dayl koa**lehkhyoa**
vacation	las vacaciones	lahss bahkah**thyo**nayss
week	la semana	lah **saymahnah**
weekday	el día de la semana	ayl **deeah** day lah **saymahnah**
weekend	el fin de semana	ayl feen day **saymahnah**
working day	el día laborable	ayl **deeah** lahbhoa**rahblay**

---

* The names of days aren't capitalized in Spanish.

Public holidays *Días festivos*

These are the main public holidays in Spain when banks, offices and shops are closed. In addition, there are various regional holidays.

January 1	**Año Nuevo**	New Year's Day
January 6	**Epifanía**	Epiphany
March 19	**San José**	St Joseph's Day
	Viernes Santo	Good Friday
	Lunes de Pascua	Easter Monday
May 1	**Día del Trabajo**	Labour Day
	Corpus Christi	Corpus Christi Day
July 25	**Santiago Apóstol**	St James's Day
August 15	**Asunción**	Assumption Day
October 12	**Día de la Hispanidad**	Columbus Day
November 1	**Todos los Santos**	All Saints' Day
December 8	**Inmaculada Concepción**	Immaculate Conception Day
December 25	**Navidad**	Christmas Day

Greetings *Saludos*

Merry Christmas!	¡Feliz Navidad!	fayleeth nahbheedhahdh
Happy New Year!	¡Feliz Año Nuevo!	fayleeth ahñoa nwaybhoa
Happy Easter!	¡Felices Pascuas!	fayleethayss pahskwahss
Happy birthday!	¡Feliz cumpleaños!	fayleeth koomplayahñoass
Best wishes!	¡Mejores deseos!	maykhoarayss dayssayoass
Congratulations!	¡Enhorabuena!	aynoarahbwaynah
Good luck!	¡Buena suerte!	bwaynah swayrtay
Have a nice trip!	¡Buen viaje!	bwayn byahkhay
All the best!	¡Qué todo salga bien!	kay toadhoa sahlgah byayn
Best regards from/to ...	Recuerdos de/a ...	raykwayrdoass day/ah
Give my love to ...	Saludos cariñosos a ...	sahloodhoass kahreeñoassoass ah

What time is it?   ¿Qué hora es?

Excuse me. Can you tell me the time?	**Perdone. ¿Puede decirme la hora?**	payrdoanay. pwaydhay daytheermay lah oarah
It's ...	**Es/Son ...**	ayss/son
five past one	**la una y cinco**	lah oonah ee theenkoa
ten past two	**las dos y diez**	lahss doss ee dyayth
a quarter past three	**las tres y cuarto**	lahss trayss ee kwahrtoa
twenty past four	**las cuatro y veinte**	lahss kwahtroa ee bayntay
twenty-five past five	**las cinco y veinti-cinco**	lahss theenkoa ee bayntee-theenkoa
half past six	**las seis y media**	lahss sayss ee maydhyay
twenty-five to seven	**las siete menos veinticinco**	lahss saytay maynoass baynteetheenkoa
twenty to eight	**las ocho menos veinte**	lahss oachoa maynoass bayntay
a quarter to nine	**las nueve menos cuarto**	lahss nwaybhay maynoass kwahrtoa
ten to ten	**las diez menos diez**	lahss dyayth maynoass dyayth
five to eleven	**las once menos cinco**	lahss onthay maynoass theenkoa
twelve o'clock	**las doce**	lahss doathay
a.m.	**de la mañana**	de lah mahñahnah
p.m.	**de la tarde**	de lah tahrday
The train leaves at ...	**El tren sale a ...**	ayl trayn sahlay ah
13.04 (1.04 p.m.)	**las trece y cuatro**	lahss traythay ee kwahtroa
0.45 (0.45 a.m.)	**las cero horas y cuarenta y cinco**	lahss thayroa oarahss ee kwahrayntah ee theenkoa
in five minutes	**en cinco minutos**	ayn theenkoa meenootoass
in a quarter of an hour	**en un cuarto de hora**	ayn oon kwahrtoa day oarah
half an hour ago	**hace media hora**	ahthay maydhyah oarah
about two hours	**aproximadamente dos horas**	ahproakseemahdhahmayntay doss oarahss
more than ten minutes	**más de diez minutos**	mahss day dyayth meenootoass
less than thirty seconds	**menos de treinta segundos**	maynoass day trayntah saygoondoass
noon	**mediodía**	maydhyoadheeah
midnight	**medianoche**	maydhyahnoachay
early	**temprano**	taymprahnoa
late	**tarde**	tahrday
in time	**a tiempo**	ah tyaympoa

Abbreviations *Abreviaturas*

A.C.	año de Cristo	A.D.
a/c	al cuidado de	c/o
a. de J.C.	antes de Jesucristo	B.C.
admón.	administración	administration
apdo.	apartado de correos	post office box
Av., Avda.	Avenida	avenue
C., Cía.	Compañía	company
C/	Calle	street
cta.	cuenta	account
cte.	corriente	of the present month
C.V.	caballos de vapor	horsepower
D.	Don	courtesy title (gentleman)
Da., Dª	Doña	courtesy title (lady)
EE.UU.	Estados Unidos	United States
f.c.	ferrocarril	railway
G.C.	Guardia Civil	police
h.	hora	hour
hab.	habitantes	population
M.I.T.	Ministerio de Información y Turismo	Ministry of Information and Tourism
Nª Sª	Nuestra Señora	Our Lady, the Virgin
Nº, núm.	número	number
p. ej.	por ejemplo	for example
P.P.	porte pagado	postage paid
pta., ptas.	peseta(s)	peseta(s)
P.V.P.	precio de venta al público	retail price
R.A.C.E.	Real Automóvil Club de España	Royal Automobile Club of Spain
R.C.	Real Club ...	Royal ... Club
RENFE	Red Nacional de Ferrocarriles Españoles	Spanish National Railway
R.N.E.	Radio Nacional de España	Spanish National Broadcasting Company
S., Sta.	San, Santa	Saint
S.A.	Sociedad Anónima	Ltd., Inc.
Sr.	Señor	Mr.
Sra.	Señora	Mrs.
Sres., Srs.	Señores	gentlemen
Srta.	Señorita	Miss
TVE	Televisión Española	Spanish Television
Ud., Vd.	Usted	you (singular)
Uds., Vds.	Ustedes	you (plural)
v.g., v.gr.	verbigracia	viz., namely

Signs and notices   *Letreros e indicaciones*

Abajo	Down
Abierto	Open
Arriba	Up
Ascensor	Lift (elevator)
Averiado	Out of order
Caballeros	Gentlemen
Caja	Cash desk
Caliente	Hot
Carretera particular	Private road
Cerrado	Closed
Cierre la puerta	Close the door
Completo	No vacancy
Cuidado	Caution
Cuidado con el perro	Beware of the dog
Empujar	Push
Entrada	Entrance
Entrada libre	Admission free
Entre sin llamar	Enter without knocking
Frío	Cold
Libre	Vacant
No molestar	Do not disturb
No obstruya la entrada	Do not block entrance
No tocar	Do not touch
Ocupado	Occupied
Peligro	Danger
Peligro de muerte	Danger of death
Pintura fresca	Wet paint
Privado	Private
Prohibido arrojar basuras	No littering
Prohibido entrar	No entry
Prohibido fumar	No smoking
Prohibida la entrada a personas no autorizadas	No trespassing
Rebajas	Sale
Reservado	Reserved
Sala de espera	Waiting room
Salida	Exit
Salida de emergencia	Emergency exit
Se alquila	To let (for rent)
Se vende	For sale
Sendero para bicicletas	Bicycle path
Señoras	Ladies
Servicios	Toilets
Tirar	Pull
Toque el timbre, por favor	Please ring

Emergency   *Urgencia*

Call the police	**Llama a la policía**	lyahmah ah lah poalee-theeah
DANGER	**PELIGRO**	payleegroa
FIRE	**FUEGO**	fway oa
Gas	**Gas**	gahss
Get a doctor	**Busque un doctor**	booskay oon doaktor
Go away	**Váyase**	bahyahssay
HELP	**SOCORRO**	sokoarroa
Get help quickly	**Busque ayuda rápido**	booskay ahyoodhah rahpeedhoa
I'm ill	**Estoy enfermo(a)**	aystoy aynfehrmoa(ah)
I'm lost	**Me he perdido**	may ay payrdeedhoa
Leave me alone	**Déjeme en paz**	daykhaymay ayn pahth
LOOK OUT	**CUIDADO**	kweedhahdhoa
POLICE	**POLICIA**	poaleetheeah
Quick	**Rápido**	rahpeedhoa
STOP	**DETENGASE**	daytayngahssay
Stop that man/ woman	**Detenga a ese(a) hombre/mujer**	daytayngah ah ayssay(ah) oambray/mookhehr
STOP THIEF	**AL LADRÓN**	ahl lahdron

Lost!   *¡Perdido!*

Where's the ...?	**¿Dónde está la ...?**	doanday aystah lah
lost property (lost and found) office	**oficina de objetos perdidos**	oafeetheenah day oabkhaytoass pehrdeedhoass
police station	**comisaría de policía**	koameessahryah day poaleetheeah
I want to report a theft.	**Quiero denunciar un robo.**	kyayroa daynoonthyahr oon roabhoa
My ... has been stolen.	**Me han robado mi ...**	may ahn roabhahdhoa mee
handbag	**bolso**	boalsoa
money	**dinero**	deenayroa
passport	**pasaporte**	passahportay
ticket	**billete**	beelyaytay
wallet	**cartera**	kahrtayrah
I've lost my ...	**He perdido mi ...**	ay pehrdeedhoa mee
I lost it in ...	**Lo perdí en ...**	loa pehrdee ayn
this morning	**esta mañana**	aystah mahñahnah
yesterday	**ayer**	ahyehr

CAR ACCIDENTS, see page 78

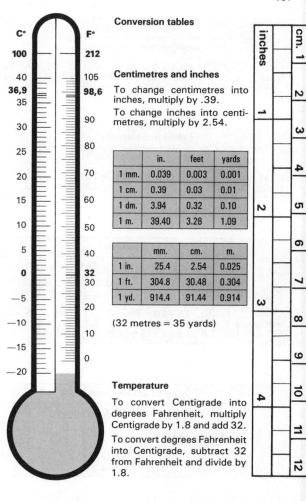

Conversion tables

Centimetres and inches

To change centimetres into inches, multiply by .39.

To change inches into centimetres, multiply by 2.54.

	in.	feet	yards
1 mm.	0.039	0.003	0.001
1 cm.	0.39	0.03	0.01
1 dm.	3.94	0.32	0.10
1 m.	39.40	3.28	1.09

	mm.	cm.	m.
1 in.	25.4	2.54	0.025
1 ft.	304.8	30.48	0.304
1 yd.	914.4	91.44	0.914

(32 metres = 35 yards)

Temperature

To convert Centigrade into degrees Fahrenheit, multiply Centigrade by 1.8 and add 32.

To convert degrees Fahrenheit into Centigrade, subtract 32 from Fahrenheit and divide by 1.8.

Kilometres into miles

1 kilometre (km.) = 0.62 miles

km.	10	20	30	40	50	60	70	80	90	100	110	120	130
miles	6	12	19	25	31	37	44	50	56	62	68	75	81

Miles into kilometres

1 mile = 1.609 kilometres (km.)

miles	10	20	30	40	50	60	70	80	90	100
km.	16	32	48	64	80	97	113	129	145	161

Fluid measures

1 litre (l.) = 0.88 imp. quarts = 1.06 U.S. quarts

1 imp. quart = 1.14 l.	1 U.S. quart = 0.95 l.
1 imp. gallon = 4.55 l.	1 U.S. gallon = 3.8 l.

l.	5	10	15	20	25	30	35	40	45	50
imp. gal.	1.1	2.2	3.3	4.4	5.5	6.6	7.7	8.8	9.9	11.0
U.S. gal.	1.3	2.6	3.9	5.2	6.5	7.8	9.1	10.4	11.7	13.0

Weights and measures

1 kilogram or kilo (kg.) = 1000 grams (g.)

100 g. = 3.5 oz.	½ kg. = 1.1 lb.
200 g. = 7.0 oz.	1 kg. = 2.2 lb.

1 oz. = 28.35 g.
1 lb. = 453.60 g.

Basic Grammar

Articles

Nouns in Spanish are either masculine or feminine. Articles agree in gender and number with the noun.

1. Definite article (the):

	singular		plural
masc.	**el tren**	the train	**los trenes**
fem.	**la casa**	the house	**las casas**

2. Indefinite article (a/an):

masc.	**un lápiz**	a pencil	**unos lápices**
fem.	**una carta**	a letter	**unas cartas**

Nouns

1. Most nouns which end in **o** are masculine. Those ending in **a** are generally feminine.

2. Normally, nouns which end in a vowel add **s** to form the plural; nouns ending in a consonant add **es**.

3. To show possession, use the preposition **de** (of).

el fin de la fiesta	the end of the party
el principio del* mes	the beginning of the month
las maletas de los viajeros	the travellers' suitcases
los ojos de las niñas	the girls' eyes
la habitación de Roberto	Robert's room

* (**del** is the contraction of **de** + **el**)

Adjectives

1. Adjectives agree with the noun in gender and number. If the masculine form ends in **o** the feminine ends in **a**. As a rule, the adjective comes after the noun.

el niño pequeño	the small boy
la niña pequeña	the small girl

If the masculine form ends in **e** or with a consonant, the feminine keeps in general the same form.

el muro/la casa grande	the big wall/house
el mar/la flor azul	the blue sea/flower

2. Most adjectives form their plurals in the same way as nouns.

un coche inglés	an English car
dos coches ingleses	two English cars

3. Possessive adjectives: They agree with the thing possessed, not with the possessor.

	sing.	plur.
my	**mi**	**mis**
your (fam.)	**tu**	**tus**
your (polite form)	**su**	**sus**
his/her/its	**su**	**sus**
our	**nuestro(a)**	**nuestros(as)**
your	**vuestro(a)**	**vuestros(as)**
their	**su**	**sus**

su hijo	*his* or *her* son
su habitación	*his* or *her* or *their* room
sus maletas	*his* or *her* or *their* suitcases

4. Comparative and superlative: These are formed by adding **más** (more) or **menos** (less) and **lo más** or **lo menos,** respectively, before the adjective.

alto	high	**más alto**	**lo más alto**

Adverbs

These are generally formed by adding **-mente** to the feminine form of the adjective (if it differs from the masculine); otherwise to the masculine.

cierto(a)	sure	**fácil**	easy
ciertamente	surely	**fácilmente**	easily

Possessive pronouns

	sing.	plur.
mine	**mío(a)**	**míos(as)**
yours (fam. sing.)	**tuyo(a)**	**tuyos(as)**
yours (polite form)	**suyo(a)**	**suyos(as)**
his/hers/its	**suyo(a)**	**suyos(as)**
ours	**nuestro(a)**	**nuestros(as)**
yours (fam. pl.)	**vuestro(a)**	**vuestros(as)**
theirs	**suyo(a)**	**suyos(as)**

Demonstrative pronouns

	masc.	fem.	neut.
this	**éste**	**ésta**	**esto**
these	**éstos**	**éstas**	**estos**
that	**ése/aquél**	**ésa/aquélla**	**eso/aquello**
those	**ésos/aquéllos**	**ésas/aquéllas**	**esos/aquellos**

The above masculine and feminine forms are also used as demonstrative adjectives, but accents are dropped. The two forms for "that" designate difference in place; **ése** means "that one", **aquél** "that one over there".

Esos libros no me gustan.	I don't like those books.
Eso no me gusta.	I don't like that.

Personal pronouns

	subject	direct object	indirect object
I	**yo**	**me**	**me**
you	**tú**	**te**	**te**
you	**usted**	**lo**	**le**
he	**él**	**lo**	**le**
she	**ella**	**la**	**le**
it	**él/ella**	**lo/la**	**le**
we	**nosotros(as)**	**nos**	**nos**
you	**vosotros(as)**	**os**	**os**
	ustedes	**los**	**les**
they	**ellos(as)**	**los**	**les**

Subject pronouns are generally omitted, except in the polite form (**usted, ustedes**) which corresponds to "you". **Tú** (sing.) and **vosotros** (plur.) are used when talking to relatives, close friends and children and between young people; **usted** and the plural **ustedes** (often abbreviated to **Vd./Vds.**) are used in all other cases.

Verbs

Here we are concerned only with the infinitive and the present tense.

	ser* (to be)	estar* (to be)	haber** (to have)
yo	soy	estoy	he
tú	eres	estás	has
usted	es	está	ha
él/ella	es	está	ha
nosotros(as)	somos	estamos	hemos
vosotros(as)	sois	estáis	habéis
ustedes	son	están	han
ellos(as)	son	están	han

* There are two verbs in Spanish for "to be". **Ser** is used to describe a permanent condition. **Estar** is used to describe location or a temporary condition.

** **haber** is used *only* in compound tenses.

Here are three of the main categories of regular verbs in the present tense:

	ends in **ar** hablar (to speak)	ends in **er** comer (to eat)	ends in **ir** reír (to laugh)
yo	hablo	como	río
tú	hablas	comes	ríes
usted	habla	come	ríe
él/ella	habla	come	ríe
nosotros(as)	hablamos	comemos	reímos
vosotros(as)	habláis	coméis	reís
ustedes	hablan	comen	ríen
ellos(as)	hablan	comen	ríen

Irregular verbs: As in all languages, these have to be learned. Here are four you will find useful.

	poder (to be able)	ir (to go)	ver (to see)	tener (to have)
yo	puedo	voy	veo	tengo
tú	puedes	vas	ves	tienes
usted	puede	va	ve	tiene
él/ella	puede	va	ve	tiene
nosotros(as)	podemos	vamos	vemos	tenemos
vosotros(as)	podéis	vais	veis	tenéis
ustedes	pueden	van	ven	tienen
ellos(as)	pueden	van	ven	tienen

Negatives

Negatives are formed by placing **no** before the verb.

Es nuevo. It's new. **No es nuevo.** It's not new.

Questions

In Spanish, questions are often formed by changing the intonation of your voice. Very often, the personal pronoun is left out, both in affirmative sentences and in questions.

| **Hablo español.** | I speak Spanish. |
| **¿Habla español?** | Do you speak Spanish? |

Note the double question mark used in Spanish.
The same is true of exclamation marks.

¡Qué tarde se hace! How late it's getting!

DICTIONARY

Dictionary
and alphabetical index

English–Spanish

f feminine   *m* masculine   *pl* plural

a un, una 159
abbey abadía *f* 81
abbreviation abreviatura *f* 154
able, to be poder 163
about *(approximately)* aproximadamente 153
above encima 15, 63
abscess flemón *m* 145
absent ausente 136
absorbent cotton algodón *m* 109
accept, to aceptar, 31, 62, 102
accessories accesorios *m/pl* 117, 125
accident accidente *m* 78, 139
accommodation alojamiento *m* 22
account cuenta *f* 131
ache dolor *m* 141
acne cream crema para el acné *f* 110
adaptor adaptador *m* 119
address señas *f/pl* 21, 102; dirección *f* 31, 76, 79
address book librito de direcciones *m* 104
adhesive adhesivo(a) 105
admission entrada *f* 82, 91, 155
admit, to admitir 149
Africa Africa *f* 146
after después de 77, 150; siguiente 150
afternoon tarde *f* 151
after-shave lotion loción para después del afeitado *f* 110
age edad *f* 149
ago hace 149, 151
air conditioner acondicionador de aire *m* 28

air conditioning aire acondicionado *m* 23
airmail por correo aéreo 133
air mattress colchón neumático *m* 92
airplane avión *m* 65
airport aeropuerto *m* 16, 21, 65
air terminal terminal aérea *f* 21
alarm clock despertador *m* 121
alcohol alcohol *m* 106
Algeria Argelia *f* 146
allergic alérgico(a) 141, 143
almond almendra *f* 53, 54
alphabet alfabeto *m* 9
alter, to *(garment)* arreglar 116
a.m. de la mañana 153
amazing asombroso(a) 84
amber ámbar *m* 122
ambulance ambulancia *f* 79
American americano(a) 105, 126
American plan pensión completa *f* 24
amethyst amatista *f* 122
amount cantidad *f* 62; suma *f* 131
amplifier amplificador *m* 119
anaesthetic anestésico *m* 144, 145
anchovy anchoa *f* 44
and y 15
animal animal *m* 85
aniseed anís *m* 51, 59
ankle tobillo *m* 139
another otro(a) 58
answer respuesta *f* 136
antibiotic antibiótico *m* 143
antidepressant antidepresivo 143
antiques antigüedades *f/pl* 83
antique shop tienda de antigüedades *f* 98

Diccionario

antiseptic antiséptico(a) 109
antiseptic antiséptico *m* 140
any alguno(a) 14
anyone alguien 11
anything algo 17, 25, 113
apartment *(flat)* apartamento *m* 22
aperitif aperitivo *m* 55
appendicitis apendicitis *f* 142
appetizer entremés *m* 41; tapa *f* 63
apple manzana *f* 54, 63
apple juice jugo de manzana *m* 60
appliance aparato *m* 119
appointment cita *f* 30, 131, 137, 145
apricot albaricoque *m* 54
April abril *m* 150
archaeology arqueología *f* 83
architect arquitecto *m* 83
area code indicativo *m* 134
arm brazo *m* 138, 139
arrival llegada *f* 16, 65
arrive, to llegar 65, 68, 130
art arte *m* 83
artery arteria *f* 138
artichoke alcachofa *f* 41, 44, 50
artificial artificial 114, 124
artist artista *m/f* 81, 83
ashtray cenicero *m* 36
Asia Asia *f* 146
ask for, to preguntar 36; pedir 24, 61, 136
asparagus espárrago *m* 41, 50
aspirin aspirina *f* 109
assorted variado(a) 41
asthma asma *m* 141
astringent astringente *m* 110
at a, en 15
at least por lo menos 24
at once ahora mismo 31
aubergine berenjena *f* 50
August agosto *m* 150
aunt tía *f* 94
Australia Australia *f* 146
automatic automático(a) 20, 122, 124
autumn otoño *m* 149
avocado aguacata *m* 41
awful horrible 84

B

baby bebé *m* 24, 111
baby food alimento para bebé *m* 111
babysitter niñera *f* 27

back espalda *f* 138
backache dolor de espalda *m* 141
bacon tocino *m* 38, 47
bacon and eggs huevos con tocino *m/pl* 38
bad malo(a) 11, 14
bag bolsa *f* 103
baggage equipaje *m* 18, 26, 31, 71
baggage car furgón de equipajes *m* 66
baggage cart carrito de equipaje *m* 18, 71
baggage check oficina de equipaje *f* 67, 71
baked al horno 46, 48
baker's panadería *f* 98
balance *(account)* balance *m* 131
balcony balcón *m* 23
ball *(inflated)* pelota *f* 128
ballet ballet *m* 87
ball-point pen bolígrafo *m* 104
banana plátano *m* 53, 63
bandage venda *f* 109
Band-Aid esparadrapo *m* 109
bangle esclava *f* 121
bangs flequillo *m* 30
bank *(finance)* banco *m* 98, 129, 130
banknote billete *m* 130
barber's barbería *f* 30, 98
basil albahaca *f* 51
basketball baloncesto *m* 90
bath *(hotel)* baño *m* 23, 25, 26
bathing cap gorro de baño *m* 117
bathing hut cabina *f* 92
bathing suit traje de baño *m* 117
bathrobe albornoz *m* 117
bath salts sales de baño *f/pl* 110
bath towel toalla de baño *f* 27
battery pila *f* 119, 121, 125; *(car)* batería *f* 75, 78
bay leaf hoja de laurel *f* 51
be, to ser, estar 13, 162
beach playa *f* 92
beach ball pelota de playa *f* 128
bean judía *f* 50
beard barba *f* 31
beautiful bonito(a) 14; hermoso(a) 84
beauty salon salón de belleza *m* 27, 30, 98
bed cama *f* 144
bed and breakfast habitación y desayuno *f* 24
bedpan silleta *f* 144

DICTIONARY

Diccionario

beef carne de buey f 47
beef steak biftec m 47
beer cerveza f 59
beet(root) remolacha f 50
before antes de 150; anterior 150, 151
begin, to empezar 80, 86, 88
beginning principio m 150
behind atrás 77
bellboy botones m 26
below debajo 14, 63
belt cinturón m 118
bend *(road)* curva f 79
berth litera f 66, 70, 71
best mejor 152
better mejor 14, 25, 101, 114
between entre 15
bicycle bicicleta f 74
big grande 14, 101
bill cuenta f 31, 62, 102; *(banknote)* billete m 130
binoculars binoculares m/pl 123
bird pájaro m 85
birth nacimiento m 25
birthday cumpleaños m 151, 152
biscuit *(Br.)* galleta f 54, 63; pasta f 54
bitter amargo(a) 61
black negro(a) 113
blackberry zarzamora f 53
blackcurrant grosella negra f 53
bladder vesícula f 138
blanket manta f 27
blazer bláser m 117
bleach aclarado m 30
bleed, to sangrar 139, 145
blind *(window)* persiana f 29
blister ampolla f 139
block *(paper)* bloc m 105
blood sangre f 142
blood pressure presión f 141, 142
blood transfusion transfusión de sangre f 144
blouse blusa f 113, 117
blow-dry modelado m 30
blue azul 113
blueberry arándano m 53
blusher colorete m 111
boar *(wild)* jabalí m 48
boarding house pensión f 19, 22
boat barco m 74
bobby pin horquilla de pinza f 111
body cuerpo m 138
boil furúnculo m 139

boiled cocido(a) 38; hervido(a) 48; en dulce 42
boiled egg huevo cocido m 38
bone hueso m 138
bonfire hoguera f 32
book libro m 11, 104
book, to reservar 69
booking office oficina de reservas f 19, 67
booklet taco m 72
bookshop librería f 98, 104
boot bota f 116
born nacido(a) 149
botanical gardens jardín botánico m 81
botany botánica f 83
bottle botella f 17, 58, 59
bottle-opener abridor de botellas m 106
bourbon whisky americano m 59
bowels intestinos m/pl 138
bow tie corbata de lazo f 117
box caja f 126
boxing boxeo m 90
boy niño m 112, 128
boyfriend amigo m 94
bra sostén m 117
bracelet pulsera f 121
braces *(suspenders)* tirantes m/pl 117
braised estofado(a) 48
brake freno m 78
brake fluid líquido de frenos m 75
brandy coñac m 59
brawn cabeza f 41
bread pan m 37, 38, 63
break, to romper 29, 119, 123, 139, 140, 145
break down, to estropear 78
breakdown avería f 78
breakdown van coche grúa m 78
breakfast desayuno m 24, 27, 34, 38
breast seno m 138
breathe, to respirar 141, 142
bridge puente m 85
briefs calzoncillos m/pl 117
bring, to traer 12
bring down, to bajar 31
broken roto(a) 29, 119, 139, 140, 145
brooch broche m 121
brother hermano m 94
brown marrón 113

bruise cardenal *m* 139
brush cepillo *m* 111
Brussels sprouts coles de bruselas *f/pl* 50
bucket cubo *m* 106, 128
buckle hebilla *f* 118
build, to construir 83
building edificio *m* 83, 85
building blocks cubos de construcción *m/pl* 128
bulb bombilla *f* 28, 75, 119
bullfight corrida *f* 89
bullfighter's cap montera *f* 127
bullfight poster cartel de toros *m* 127
bullring plaza de toros *f* 81
burn quemadura *f* 139
burn out, to *(bulb)* fundir 29
bus autobús *m* 18, 19, 65, 72, 73
business negocios *m/pl* 16, 131
business trip viaje de negocios *m* 94
bus stop parada de autobús *f* 72, 73
busy ocupado(a) 96
butane gas gas butano *m* 32, 106
butcher's carnicería *f* 98
butter mantequilla *f* 37, 38, 63
button botón *m* 29, 118
buy, to comprar 82, 104

C

cabbage berza *f*, repollo *m* 50
cabin *(ship)* camarote *m* 74
cable telegrama *m* 133
cable car funicular *m* 74
cable release cable del disparador *m* 125
caffein-free descafeinado(a) 38, 60
cake pastel *m* 54, 63; bollo *m* 63
cake shop pastelería *f* 98
calculator calculadora *f* 105
calendar calendario *m* 104
call *(phone)* llamada *f* 135, 136
call, to llamar 10, 31, 71, 78, 136, 156
cambric batista *f* 114
camel-hair pelo de camello *m* 114
camera cámara *f* 124, 125
camera shop tienda de fotografía *f* 98
camp, to acampar 32
campbed cama de campaña *f* 106
camping camping *m* 32
camping equipment equipo de camping *m* 106

camp site camping *m* 32
can *(of peaches)* lata *f* 120
can *(to be able)* poder 12, 163
Canada Canadá *m* 146
cancel, to anular 65
candle vela *f* 106
candy caramelo *m* 63, 126
candy store bombonería *f* 98
can opener abrelatas *m* 106
cap gorra *f* 116
caper alcaparra *f* 51
capital *(finance)* capital *m* 131
car coche *m* 20, 75, 76, 78
carafe garrafa *f* 58
carat quilate *m* 121
caravan caravana *f* 32
caraway comino *m* 51
carbon paper papel carbón *m* 104
carburetor carburador *m* 78
card tarjeta *f* 131
card game juego de cartas *m* 128
cardigan chaqueta de punto *f* 117
car hire alquiler de coches *m* 20
car park estacionamiento *m* 77
car radio radio para coche *f* 119
car rental alquiler de automóviles *m* 20
carrot zanahoria *f* 50
carry, to llevar 21
cart carrito *m* 18
carton *(cigarettes)* cartón (de cigarrillos) *m* 17
cartridge *(camera)* cartucho *m* 124
case *(instance)* caso *m* 143; *(glasses etc.)* estuche *m* 123; funda *f* 125
cash, to cobrar 129, 130
cash desk caja *f* 155
cashier cajero(a) *m/f* 103
cassette casette *f* 119, 127
castanets castañuelas *f/pl* 127
castle castillo *m* 81
catalogue catálogo *m* 82
cathedral catedral *f* 81
Catholic católico(a) 84
cauliflower coliflor *f* 50
caution cuidado *m* 79, 155; atención *f* 79
cave cueva *f* 81
celery apio *m* 50
cellophane tape cinta adhesiva *f* 104
cemetery cementerio *m* 81
centimetre centímetro *m* 112
centre centro *m* 19, 21, 72, 76, 81
century siglo *m* 149

ceramics cerámica f 83
cereal cereales m/pl 38
certificate certificado m 144
chain (jewellery) cadena f 121
chair silla f 36, 106
chamber music música de cámara f 128
champagne champán m 56
change (money) suelto m 77; moneda f 130
change, to cambiar 18, 61, 65, 68, 73, 75, 123, 130; hacer transbordo 73
chapel capilla f 81
charcoal carbón m 106
charge precio m 32; tarifa f 136
charge, to cobrar 24, 124; (commission) cargar 130
charm (trinket) amuleto m 121
charm bracelet pulsera de fetiches f 121
cheap barato(a) 14, 24, 25, 101
check cheque m 129; (restaurant) cuenta f 62
check, to controlar 75, 123; (luggage) facturar 71
check book chequera f 131
check in, to (airport) presentarse 65
check out, to marcharse 31
checkup (medical) reconocimiento general m 142
cheers! ¡salud! 55
cheese queso m 52, 63
cheesecake pastel de queso m 54
chemist's farmacia f 98, 108
cheque cheque m 130
cheque book chequera f 131
cherry cereza f 53
chervil perifollo m 51
chess ajedrez m 128
chest pecho m 138, 141
chestnut castaña f 53
chewing gum chicle m 126
chicken pollo m 49, 63
chicken breast pechuga de pollo f 49
chicken liver higadito de pollo m 41, 48
chickpea garbanzo m 50
chicory (Am.) achicoria f 50
chiffon gasa f 114
child niño(a) m/f 24, 61, 92, 139, 149
children's doctor pediatra m/f 137
chips patatas fritas f/pl 63; (Am.) patatas fritas f/pl, chips m/pl 63

chives cebolleta f 51
chocolate chocolate m 54, 63, 126; (hot) chocolate (caliente) m 38, 60
chop chuleta f 47
Christmas Navidad f 152
church iglesia f 81, 84, 85
cigar puro m 126
cigarette cigarrillo m 17, 95, 126
cigarette case pitillera f 121
cigarette lighter encendedor m 121, 126
cigarette paper papel para cigarrillos m 126
cine camera cámara de filmar f 124
cinema cine m 86, 96
cinnamon canela f 51
circle (theatre) anfiteatro m 87
city ciudad f 81
clam almeja f 41, 45
classical clásico(a) 128
clean limpio(a) 61
clean, to limpiar 29, 76
cleansing cream crema limpiadora f 110
cliff acantilado m 85
clip clip m 121
clock reloj m 121, 153
clog, to atascar 28
close (near) cercano(a) 78, 98
close, to cerrar 11, 82, 108, 129, 132, 155
closed cerrado(a) 155
clothes ropa f 29, 117
clothes peg percha f 106
clothing prendas de vestir f/pl 112
cloud nube f 95
clove clavo m 50
coach (bus) autocar m 72, 80
coat abrigo m 117
coconut coco m 53
cod bacalao m 45
coffee café m 38, 60, 64
coin moneda f 83
cold frío(a) 14, 25, 38, 61, 95
cold (illness) resfriado m 108, 141
cold cuts fiambres m/pl 41, 64
collar cuello m 118
collect call llamada a cobro revertido f 135
cologne agua de colonia f 110
colour color m 103, 112, 124, 125
colour chart muestrario m 30
colour fast color fijo 113
colourful colorido(a) 101

colour negative negativo de color *m* 124

colour rinse reflejos *m/pl* 30

colour shampoo champú colorante *m* 111

colour slide diapositiva *f* 124

comb peine *m* 111

come, to venir 34, 61, 93, 95, 137, 146

comedy comedia *f* 86

commission comisión *f* 130

compact disc disco compacto *m* 127

compartment departamento *m* 71

compass brújula *f* 106

complaint reclamación *f* 61

concert concierto *m* 87

concert hall sala de conciertos *f* 81, 87

condition condición *f* 91

conductor *(orchestra)* director *m* 88

confectioner's confitería *f* 98

confirm, to confirmar 65

confirmation confirmación *f* 23

congratulation enhorabuena *f* 152

connection *(plane)* conexión *f* 65; *(train)* transbordo *m* 68

constipated estreñido(a) 140

contact lens lente de contacto *m* 123

contain, to contener 37

contraceptive contraceptivo *m* 109

control control *m* 16

convent convento *m* 81

convention hall palacio de convenciones *m* 81

cookie galleta *f* 54, 64; pasta *f* 54

cool box nevera portátil *f* 106

copper cobre *m* 122

copperware objetos de cobre *m/pl* 127

coral coral *m* 122

corduroy pana *f* 114

cork corcho *m* 61

corkscrew sacacorchos *m* 106

corn *(Am.)* maíz *m* 50

corner rincón *m* 36; *(street)* esquina *f* 21, 77

corn plaster callicida *m* 109

correct correcto(a) 11

cost precio *m* 131; coste *m* 135, 136

cost, to costar 10, 80

cotton algodón *m* 114

cotton wool algodón *m* 109

cough tos *f* 108, 141

cough, to toser 142

cough drops gotas para la tos *f/pl* 109

counter mostrador *m* 132

countryside campo *m* 85

court house palacio de justicia *m* 81

courtyard patio *m* 23, 36

cousin primo(a) *m/f* 94

cover charge cubierto *m* 62

crab cangrejo *m* 46

cracker galleta salada *f* 64

cramp calambre *m* 141

crayfish cangrejo *m* 46

crayon lápiz de color *m* 104

cream crema 113

cream nata *f* 54, 64; crema *f* 60, 110

creamy cremoso(a) 52

credit crédito *m* 130

credit, to acreditar 131

credit card tarjeta de crédito *f* 20, 31, 62, 102, 129, 130

crepe crepé *m* 114

crisps patatas fritas *f/pl*, chips *m/pl* 64

crockery vajilla *f* 106, 107

cross cruz *f* 121

crossing *(by sea)* travesía *f* 74

crossroads cruce *m* 77, 79

cruise crucero *m* 74

crystal cristal *m* 122

cucumber pepino *m* 42, 50, 64

cuff link gemelo *m* 121

cuisine cocina *f* 34

cup taza *f* 36, 60, 107

cured en salazón 46; serrano 42

currency moneda *f* 129

currency exchange office oficina de cambio *f* 18, 67, 129

current corriente *f* 92

curtain cortina *f* 28

curve *(road)* curva *f* 79

customs aduana *f* 16, 79, 102

cut *(wound)* cortadura *f* 139

cut, to cortar 139

cut glass cristal tallado *m* 122

cuticle remover quitacutículas *m* 110

cutlery cubiertos *m/pl* 106, 107, 121

cycling ciclismo *m* 90

cystitis cistitis *f* 142

D

dairy lechería f 98
dance baile m 88
dance, to bailar 88, 96
danger peligro m 79, 155, 156
dangerous peligroso(a) 79, 92
dark oscuro(a) 25, 101, 112, 113
date fecha f 25, 150; (fruit) dátil m
    53
daughter hija f 94
day día m 16, 20, 24, 32, 80, 151
daylight luz del día f 124
day off día libre m 151
death muerte f 155
decade década f 149
December diciembre m 150
decision decisión f 24, 102
deck (ship) cubierta f 74
deck-chair silla de lona f 92, 106
declare, to declarar 16, 17
deer corzo m 48
delay demora f 69
delicatessen mantequería f 98
deliver, to enviar 102
delivery envío m 102
denim algodón asargado m 114
dentist dentista m/f 98, 145
denture dentadura f 145
deodorant desodorante m 110
department departamento m 83, 100
department store grandes almace-
    nes m/pl 98
departure salida f 65, 80
deposit depósito m 20, 131
deposit, to (bank) depositar 131
dessert postre m 37, 54
detour (traffic) desviación f 79
develop, to revelar 124
diabetic diabético(a) 141
diabetic diabético(a) m/f 37
dialling code indicativo m 134
diamond diamante m 122
diaper pañal m 111
diarrhoea diarrea f 140
dice dado m 128
dictionary diccionario m 104
diet dieta f 37
difficult difícil 14
difficulty dificultad f 28, 102, 141
dill eneldo m 51
dining-car coche restaurante m 66,
    68
dining-room comedor m 27
dinner cena f 34, 95

dinner jacket smoking m 117
direct directo(a) 68, 134
direct, to indicar 12
direction dirección f 76
directory (phone) guía de teléfonos f
    134
disabled minusválido(a) 82
disc disco m 77, 127, 128
disc film disco-película m 124
discotheque discoteca f 88
disease enfermedad f 142
dish plato m 37
dishwashing detergent detergente
    para vajilla m 106
disinfectant desinfectante m 109
dislocate, to dislocar 140
display case vitrina f 100
dissatisfied descontento(a) 103
district (country) comarca f 76
disturb, to molestar 155
diversion (traffic) desviación f 79
dizzy mareado(a) 140
doctor doctor(a) m/f 79, 137, 145;
    médico(a) m/f 137, 144
doctor's office consultorio m 137
dog perro m 155
doll muñeca f 127
dollar dólar m 18, 102, 130
door puerta f 155
dose dosis f 143
double doble 59, 74
double bed cama matrimonial f 23
double room habitación doble f 19,
    23
down abajo 15
downstairs abajo 15
downtown centro de la ciudad m 81
dozen docena f 148
drawing paper papel de dibujo m
    104
drawing pin chincheta f 104
dress vestido m 117
dressing gown bata f 117
drink bebida f 60, 61; copa f 95
drink, to beber 13, 35, 36
drinking water agua potable f 32
drip, to (tap) gotear 28
drive, to conducir 76
driving licence permiso de conducir
    m 20, 79
drop (liquid) gota f 109
drugstore farmacia f 98, 108
dry seco(a) 30, 58, 111
dry cleaner's tintorería f 29, 98

dry shampoo champú seco *m* 111
Dublin bay prawn cigala *f* 41, 46
duck pato *m* 49
dummy chupete *m* 111
during durante 150, 151
duty *(customs)* impuestos *m/pl* 17
duty-free shop tienda libre de impuestos *f* 19
dye tintura *f* 30, 111

E

each cada 149
ear oreja *f* 138
earache dolor de oídos *m* 141
ear drops gotas para los oídos *f/pl* 109
early temprano 14
earring pendiente *m* 121, 127
earthenware loza de barro *f* 127
east este *m* 77
Easter Pascua *f* 152
easy fácil 14
eat, to comer 13, 36, 144, 162
eel anguila *f* 41
egg huevo *m* 38, 42, 44, 64
eggplant berenjena *f* 50
eight ocho 147
eighteen dieciocho 147
eighth octavo(a) 148
eighty ochenta 147
elastic elástico(a) 109
elastic elástico *m* 118
Elastoplast esparadrapo *m* 109
electrical eléctrico(a) 119
electrical appliance aparato eléctrico *m* 119
electrician electricista *m* 98
electricity electricidad *f* 32
electronic electrónico(a) 125, 128
elevator ascensor *m* 27, 100
eleven once 147
embarkation embarco *m* 74
embroidery bordado *m* 127
emerald esmeralda *f* 122
emergency urgencia *f* 156
emergency exit salida de emergencia *f* 27, 99, 155
emery board lima de papel *f* 110
empty vacío(a) 14
enamel esmalte *m* 122
end final *m* 150
endive *(Br.)* achicoria *f* 50
engagement ring sortija de pedida *f* 121

engine *(car)* motor *m* 78
England Inglaterra *f* 146
English inglés(esa) 11, 80, 82, 84, 104, 105, 126
enjoy, to gustar 62
enjoyable agradable 31
enjoy oneself, to divertirse 96
enlarge, to amplificar 125
enough bastante 14
enquiry información *f* 68
enter, to entrar 155
entrance entrada *f* 68, 99, 155
entrance fee entrada *f* 82
envelope sobre *m* 27, 104
equipment equipo *m* 92, 106
eraser goma de borrar *f* 104
escalator escalera mecánica *f* 100
espresso coffee café exprés *m* 60
estimate estimación *f* 131
Europe Europa *f* 146
evening tarde *f* 9, 96, 151; noche *f* 86, 95
evening dress traje de noche *m* 88, 117
everything todo 31
excellent excelente 62
exchange, to cambiar 103
exchange rate cambio *m* 18, 130
exclude, to excluir 24
excursion excursión *f* 80
excuse, to perdonar 10
exercise book cuaderno *m* 104
exhaust pipe tubo de escape *m* 78
exhibition exhibición *f* 81
exit salida *f* 68, 79, 99, 155
expect, to esperar 130
expensive caro(a) 14, 19, 23, 101
exposure *(photography)* exposición *f* 124
exposure counter escala de exposición *f* 125
express urgente 133
expression expresión *f* 10
expressway autopista *f* 76, 79
external externo(a) 109
extra más 27, 36
extract, to *(tooth)* sacar 145
eye ojo *m* 123, 138, 139
eye drops gotas para los ojos *f/pl* 109
eye liner perfilador de ojos *m* 110
eye pencil lápiz de ojos *m* 110
eye shadow sombra de ojos *f* 110
eye specialist oculista *m/f* 137

F

face cara f 138
face powder polvo de la cara m 110
factory fábrica f 79, 81
fair feria f 81
fall caída f 139; (autumn) otoño m 149
family familia f 94
fan ventilador m 28; (folding) abanico m 127
fan belt correa de ventilador f 75
far lejos 14, 100
fare tarifa f 21, 65, 67, 72
farm granja f 85
fast rápido(a) 124
fat (meat) grasa f 37
father padre m 94
faucet grifo m 28
February febrero m 150
fee (doctor) honorarios m/pl 144
feeding bottle biberón m 111
feel, to (physical state) sentirse 140
felt fieltro m 114
felt-tip pen rotulador m 114
ferry transbordador m 74
fever fiebre f 140
few pocos(as) 14; (a) (alg)unos(as) 14
field campo m 85
fifteen quince 147
fifth quinto(a) 148
fig higo m 53
file (tool) lima f 110
fill in, to llenar 25, 144
filling (tooth) empaste m 145
filling station gasolinera f 75
film película f 86, 124, 125; rollo m 124
film winder enrollador m 125
filter filtro m 125
filter-tipped con filtro 126
find, to encontrar 10, 12, 100, 137
fine (OK) muy bien 25
fine arts bellas artes f/pl 83
finger dedo m 138
fire fuego m 156
first primero(a) 68, 72, 148
first class primera clase f 66, 69
first name nombre (de pila) m 25
fish pescado m 45
fish, to pescar 91
fishing pesca f 91
fishing tackle aparejo de pesca m 106

fishmonger's pescadería f 98
fit, to quedar bien 115, 116
fitting room probador m 115
five cinco 147
fix, to arreglar 75, 145
flannel franela f 114
flash (photography) flash m 125
flashlight linterna f 106
flat plano(a) 116
flat (apartment) apartamento m 22
flat tyre pinchazo m 75, 78
flea market mercado de cosas viejas m 81
flight vuelo m 65
flint piedra de mechero f 126
flippers aletas para nadar f/pl 128
floor piso m 26
floor show atracciones m/pl 88
flour harina f 37
flower flor f 85
flower shop florería f 98
flu gripe f 142
fluid líquido m 75
folding chair silla plegable f 107
folding table mesa plegable f 107
folk music música folklórica f 128
food alimento m 37, 111; comida f 61
food box fiambrera f 106
food poisoning intoxicación f 142
foot pie m 138
football fútbol m 90
foot cream crema para los pies f 110
footpath sendero m 85
for por, para 15
forbid, to prohibir 155
foreign extranjero(a) 59
forest bosque m 85
fork tenedor m 36, 107
form (document) impreso m 133; ficha f 23
fortnight quincena f 151
fortress fortaleza f 81, 85
forty cuarenta 147
foundation cream maquillaje m 110
fountain fuente f 81
fountain pen pluma estilográfica f 104
four cuatro 147
fourteen catorce 147
fourth cuarto(a) 148
France Francia f 146
free libre 14, 71, 82, 96, 155
french fries patatas fritas f/pl 64
fresh fresco(a) 53, 61

Friday viernes *m* 151
fried frito(a) 46, 48
fried egg huevo frito *m* 38, 64
friend amigo(a) *m/f* 93, 95
fringe flequillo *m* 30
frock vestido *m* 117
from de, desde 15
front delantero(a) 23, 75
fruit fruta *f* 53
fruit cocktail ensalada de fruta *f* 53
fruit juice jugo de fruta *m* 38, 60;
  zumo de fruta *m* 42
fruit stand frutería *f* 98
frying-pan sartén *f* 106
full lleno(a) 14
full board pensión completa *f* 24
full insurance seguro a todo riesgo *m*
  20
furnished amueblado(a) 22
furniture muebles *m/pl* 83
furrier's peletería *f* 98

G

gabardine gabardina *f* 114
gallery galería *f* 81, 98
game juego *m* 128; *(food)* caza *f* 48
garage garaje *m* 26, 78
garden jardín *m* 85
gardens jardines públicos *m/pl* 81
garlic ajo *m* 51
garment prenda *f* 29
gas gas *m* 156
gasoline gasolina *f* 75, 78
gastritis gastritis *f* 142
gauze gasa *f* 109
general general 26
general delivery lista de correos *f* 133
general practitioner generalista *m/f*
  137
gentleman caballero *m* 155
geology geología *f* 83
Germany Alemania *f* 146
get, to *(find, call)* conseguir 10, 32,
  90, 134; coger 19, 21; llamar
  137; buscar 156; *(go)* llegar 100
get back, to volver 80; regresar 85
get by, to pasar 70
get off, to apear 73
get to, to llegar a 10, 70; ir a 19
get up, to levantarse 144
gherkin pepinillo *m* 42, 50, 64
gift *(present)* regalo *m* 120
gin ginebra *f* 59
gin and tonic ginebra con tónica *f* 60

ginger jengibre *m* 51
girdle faja *f* 117
girl niña *f* 112, 128
girlfriend amiga *f* 94
give, to dar 12, 136, 140
give way, to *(traffic)* ceder el paso 79
glad *(to know you)* tanto gusto 93
gland glándula *f* 138
glass vaso *m* 36, 58, 59, 61, 143
glasses gafas *f/pl* 123
gloomy lúgubre 84
glossy *(finish)* acabado de brillo 125
glove guante *m* 117
glue cola de pegar *f* 104
go, to ir 77, 96, 163
go away, to irse 156
go back, to regresar 77
gold oro *m* 121, 122
golden dorado(a) 113
gold plate lámina de oro *f* 122
golf golf *m* 91
golf club palo de golf *m* 91
golf course campo de golf *m* 91
good bueno(a) 14, 101
good-bye adiós 9
Good Friday Viernes Santo *m* 152
goods artículos *m/pl* 16
goose ganso *m* 48
go out, to salir 96
gram gramo *m* 120
grammar book libro de gramática *m*
  105
grape uva *f* 53, 64
grapefruit pomelo *m* 53
grapefruit juice jugo de pomelo *m*
  38, 60; zumo de pomelo *m* 42
gray gris 113
graze arañazo *m* 139
greasy graso(a) 30, 111
great *(excellent)* estupendo(a) 95
Great Britain Gran Bretaña *f* 146
green verde 113
green bean judía verde *m* 50
greengrocer's verdulería *f* 98
green salad ensalada de lechuga *f* 43
greeting saludo *m* 9
grey gris 113
grilled a la parrilla 46, 48;
  a la plancha 41
grocery tienda de comestibles *f* 98,
  120
groundsheet alfombra (de hule) *f* 106
group grupo *m* 82
guide guía *m/f* 80

guidebook guía f 82, 104, 105
guitar guitarra f 127
gum *(teeth)* encía 145
gynaecologist ginecólogo m/f 137

H

hair cabello m 30, 111
hairbrush cepillo para el pelo m 111
haircut corte de pelo m 30
hairdresser's peluquería f 27, 30, 98
hair dryer secador de pelo m 119
hairgrip horquilla de pinza f 111
hair lotion loción capilar f 111
hairpin horquilla f 111
hairspray laca para el pelo f 30, 111
hake merluza f 46
half mitad f 148
half a day medio día m 80
half an hour media hora f 153
half board media pensión f 24
half price *(ticket)* media tarifa f 69
hall *(large room)* sala f 81, 87
hall porter conserje m 26
ham jamón m 38, 42, 44, 47, 64
ham and eggs huevos con jamón m/pl 38
hamburger hamburguesa f 64
hammer martillo m 106
hand mano f 138
handbag bolso de mano m 117, 156
hand cream crema para las manos f 110
handicrafts artesanía f 83
handkerchief pañuelo m 117
hand lotion loción para las manos f 110
handmade hecho(a) a mano 113
hanger percha f 27
hangover resaca f 108
happy feliz 152
harbour puerto m 81
hard duro(a) 52, 123
hard-boiled *(egg)* duro 38, 42
hardware shop ferretería f 98
hare liebre f 49
hat sombrero m 117
have, to haber 162; tener 163
hay fever fiebre del heno f 108
hazelnut avellana f 53
he él 161
head cabeza f 138, 139
headache dolor de cabeza m 141
headcheese cabeza f 41
headlight luz f 79

headphones casco con auriculares m 119
head waiter jefe m 61
health salud f 55
health food shop tienda de alimentos dietéticos f 98
health insurance seguro m 144
health insurance form hoja de seguro f 144
heart corazón m 47, 138
heart attack ataque al corazón m 141
heating calefacción f 23, 28
heavy pesado(a) 14, 101
heel tacón m 116
height altura f 85
helicopter helicóptero m 74
hello! *(phone)* oiga 135
help ayuda f 156
help! ¡socorro! 156
help, to ayudar 12, 21, 71; atender 100; *(oneself)* servirse 120
hen gallina f 48
her su 160
herbs hierbas finas f/pl 51
here aquí 13, 15
herring arenque m 41, 45
high alto(a) 92, 141
high season alta estación f 149
high-speed rápido(a) 124
high tide marea alta f 92
hill colina f 85
hire alquiler m 20
hire, to alquilar 20, 91, 92, 119, 155
his su 160
history historia f 83
hitchhike, to hacer auto-stop 74
hold on! *(phone)* espere 136
hole hoyo m 29
holiday día festivo m 151
holidays vacaciones f/pl 16, 151
home address domicilio m 25
honey miel f 38
hope, to esperar 94
hors d'œuvre entremés m 41
horse riding equitación f 90
hospital hospital m 98, 144
hot caliente 14, 24, 38, 60, 95
hotel hotel m 19, 21, 22, 80
hotel guide guía de hoteles f 19
hotel reservation reserva de hotel f 19
hot water agua caliente f 23, 28

hot-water bottle botella de agua caliente *f* 27
hour hora *f* 153
house casa *f* 83, 85
hovercraft aerodeslizador *m* 74
how cómo 10
how far a qué distancia 10, 76
how long cuánto tiempo 10
how many cuántos(as) 10
how much cuánto 10
hundred cien, ciento 147
hungry, to be tener hambre 13, 35
hunt, to cazar 91
hurry *(to be in a)* tener prisa 21
hurry up! ¡dése prisa! 13
hurt, to doler 139, 140, 145
husband marido *m* 94
hut cabaña *f* 85
hydrofoil hidroplano *m* 74

I

I yo 161
ice-cream helado *m* 54, 64
ice cube cubito de hielo *m* 27
ice pack elemento congelable *m* 106
iced tea té helado *m* 60
ill enfermo(a) 140, 156
illness enfermedad *f* 140
immediately inmediatamente 137
important importante 13
in en 15
include, to incluir 20, 24, 31, 62, 80
indigestion indigestión *f* 141
indoor *(swimming pool)* cubierto(a) 91
inexpensive barato(a) 35, 124
infect, to infectar 140
infection infección *f* 141
inflammation inflamación *f* 142
inflation inflación *f* 131
inflation rate tasa de inflación *f* 131
influenza gripe *f* 142
information información *f* 67, 80
injection inyección *f* 142, 144
injure, to herir 139
injured herido(a) 79, 139
injury herida *f* 139
ink tinta *f* 105
inn fonda *f*, posada *f* 33
inquiry información *f* 68
insect bite picadura de insecto *f* 108, 139
insect repellent repelente para insectos *m* 109

insect spray spray para insectos *m* 109
inside dentro 15
instead en lugar de 37
insurance seguro *m* 20, 79, 144
insurance company compañía de seguros *f* 79
interest interés *m* 80, 131
interested, to be interesarse 83
interesting interesante 84
international internacional 132, 134
interpreter intérprete *m* 131
intersection cruce *m* 77, 79
introduce, to presentar 93
introduction presentación *f* 93; formulario de presentación *m* 130
investment inversión *f* 131
invitation invitación *f* 94
invite, to invitar 94
invoice factura *f* 131
iodine yodo *f* 109
Ireland Irlanda *f* 146
iron *(laundry)* plancha *f* 119
iron, to planchar 29
ironmonger's ferretería *f* 99
Italy Italia *f* 146
its su 160
ivory marfil *m* 122

J

jacket chaqueta *f* 117
jade jade *m* 122
jam mermelada *f* 38
jam, to atrancar 28, 125
January enero *m* 150
jar tarro *m* 120
jaundice ictericia *f* 142
jaw mandíbula *f* 138
jeans tejanos *m/pl* 117
jersey jersey *m* 117
jewel box joyero *m* 121
jeweller's joyería *f* 99, 121
jewellery joyas *f/pl* 127
joint articulación *f* 138
journey viaje *m* 73
juice jugo *m* 38, 40, 60; zumo *m* 42
July julio *m* 150
June junio *m* 150
just *(only)* sólo 16, 100

K

kerosene petróleo *m* 106
ketchup salsa de tomate *f* 37, 64

key llave f 26
kid (goat) cabrito m 47
kidney riñón m 47, 48, 138
kilogram kilogramo m 120
kilometre kilómetro m 20, 79
kind amable 95
kind (type) clase f 140
knee rodilla f 138
knife cuchillo m 36, 107
knock, to llamar 155
know, to saber 16, 24; conocer 114

L

label etiqueta f 105
lace encaje m 114, 127
lady señora f 155
lake lago m 85, 91
lamb cordero m 47
lamp lámpara f 29, 106, 119
lamprey lampresa f 46
landmark punto de referencia m 85
large grande 101, 116
last último(a) 14, 68, 72, 74; pasado(a) 149, 150
late tarde 14
later más tarde 135
laugh, to reír 11, 162
launderette launderama f 99
laundry (place) lavandería f 29, 99; (clothes) ropa f 29
laundry service servicio de lavado m 23
laxative laxante m 109
lead, to llevar 76
leap year año bisiesto m 149
leather cuero m 114, 116
leather goods store tienda de artículos de cuero f 99
leave, to marcharse 31, 95; salir 68, 74; (deposit) dejar 27, 71
leek puerro m 50
left izquierda 21, 63, 69, 77
left-luggage office oficina de equipaje f 67, 71
leg pierna f 47, 138
lemon limón m 37, 38, 53, 60, 64
lemonade limonada f 60
lemon juice jugo de limón m 60
lens (glasses) lente f 123; (camera) objetivo m 125
lens cap capuchón para el objetivo m 125
lentil lenteja f 50

less menos 14
let, to (hire out) alquilar 155
letter carta f 132
letter box buzón m 133
letter of credit carta de crédito f 130
lettuce lechuga f 50, 64
level crossing paso a nivel m 79
library biblioteca f 81, 99
licence (permit) permiso m 20, 79
lie down, to acostarse 142
life belt cinturón salvavidas m 74
life boat bote salvavidas m 74
lifeguard vigilante m 92
lift ascensor m 27, 100
light luz f 28, 124; (cigarette) lumbre f 95
light ligero(a) 14, 54, 101, 128; liviano(a) 58; (colour) claro(a) 101, 112, 113
light, to (fire) encender 32
lighter encendedor m 126
lighter fluid gasolina para encendedor m 126
lighter gas gas para encendedor m 126
light meter exposímetro m 125
like, to querer 12, 20, 23; gustar 24, 27, 93, 102, 112
lime (fruit) lima f 53
line línea f 73
linen (cloth) hilo m 114
lip labio m 138
lipsalve cacao para los labios m 110
lipstick lápiz de labios m 110
liqueur licor m 59, 60
listen, to escuchar 128
litre litro m 58, 75, 120
little (a) un poco 14
live, to vivir 83
liver hígado m 47, 138
lobster (spiny) langosta f 42, 46
local local 36, 43, 59
long largo(a) 30, 116, 117
long-sighted présbite 123
look, to mirar 100; ver 123
look for, to buscar 13
look out! ¡cuidado! 156
lose, to perder 123, 156
loss pérdida f 131
lost perdido(a) 13, 156
lost and found office oficina de objetos perdidos f 67, 156
lost property office oficina de objetos perdidos f 67, 156

lot *(a)* mucho 14
lotion loción *f* 110
lovely bonito(a) 94
low bajo(a) 92,
lower inferior 70
low season baja estación *f* 149
low tide marea baja *f* 92
luck suerte *f* 135, 152
luggage equipaje *m* 18, 26, 31, 71
luggage locker consigna automática *f* 18, 67, 71
luggage trolley carrito de equipaje *m* 18, 71
luggage van furgón de equipajes *m* 66
lump *(bump)* chichón *m* 139
lunch almuerzo *m* 34, 80
lunch, to almorzar 95
lung pulmón *m* 138

M

machine máquina *f* 113
mackerel caballa *f* 45
magazine revista *f* 105
magnificent magnífico(a) 84
maid camarera *f* 26
mail, to mandar por correo 28
mail correo *m* 28, 133
mailbox buzón *m* 133
main principal 80
make, to hacer 104
make up, to hacer 28, 71; preparar 108
make-up remover pad toallita de maquillaje *f* 110
man caballero *m* 115; hombre *m* 156
manager director *m* 26
manicure manicura *f* 30
many muchos(as) 14
map mapa *m* 76, 105
March marzo *m* 150
marinated en escabeche 46
market mercado *m* 81, 99
marmalade mermelada amarga de naranjas *f* 38
married casado(a) 94
mascara pintura de pestañas *f* 110
mass *(church)* misa *f* 84
mat *(finish)* mate 125
match cerilla *f* 106, 126; *(sport)* partido *m* 90
match, to *(colour)* hacer juego 112
material *(cloth)* tejido *m* 113
matinée sesión de la tarde *f* 87

mattress colchón *m* 106
mauve malva 113
May mayo *m* 150
may *(can)* poder 12, 163
meadow prado *m* 85
meal comida *f* 24, 34, 35, 62, 143
mean, to querer decir 11, 25
means medio *m* 74
measles sarampión *m* 142
measure, to medir 114
meat carne *f* 47, 61
mechanic mecánico *m* 78
mechanical pencil lapicero *m* 121
medical médico(a) 144
medicine medicina *f* 83, 143
medium *(meat)* regular 48
meet, to encontrar 96
melon melón *m* 42, 53, 64
mend, to arreglar 75; *(clothes)* remendar 29
menthol *(cigarettes)* mentolado(a) 126
menu menú *m* 37, 39; *(printed)* carta *f* 36, 40
message recado *m* 28, 136
methylated spirits alcohol de quemar *m* 106
metre metro *m* 112
mezzanine *(theatre)* anfiteatro *m* 87
middle medio *m* 69, 87, 150
midnight medianoche *f* 153
mild suave 52
mileage kilometraje *m* 20
milk leche *f* 38, 60, 64
milkshake batido *m* 60
million millón *m* 148
minced meat carne picada *f* 47
mineral water agua mineral *f* 60
minister *(religion)* ministro *m* 84
mint menta *f* 51
minute minuto *m* 153
mirror espejo *m* 115, 123
miscellaneous diverso(a) 127
Miss señorita *f* 9
miss, to faltar 18, 29, 61
mistake error *m* 61; *(to make a mistake)* equivocarse 31, 62, 103
modified American plan media pensión *f* 24
moisturizing cream crema hidratante *f* 110
moment momento *m* 136
monastery monasterio *m* 81
Monday lunes *m* 151

money dinero *m* 129, 156
money order giro postal *m* 132
month mes *m* 150
monument monumento *m* 81
moped velomotor *m* 74
more más 14
morning mañana *f* 151
Morocco Marruecos *m* 146
mortgage hipoteca *f* 131
mosque mezquita *f* 81
mosquito net red para mosquitos *f* 106
mother madre *f* 94
motorbike motocicleta *f* 74
motorboat motora *f* 92
motorway autopista *f* 76, 79
mountain montaña *f* 85
moustache bigote *m* 31
mouth boca *f* 138
mouthwash gargarismo *m* 109
move, to mover 139, 140
movie película *f* 86
movie camera cámara de filmar *f* 124
movies cine *m* 86, 96
Mr. Señor *m* 9
Mrs. Señora *f* 9
much mucho 14
mug taza alta *f* 107
muscle músculo *m* 138, 139
museum museo *m* 81
mushroom seta *f* 44, 50; champiñon *m* 41, 50
music música *f* 83, 128
mussel mejillón *m* 42
must, to deber 31, 37, 61; tener que 23, 95
mustard mostaza *f* 37, 51, 64
mutton carnero *m* 47
my mi 160
myself mismo(a) 120

N

nail *(human)* uña *f* 110
nail clippers alicates de uñas *m/pl* 110
nail file lima de uñas *f* 110
nail polish esmalte de uñas *m* 110
nail polish remover acetona quita-esmalte de uñas *f* 110
nail scissors tijeras de uñas *f/pl* 110
name nombre *m* 23, 25, 79, 93
napkin servilleta *f* 36, 105
nappy pañal *m* 111
narrow estrecho(a) 116

nationality nacionalidad *f* 25
natural natural 83
natural history historia natural *f* 83
nausea náusea *f* 140
near cerca 14
near to cerca de 15
nearby cerca de aquí 77, 84
nearest más cercano(a) 78, 98
necessary necesario(a) 88
neck cuello *m* 30, 138
necklace collar *m* 121
need, to necesitar 29, 116
needle aguja *f* 27
negative negativo *m* 124
nephew sobrino *m* 94
nerve nervio *m* 138
nervous nervioso(a) 138
nervous system sistema nervioso *m* 138
Netherlands Países Bajos *m/pl* 146
never nunca 15
new nuevo(a) 14
newspaper periódico *m* 104, 105
newsstand quiosco de periódicos *m* 19, 67, 99, 104
New Year Año Nuevo *m* 152
New Zealand Nueva Zelandia *f* 146
next próximo(a) 14, 68, 73, 76, 149, 151
next to junto a 15, 77
niece sobrina *f* 94
night noche *f* 24, 26, 151
nightclub centro nocturno *m* 88
night cream crema de noche *f* 110
nightdress camisón *m* 117
nine nueve 147
nineteen diecinueve 147
ninety noventa 147
ninth noveno(a) 148
nipple *(feeding bottle)* tetina *f* 111
no no 9
noisy ruidoso(a) 25
nonalcoholic sin alcohol 60
none ninguno(a) 15
nonsmoker no fumadores *m/pl* 36, 69, 70
noon mediodía *m* 153
normal normal 30
north norte *m* 77
North America América del Norte *f* 146
nose nariz *f* 138
nosebleed hemorragia nasal *f* 141
not no 15, 163

note *(banknote)* billete m 130
notebook cuaderno m 105
note paper papel de cartas m 105
nothing nada 15, 17
notice *(sign)* indicación f 155
November noviembre m 150
now ahora 15
number número m 26, 65, 134, 136, 147
nurse enfermera f 144
nutmeg nuez moscada f 51

O

occupation ocupación f 94
occupied ocupado(a) 14, 70, 155
October octubre m 150
octopus pulpo m 46
office oficina f 19, 67, 99, 132, 156
oil aceite m 30, 37, 75, 111
oily graso(a) 30, 111
old viejo(a) 14
old town ciudad vieja f 81
olive aceituna f 41
olive oil aceite de oliva m 37
omelet tortilla f 44
on sobre, en 15
once una vez 148
one uno(a) 147
one-way *(ticket)* ida 65, 69
one-way street dirección única f 79
onion cebolla f 50
only sólo 80, 109
on request a petición 73
on time a la hora 68
onyx ónix m 122
open abierto(a) 14, 82, 155
open, to abrir 11, 17, 82, 108, 129, 131, 132, 142
open-air al aire libre 91
opera ópera f 87
opera house teatro de la ópera m 87
operation operación f 144
operator telefonista m/f 134
operetta opereta f 87
opposite enfrente 77
optician óptico m 99, 123
or o 15
orange naranja 113
orange naranja f 53, 64
orange juice jugo de naranja m 38, 60; zumo de naranja m 42
orangeade naranjada f 60
orchestra orquesta f 88; *(seats)* platea f 87

order, to *(meal)* pedir 36, 61; *(goods)* encargar 102, 103
oregano orégano m 51
ornithology ornitología f 83
our nuestro(a) 160
out of order estropeado(a) 78; averiado(a) 155
out of stock agotado(a) 103
outlet *(electric)* enchufe m 26
outside fuera 15, 36
overdone demasiado hecho(a) 61
overheat, to *(engine)* calentar demasiado 78
overtake, to adelantar 79
owe, to deber 144
oxtail rabo de buey m 47
oyster ostra f 42, 46

P

pacifier chupete m 111
packet paquete m 120; *(cigarettes)* cajetilla f 126
page *(hotel)* botones m 26
pail cubo m 128
pain dolor m 140, 141, 144
painkiller analgésico m 140, 144
paint pintura f 155
paint, to pintar 83
paintbox caja de pinturas f 105
painter pintor m 83
painting pintura f 83
pair par m 116
pajamas pijama m 118
palace palacio m 81
palpitation palpitación f 141
panties bragas f/pl 117
pants *(trousers)* pantalón m 117
panty girdle faja braga f 117
panty hose leotardos m/pl 117
paper papel m 104, 105
paperback rústica f 105
paper napkin servilleta de papel f 105
paraffin *(fuel)* petróleo m 106
parcel paquete m 132
pardon perdone 10
parents padres m/pl 94
park parque m 81
park, to aparcar 26, 77
parking aparcamiento m 77; estacionamiento m 79
parking disc disco de aparcamiento m 77
parking meter parquímetro m 77

parliament cortes f/pl 81
parsley perejil m 51
parsnip chirivía f 50
part parte f 138; (hair) raya f 30
parting raya f 30
partridge perdiz f 48, 49
pass (rail, bus) pase m 72
pass, to (car) adelantar 79
passport pasaporte m 16, 17, 25, 156
passport photo foto para pasaporte f 124
pass through, to estar de paso 16
pasta pastas f/pl 40
paste (glue) engrudo m 105
pastry pastel m 64
pastry shop pastelería f 33, 99
path sendero m 155
patient paciente m/f 144
pay, to pagar 17, 62, 100, 102
payment pago m 131
pea guisante m 50
peach melocotón m 53, 54
peanut cacahuete m 53
pear pera f 53
pearl perla f 122
people gente f 79
pedestrian peatón m 79
peg (tent) estaca f 107
pen pluma f 105
pencil lápiz m 105
pencil sharpener sacapuntas m 105
pendant medallón m 121
penicilline penicilina f 143
penknife cortaplumas m 106
pensioner jubilado(a) m/f 82
pepper pimienta f 37, 38, 51, 64
peppers pimientos m/pl 42, 48, 50
per cent por ciento 148
perch perca f 46
performance (session) función f 86
perfume perfume m 110
perfume shop perfumería f 108
perhaps quizá, tal vez 15
per hour por hora 77, 91
period (monthly) reglas f/pl 141
period pains dolores menstruales m/pl 141
permanent wave permanente f 30
permit permiso m 91
per night por noche 24
per person por persona 32
person persona f 32

personal personal 17
personal call llamada personal f 135
personal cheque cheque personal m 130
person-to-person call llamada personal f 135
per week por semana 20, 24
peseta peseta f 129
petrol gasolina f 75, 78
pewter peltre m 122
pheasant faisán m 48
phone teléfono m 28, 134
phone, to telefonear 134
phone booth cabina de teléfono f 134
phone call llamada 135, 136
phone number número de teléfono m 96
photo foto(grafía) f 82, 124, 125
photocopy fotocopia f 104
photograph, to fotografiar, tomar fotografías 82
photographer fotógrafo m 99
photography fotografía f 124
phrase expresión f 11
pickles pepinillos m/pl 50, 64
pick up, to recoger 80
picnic merienda f 63
picnic basket bolsa para merienda f 106
picture cuadro m 83; (photo) fotografía f 82
piece (slice) trozo m 52, 120
pigeon pichón m 49
pill píldora f 141, 143
pillow almohada f 27
pin alfiler m 121
pineapple piña f 53
pineapple juice zumo de piña m 42
pink rosa 113
pipe pipa f 126
pipe cleaner limpiapipas m 126
pipe tobacco tabaco para pipa m 126
pipe tool utensilios para pipa m/pl 126
pitcher botijo m 127
place lugar m 25
place of birth lugar de nacimiento m 25
plane avión m 65
plaster yeso m 140
plastic plástico m 107
plastic bag bolsa de plástico f 107
plate plato m 36, 61, 107
platform (station) andén m 67, 68, 69, 70

DICTIONARY

platinum platino m 122
play *(theatre)* pieza f 86
play, to jugar 90; *(music)* tocar 88
playground campo de juego m 32
playing card naipe f 105
please por favor 9
plimsolls zapatos de lona m/pl 116
plug *(electric)* clavija de enchufe f 29, 119
plum ciruela f 53
p.m. de la tarde 133
pneumonia neumonía f 142
poached hervido(a) 46
pocket bolsillo m 118
pocket watch reloj de bolsillo m 121
point punto m 80
point, to *(show)* señalar 11
poison veneno m 109
poisoning intoxicación f 142
police policía f 78, 156
police station comisaría de policía f 99, 156
pomegranate granada f 53
poplin popelín m 114
popular popular 80
pork cerdo m 47
port puerto m 74; *(wine)* oporto m 60
portable portátil 119
porter mozo m 18, 26, 71
portion porción f 61; ración f 54
Portugal Portugal m 146
possible posible 137
post *(letters)* correo m 133
post, to mandar por correo 28
postage franqueo m 132
postage stamp sello m 28, 126, 132
postcard tarjeta postal f 105, 126, 132
poste restante lista de correos f 133
post office oficina de correos f 99, 132
potato patata f 50, 64
pottery alfarería f 83
poultry aves f/pl 48
pound *(money)* libra f 18, 102, 130; *(weight)* libra f 120
powder polvo m 110
powder compact polvera f 121
prawn gamba f 41, 43; quisquilla f 42, 46; langostino m 42, 46
preference preferencia f 101
pregnant embarazada 141
premium *(gasoline)* super 75

prescribe, to recetar 143
prescription receta f 108, 143
present *(gift)* regalo m 120
press, to *(iron)* planchar 29
press stud broche de presión m 118
pressure presión f 75
price precio m 24
priest sacerdote m 84
print *(photo)* copia f 125
print, to imprimir 124
private privado(a) 155; particular 80, 92, 155
private toilet water particular m 23
processing *(photo)* revelado m 124
profession profesión f 25
profit ganancia f 131
programme programa m 87, 88
prohibit, to prohibir 32, 79, 92, 155
pronunciation pronunciación f 6, 11
propelling pencil lapicero m 121
Protestant protestante 84
provide, to conseguir 131
prune ciruela pasa f 53
public holiday día festivo m 152
pull, to tirar 155
pullover pullover m 117
puncture pinchazo m 75
purchase compra f 131
pure puro(a) 113
purple purpúreo(a) 113
push, to empujar 155
pyjamas pijama m 118

Q

quail codorniz f 48
quality calidad f 103, 114
quantity cantidad f 14, 103
quarter cuarto m 148; *(part of town)* barrio m 81
quarter of an hour cuarto de hora m 153
quartz cuarzo m 122
question pregunta f 10, 76
quick rápido(a) 14, 156
quickly rápidamente 137
quiet tranquilo(a) 23, 25

R

rabbi rabino m 84
rabbit conejo m 48, 49
race course/track pista de carreras f 91
racket *(sport)* raqueta f 91
radiator radiador m 78

radio *(set)* radio f 23, 28, 119
radish rábano m 42, 50
railroad crossing paso a nivel m 79
railway ferrocarril m 154
railway station estación (de ferrocarril) f 19, 21, 67, 70
rain, to llover 94
rain boot bota par la lluvia f 116
raincoat impermeable m 118
raisin pasa f 53
rangefinder telémetro m 125
rare *(meat)* poco hecho(a) 48
rash sarpullido m 139
raspberry frambuesa f 53
rate tarifa f 20; tasa f 131
razor máquina (navaja) de afeitar f 111
razor blade hoja de afeitar f 111
reading-lamp lámpara para leer f 27
ready listo(a) 29, 116, 123, 125
real auténtico(a) 121
rear trasero(a) 75
receipt recibo m 103, 144
recent reciente 149
reception recepción f 23
receptionist recepcionista m/f 26
recommend, to recomendar 35, 80, 86, 88, 137, 145; aconsejar 36, 41, 43, 50, 54
record *(disc)* disco m 127, 128
record player tocadiscos m 119
rectangular rectangular 101
red rojo(a) 113; *(wine)* tinto 58
redcurrant grosella roja f 53
red mullet salmonete m 46
reduction descuento m 24, 82
refill recambio m 105
refund, to devolver 103
regards recuerdos m/pl 152
register, to facturar 71
registered mail registrado(a) 133
registration inscripción f 25
registration form ficha f 25
regular *(petrol)* normal 75
religion religión f 83
religious service servicio religioso m 84
rent, to alquilar 20, 91, 92, 119, 155
rental alquiler m 20
repair reparación f 125
repair, to arreglar 29, 119, 121, 123, 145; reparar 116, 125
repeat, to repetir 11
report, to denunciar 156

reservation reserva f 19, 23, 65, 69
reservation office oficina de reservas f m 19, 67
reserve, to reservar 19, 23, 35, 86
restaurant restaurante m 19, 32, 34, 35, 67
return *(ticket)* ida y vuelta 65, 69
return, to *(give back)* devolver 103
reversed charge call llamada a cobro revertido f 135
rheumatism reumatismo m 141
rhubarb ruibarbo m 53
rib costilla f 138
ribbon cinta f 105
rice arroz m 45, 50, 54
ride, to *(horse)* montar a caballo 74
right derecho(a) 21, 63, 69, 77; *(correct)* correcto(a) 14
ring *(on finger)* sortija f 121
ring, to tocar el timbre 155; telefonear 134
river río 85, 91
road carretera f 76, 77, 79, 85
road map mapa de carreteras m 105
road sign señal de circulación f 79
roast asado(a) 48, 49
roll *(bread)* panecillo m 37, 64
roller skate patín de ruedas m 128
roll film carrete m, rollo m 124
roll-neck cuello vuelto m 117
room habitación f 19, 23, 24, 25, 27; *(space)* sitio m 32
room number número de la habitación m 26
room service servicio de habitación m 23
rope cuerda f 107
rosary rosario m 122, 127
rosé rosé 58
rosemary romero m 51
rouge colorete m 111
round redondo(a) 101
round *(golf)* juego m 91
round-neck cuello redondo m 117
roundtrip *(ticket)* ida y vuelta 65, 69
rowing-boat barca f 92
royal palace palacio real m 82
rubber *(eraser)* goma de borrar f 105
ruby rubí m 122
rucksack mochila f 107
ruin ruina f 82
ruler regla f 105
rum ron m 44, 60
running water agua corriente f 23

DICTIONARY

S

safe *(not dangerous)* sin peligro 92
safe caja fuerte *f* 27
safety pin imperdible *m* 111
saffron azafrán *m* 51
sage salvia *f* 51
sailing-boat velero *m* 92
salad ensalada *f* 43, 64
salami salchichón *m* 42, 64
sale venta *f* 131; *(bargains)* rebajas *f/pl* 101
sales tax impuesto *m* 102
salmon salmón *m* 42, 46
salt sal *f* 37, 38, 51, 64
salty salado(a) 61
sand arena *f* 91
sandal sandalia *f* 116
sandwich bocadillo *m* 64
sanitary towel/napkin compresa *f* 109
sapphire zafiro *m* 122
sardine sardina *f* 42, 46
satin raso *m* 114
Saturday sábado *m* 151
sauce salsa *f* 49
saucepan cazo *m* 107
saucer platillo *m* 107
sausage salchicha *f* 47, 64
sautéed salteado(a) 46, 48
scallop venera *f* 46
scarf bufanda *f* 118
scarlet escarlata 113
school escuela *f* 79
scissors tijeras *f/pl* 107, 110
scooter escúter *m* 74
Scotch whisky escocés *m* 60
Scotland Escocia *f* 146
scrambled egg huevo revuelto *m* 38, 44
screwdriver destornillador *m* 107
sculptor escultor *m* 83
sculpture escultura *f* 83
sea mar *m* 23, 85
sea bass mero *m* 46
sea bream besugo *m* 45
seafood mariscos *m/pl* 45
season estación *f* 149
seasoning condimento *m* 37
seat asiento *m* 69, 70, 87; *(theatre, etc.)* localidad *f*, entrada *f* 86, 87, 89
seat belt cinturón de seguridad *m* 75
second segundo(a) 148
second segundo *m* 153
second class segunda clase *f* 66, 69

second hand segundero manecilla *m* 122
second-hand de segunda mano 104
secretary secretario(a) *m/f* 27, 131
see, to ver 12, 163
sell, to vender 100
send, to mandar 31, 78, 102, 132, 133; enviar 103
send up, to subir 26
sentence frase *f* 11
separately separadamente 62
September septiembre *m* 150
serge estameña *f* 114
serious serio(a) 139
service servicio *m* 24, 62, 98, 100; *(religion)* servicio *m* 84
serviette servilleta *f* 36
set *(hair)* marcado *m* 30
set menu plato combinado *m* 36, 39
setting lotion fijador *m* 30, 111
seven siete 147
seventeen diecisiete 147
seventh séptimo(a) 148
seventy setenta 147
sew, to coser 29
shade sombra *f* 89; *(colour)* tono *m* 112
shampoo lavado *m* 30; champú *m* 30, 111
shape forma *f* 103
sharp *(pain)* agudo(a) 140
shave, to afeitar 30
shaver máquina de afeitar (eléctrica) *f* 26, 119
shaving cream crema de afeitar *f* 111
she ella 161
shelf estante *m* 120
sherry jerez *m* 43, 48, 55, 60
ship embarcación *f* 74
shirt camisa *f* 118
shirt-maker's camisería *f* 99
shiver escalofrío *m* 140
shoe zapato *m* 116
shoelace cordón (para zapato) *m* 116
shoemaker's zapatero *m* 99
shoe polish crema para zapatos *f* 116
shoe shop zapatería *f* 99
shop tienda *f*, comercio *m* 98, 99; *(big)* almacén *m* 98
shopping compras *f/pl* 97
shopping area zona de tiendas *f* 82, 100

Diccionario

shopping centre centro comercial *m* 99

short corto(a) 30, 116, 117

shorts pantalón corto *m* 118

short-sighted miope 123

shoulder espalda *f* 138

shovel pala *f* 128

show *(theatre)* función *f* 86; *(night-club)* atracciones *f/pl* 88

show, to enseñar 12, 13, 76, 100, 124; mostrar 119

shower ducha *f* 23, 32

shrimp quisquilla *f* 42, 46; gamba *f* 41, 43; langostino *m* 42, 46

shrink, to encoger 113

shut cerrado(a) 14

shutter *(window)* postigo *m* 29; *(camera)* obturador *m* 125

sick *(ill)* enfermo 140, 156

sickness *(illness)* enfermedad *f* 140

side lado *m* 30

sideboards/burns patillas *f/pl* 31

sightseeing tour recorrido turístico *m* 80

sign *(notice)* letrero *m* 155; *(road)* señal *f* 79

sign, to firmar 25

signature firma *f* 25

signet ring sortija de sello *f* 121

silk seda *f* 114

silver plateado(a) 113

silver plata *f* 121, 122

silver plate plata chapada *f* 122

silverware objetos de plata *m/pl* 122

simple sencillo(a) 124

since desde 15, 150

sing, to cantar 88

single soltero(a) 94; *(ticket)* ida 65, 69

single room habitación sencilla *f* 19, 23

sister hermana *f* 94

sit down, to sentarse 96

six seis 147

sixteen dieciséis 147

sixth sexto(a) 148

sixty sesenta 147

size tamaño *m* 124; *(clothes, shoes)* talla *f* 114, 115, 116

sketching block bloc de dibujo *m* 105

ski, to esquiar 91

skiing esquí *m* 90

ski lift telesquí *m* 91

skin piel *f* 138

skin-diving natación submarina *m* 92

skirt falda *f* 118

sleep, to dormir 71, 144

sleeping bag saco de dormir *m* 107

sleeping-car coche cama *m* 66, 68, 71

sleeping pill somnífero *m* 109, 143, 144

sleeve manga *f* 117

slice rebanada *f* 120

slide *(photo)* diapositiva *f* 124

slip combinación *f* 118

slipper zapatilla *f* 116

slow lento(a) 14; despacio(a) 11, 21, 79, 135

small pequeño(a) 14, 25, 54, 61, 101, 116

smoke, to fumar 155

smoked ahumado(a) 41, 42, 46

smoker fumadores *m/pl* 69, 70

snack tentempié *m* 63

snail caracol *m* 41

snap fastener broche de presión *m* 118

sneakers zapatos de lona *m/pl* 116

snorkel espantasuegras *m/pl* 128

snow, to nevar 94

snuff rapé *m* 126

soap jabón *m* 27, 111

soccer fútbol *m* 90

sock calcetín *m* 118

socket *(outlet)* enchufe *m* 26

soda water soda *f* 60

soft blando(a) 52; suave 123

soft-boiled *(egg)* pasado por agua 38

sold out *(theatre)* agotado(a) 87

sole suela *f* 116; *(fish)* lenguado *m* 46

solution solución *f* 123

some unos(as) 14

someone alguien 96

something algo 36, 54, 108, 112, 114, 125, 139

son hijo *m* 94

soon pronto 15

sore throat angina *f* 141

sorry *(I'm)* lo siento 10, 16, 87

sort clase *f* 52, 120

soup sopa *f* 43

south sur *m* 77

South Africa Africa del Sur *f* 146

South America América del Sur *f* 146

souvenir recuerdo *m* 127

souvenir shop tienda de objetos de regalo *f* 99

Soviet Union Unión Soviética *f* 146
spade pala *f* 128
spaghetti espaguetis *m/pl* 64
Spain España *f* 146
Spanish español(a) 11, 114, 104
spare tyre rueda de repuesto *f* 75
sparking plug bujía *f* 75
sparkling *(wine)* espumoso(a) 58
spark plug bujía *f* 75
speak, to hablar 11, 135, 162
speaker *(loudspeaker)* altavoz *m* 119
special especial 20, 37
special delivery urgente 133
specialist especialista *m/f* 142
speciality especialidad *f* 40, 43, 59
specimen *(medical)* muestra *f* 142
spectacle case estuche para gafas *m* 123
spend, to gastar 101
spice especia *f* 51
spinach espinaca *f* 50
spine espina dorsal *f* 138
spiny lobster langosta *f* 46
sponge esponja *f* 111
spoon cuchara *f* 36, 107
sport deporte *m* 90
sporting goods shop tienda de artículos de deporte *f* 99
sprain, to torcer 140
spring *(season)* primavera *f* 149
square cuadrado(a) 101
squid calamar *m* 41, 46
stadium estadio *m* 82
staff personal *m* 26
stain mancha *f* 29
stainless steel acero inoxidable *m* 107, 122
stalls *(theatre)* platea *f* 87
stamp *(postage)* sello *m* 28, 126, 132
staple grapa *f* 105
start, to empezar 80, 86, 88; *(car)* arrancar 78
starter entremés *m* 41; tapa *f* 63
station *(railway)* estación (de ferro-carril) *f* 21, 67, 70; *(underground, subway)* estación de metro *f* 73
stationer's papelería *f* 99, 104
statue estatua *f* 82
stay estancia *f* 31, 93
stay, to quedarse 16, 24, 25; hospe-darse 93
steak filete *m* 47
steal, to robar 156
steamed cocido(a) al vapor 46

stewed estofado(a) 48
stew pot cacerola *f* 107
stiff neck tortícolis *f* 141
sting picadura *f* 139
sting, to picar 139
stock exchange bolsa *f* 82
stocking media *f* 118
stomach estómago *m* 138
stomach ache dolor de estómago *m* 141
stools heces *f/pl* 142
stop *(bus)* parada *f* 72, 73
stop! alto 79; deténgase 156
stop, to parar 21, 68, 70; detenerse 74
stop thief! al ladrón 156
store tienda *f* 98, 99; *(big)* almacén *m* 98
straight ahead (todo) derecho 21, 77
strange extraño(a) 84
strawberry fresa *f* 53, 54
street calle *f* 25, 76
street map mapa de la ciudad *m* 105
string cuerda *f* 105
strong fuerte 52, 143
student estudiante *m/f* 82, 94
stuffed relleno(a) 41
subway metro *m* 73
suede ante *m* 114, 116
sufficient suficiente 68
sugar azúcar *m* 37, 64
suit *(man)* traje *m* 118; *(woman)* vestido *m* 118
suitcase maleta *f* 18
summer verano *m* 149
sun sol *m* 89, 94
sunburn quemadura de sol *f* 108
Sunday domingo *m* 151
sunglasses gafas de sol *f/pl* 123
sunny soleado(a) 94
sunshade *(beach)* sombrilla *f* 92
sunstroke insolación *f* 141
sun-tan cream crema solar *f* 111
super *(petrol)* super 75
superb soberbio(a) 84
supermarket supermercado *m* 99
suppository supositorio *m* 109
surcharge suplemento *m* 69
sure *(fact)* cierto(a) 160
surfboard plancha de deslizamiento *f* 92
surgery *(consulting room)* consulta *f* 137

surgical dressing hilas *f/pl* 109
suspenders *(Am.)* tirantes *m/pl* 118
sweater suéter *m* 118
sweatshirt suéter de tela de punto *m* 118
sweet dulce 58, 61
sweet caramelo *m* 64, 126
sweet corn maíz *m* 50
sweetener edulcorante *m* 37, 64
sweet shop bombonería *f* 99
swell, to hinchar 139
swelling hinchazón *f* 139
swim, to nadar 91, 92; bañarse 92
swimming natación *f* 90
swimming pool piscina *f* 32, 91
swimming trunks bañador *m* 118
swimsuit traje de baño *m* 118
switch interruptor *m* 29
switchboard operator telefonista *m/f* 26
switch on, to *(light)* encender 79
swollen hinchado(a) 139
swordfish pez espada *m* 46
synagogue sinagoga *f* 84
synthetic sintético(a) 114
system sistema *m* 138

T

table mesa *f* 35, 36, 107
tablet tableta *f* 109
taffeta tafetán *m* 114
tailor's sastre *m* 99
take, to llevar 18, 21, 67, 102; tomar 25, 72
take away, to *(carry)* llevar 63, 103
take off, to *(plane)* despegar 65
talcum powder polvo de talco *m* 111
tambourine pandereta *f* 127
tampon tampon higiénico *m* 109
tangerine mandarina *f* 53
tap *(water)* grifo *m* 28
tape recorder magnetófono *m* 119
tarragon estragón *m* 51
tart tarta *f* 54; tartaleta *f* 42
tax impuesto *m* 24, 102
taxi taxi *m* 19, 21, 31, 67
tea té *m* 38, 60, 64
tear, to desgarrar 140
tearoom salón de té *m* 34
teaspoon cucharilla *f* 107, 143
teat *(feeding bottle)* tetina *f* 111
telegram telegrama *m* 133
telephone teléfono *m* 28, 134

telephone, to telefonear 134
telephone booth cabina de teléfonos *f* 134
telephone call llamada *f* 135, 136
telephone directory guía de teléfonos *f* 134
telephone number número de teléfono *m* 96, 134, 136
telephoto lens lente de acercamiento *f* 125
television televisión *f* 23; *(set)* televisor *m* 28
telex télex *m* 133
telex, to mandar un télex 130
tell, to decir 12, 73, 76, 135, 136, 153
temperature temperatura *f* 92, 140, 142
temporary temporal 145
ten diez 147
tendon tendón *m* 138
tennis tenis *m* 91
tennis court pista de tenis *f* 91
tennis racket raqueta de tenis *f* 91
tent tienda (de campaña) *f* 32, 107
tent peg estaca *f* 107
tent pole mástil *m* 107
tenth décimo(a) 148
term *(word)* expresión *f* 131
terminus terminal *f* 72
terrible terrible 84
terrycloth tela de toalla *f* 114
tetanus tétanos *m* 140
than que 14
thank you gracias 10
that ése(a), aquél(la) 161
the el, la 159
theatre teatro *m* 86
theft robo *m* 156
their su 160
then entonces 15
there allí 14
thermometer termómetro *m* 109, 144
these éstos(as) 161
they ellos(as) 161
thief ladrón *m* 156
thigh muslo *m* 138
thin tenue 114
think, to *(believe)* creer 62, 95
third tercero(a) 148
third tercio *m* 148
thirsty, to be tener sed 13, 35
thirteen trece 147

thirty treinta 147
this éste(a) 161
those ésos(as), aquéllos(as) 161
thousand mil 148
thread hilo *m* 27
three tres 147
throat garganta *f* 138
throat lozenge pastilla para la garganta *f* 109
through train tren directo *m* 68, 69
thumb pulgar *m* 138
thumbtack chincheta *f* 105
Thursday jueves *m* 151
thyme tomillo *m* 51
ticket billete *m* 65, 69, 72, 156; *(theatre, etc.)* localidad *f*, entrada *f* 86, 87, 90
ticket office taquilla *f* 67
tide marea *f* 92
tie corbata *f* 118
tie clip sujetador de corbata *m* 122
tight ajustado(a) 116
tights leotardos *m/pl* 118
time tiempo *m* 80; *(clock)* hora *f* 137, 153; *(occasion)* vez *f* 143
timetable *(railway guide)* guía de ferrocarriles *f* 68
tin *(can)* lata *f* 120
tinfoil papel de estaño *m* 107
tin opener abrelatas *m* 107
tint tinte *m* 111
tinted ahumado(a) 123
tire neumático *m* 75
tired cansado(a) 13
tissue *(handkerchief)* pañuelo de papel *m* 111
tissue paper papel de seda *m* 105
to a, para 15
toast tostada *f* 38, 64
tobacco tabaco *m* 126
tobacconist's tabacos *m/pl* 99, 126; estanco *m* 99
today hoy 29, 151
toe dedo del pie *m* 138
toilet paper papel higiénico *m* 111
toiletry artículos de tocador *m/pl* 110
toilets servicios *m/pl* 27, 28, 32, 67
toll peaje *m* 79
tomato tomate *m* 50, 64
tomato juice zumo de tomate *m* 42; jugo de tomate *m* 60
tomb tumba *f* 82
tomorrow mañana 29, 151
tongue lengua *f* 138

tonic water tónica *f* 60
tonight esta noche 29, 86, 87, 96
tonsil amígdala *f* 138
too demasiado 14; *(also)* también 15
tool kit caja de herramientas *f* 107
tooth diente *m* 145
toothache dolor de muelas *m* 145
toothbrush cepillo de dientes *m* 111, 119
toothpaste pasta de dientes *m* 111
topaz topacio *m* 122
torch *(flashlight)* linterna *f* 107
torn desgarrado(a) 140
touch, to tocar 155
tough duro(a) 61
tourist information información turística *f* 67
tourist office oficina de turismo *f* 80
towel toalla *f* 27
tower torre *f* 82
town ciudad *f* 21, 76, 105
town hall ayuntamiento *m* 82
tow truck grúa *f* 78
toy juguete *m* 128
toy shop juguetería *f* 99
tracing paper papel transparente *m* 105
tracksuit chandal de entrenamiento *m* 118
traffic *(car)* tráfico *m* 76
traffic light semáforo *m* 77
trailer caravana *f* 32
train tren *m* 66, 68, 69, 70, 73
tranquillizer sedante *m* 109
transfer *(bank)* transferencia *f* 131
transformer transformador *m* 119
translate, to traducir 11
transport transporte *m* 74
travel agency agencia de viajes *f* 99
traveller's cheque cheque de viajero *m* 18, 62, 102, 129, 130
travel sickness mareo *m* 108
treatment tratamiento *m* 143
tree árbol *m* 85
tremendous tremendo 84
trim, to *(beard)* recortar 31
trip viaje *m* 73, 94, 152
tripe callos *m/pl* 41, 47
trolley carrito *m* 18, 71
trousers pantalón *m* 118
trout trucha *f* 46
truffle trufa *f* 50
try, to probar 115; intentar 135
T-shirt camiseta *f* 118

DICTIONARY

Diccionario

tube tubo m 120
Tuesday martes m 151
tulle tul m 114
tuna atún m 41, 45
Tunisia Túnez m 146
tunny atún m 41, 45
turbot rodaballo m 46
turkey pavo m 48
turn, to (change direction) doblar 21, 77
turquoise turquesa 113
turquoise turquesa f 122
turtleneck cuello vuelto m 117
tuxedo smoking m 117
tweezers pinzas f/pl 111
twelve doce 147
twenty veinte 147
twice dos veces 148
twin bed dos camas f/pl 23
two dos 147
type (kind) clase f 66
typewriter máquina de escribir f 27
typewriter ribbon cinta para máquina f 105
typical típico(a) 35
typing paper papel de máquina m 105
tyre neumático m 75

U

ugly feo(a) 14, 84
umbrella paraguas m 118; (beach) sombrilla f 92
uncle tío m 94
unconscious inconsciente 139
under debajo 15
underdone (meat) poco hecho(a) 48, 61
underground (railway) metro m 73
underpants calzoncillos m/pl 118
undershirt camiseta f 118
understand, to comprender 12, 16; entender 12
undress, to desvestir 142
United States Estados Unidos m/pl 146
university universidad f 82
unleaded sin plomo 75
until hasta 150
up arriba 15
upper superior 70
upset stomach molestias de estómago f/pl 108
upstairs arriba 15, 69
urgent urgente 13, 145

urine orina f 142
use uso m 17, 109
use, to usar 134
useful útil 15

V

vacancy habitación libre f 23
vacant libre 14, 155
vacation vacaciones f/pl 151
vaccinate, to vacunar 140
vacuum flask termo m 107
vaginal vaginal 141
valley valle m 85
value valor m 131
vanilla vainilla f 51, 54
veal ternera f 47
vegetable verdura f, legumbre f 50
vegetable store verdulería f 99
vegetarian vegetariano(a) 37
vein vena f 138
velvet terciopelo m 114
venereal disease enfermedad venérea f 142
venison venado m 49
vermouth vermut m 55, 60
very muy 15
vest camiseta f 118; (Am.) chaleco m 118
veterinarian veterinario m 99
video cassette video-cassette f 119, 127
video-recorder video-grabadora f 119
video tape cinta video f 124
view vista f 23, 25
village pueblo m 76, 85
vinegar vinagre m 37
vineyard viñedo m 85
visit visita f 144
visit, to visitar 84
visiting hours horas de visita f/pl 144
V-neck cuello en forma de V m 117
volleyball balonvolea m 90
voltage voltaje m 119
vomit, to vomitar 140

W

waistcoat chaleco m 118
wait, to esperar 21, 96, 108
waiter camarero m 26, 36
waiting-room sala de espera f 67
waitress camarera f 26, 36
wake, to despertar 27; llamar 71
Wales País de Gales m 146

walk, to caminar 74; ir a pie 85
wall muro *m* 85
wallet cartera *f* 156
walnut nuez *f* 53
want, to *(wish)* desear, querer 12
wash, to lavar 29
washable lavable 113
wash-basin lavabo *m* 28
washing powder jabón en polvo *m* 107
watch reloj *m* 121, 122
watchmaker's relojería *f* 99, 121
watchstrap correa de reloj *f* 122
water agua *f* 23, 28, 32, 38, 75, 92
waterfall cascada *f* 85
water flask cantimplora *f* 107
watermelon sandía *f* 53
water-ski esquí acuático *m* 92
wave ola *f* 92
way camino *m* 76
we nosotros(as) 161
weather tiempo *m* 94
wedding ring anillo de boda *m* 121
Wednesday miércoles *m* 151
week semana *f* 16, 20, 24, 151
weekday día de la semana *m* 151
weekend fin de semana *m* 151
well *(healthy)* bien 10, 140
well-done *(meat)* muy hecho(a) 48
west oeste *m* 77
western *(film)* película del Oeste *f* 86
what qué 10; cómo 11; cuál 20
wheel rueda *f* 78
when cuándo 10
where dónde 10
which cuál 10
whisky whisky *m* 17, 60
white blanco(a) 58, 113
whitebait boquerón *m* 45
whiting pescadilla *f* 46
who quién 10
why por qué 10
wick mecha *f* 126
wide ancho(a) 116
wide-angle lens gran angular *m* 125
wife mujer *f* 94
wild boar jabalí *m* 49
wind viento *m* 95
windmill molino de viento *m* 85
window ventana *f* 28, 36, 69;
   (shop) escaparate *m* 100, 112
windscreen/shield parabrisas *m* 76
wine vino *m* 17, 56, 58, 61
wine list carta de vinos *f* 58

wine merchant's tienda de vinos *f*, bodega *f* 99
wine skin bota *f* 127
winter invierno *m* 149
wiper limpiaparabrisas *m* 75
wish deseo *m* 152
with con 15
withdraw, to *(bank)* retirar 131
without sin 15
woman señora *f* 115; mujer *f* 141, 156
wood alcohol alcohol de quemar *m* 107
woodcarving talla en madera *f* 127
woodcock becada *f* 48
wool lana *f* 114
word palabra *f* 11, 15, 133
work, to *(function)* funcionar 28, 119
working day día laborable *m* 151
worse peor 14
wound herida *f* 139
wrap, to envolver 102
wrapping paper papel de envolver *m* 105
wristwatch reloj de pulsera *m* 122
write, to escribir 11, 101
writing pad bloc de papel *m* 105
writing-paper papel de escribir *m* 27
wrong incorrecto(a) 14; equivocado(a) 77, 136

X

X-ray *(photo)* radiografía *f* 140

Y

year año *m* 149
yellow amarillo(a) 113
yes sí 9
yesterday ayer 151
yet todavía 15
yield, to *(traffic)* ceder el paso 79
yoghurt yogur *m* 64
you tú, usted 161
young joven 14
your tu, su, vuestro(a) 160
youth hostel albergue de juventud *m* 22

Z

zero cero *m* 147
zip(per) cremallera *f* 118
zoo zoo(lógico) *m* 82
zoology zoología *f* 83
zucchini calabacín *m* 50

Índice en español